THE
COMPLETE
IDIOT'S
GUIDE® TO

Cooking Techniques and Science

by Sarah Labensky, CCP, CPFM,
and James Fitzgerald, Ph.D., CCP

ALPHA
A Pearson Education Company

For all the great-grandmas, grandmas, and moms of this world who were the first real pioneers of culinary science. Thanks for teaching us the foundation—if you can boil water, you can cook.

Copyright © 2003 by CWL Publishing Enterprises, Inc., John Woods, President

This is a CWL Publishing Enterprises book, developed for Alpha Books by CWL Publishing Enterprises, Inc., Madison, Wisconsin, WI, www.cwlpub.com.

International Standard Book Number: 0-02-864426-3
Library of Congress Catalog Card Number: 2002113244

04 03 02   8 7 6 5 4 3 2 1

Interpretation of the printing code: The rightmost number of the first series of numbers is the year of the book's printing; the rightmost number of the second series of numbers is the number of the book's printing. For example, a printing code of 02-1 shows that the first printing occurred in 2002.

Printed in the United States of America

For marketing and publicity, please call: 317-581-3722

The publisher offers discounts on this book when ordered in quantity for bulk purchases and special sales.

For sales within the United States, please contact: Corporate and Government Sales, 1-800-382-3419 or corpsales@pearsontechgroup.com

Outside the United States, please contact: International Sales, 317-581-3793 or international@pearsontechgroup.com

Publisher: *Marie Butler-Knight*
Product Manager: *Phil Kitchel*
Managing Editor: *Jennifer Chisholm*
Acquisitions Editor: *Renee Wilmeth*
Development Editor: *Nancy D. Lewis*
Production Editor: *Katherin Bidwell*
Copy Editor: *Jan Zunkel*
Illustrator: *Chris Eliopoulos*
Cover/Book Designer: *Trina Wurst*
Indexer: *Julie Bess*
Layout/Proofreading: *Angela Calvert, Mary Hunt, Sherry Taggart*

Contents at a Glance

Contents

Foreword

Cooking has become a fundamental facet of human life. It is not merely taking food ingredients and heating or cooling to them to make them edible; it is the complete transformation of raw food ingredients, herbs, spices, wines, and other flavoring agents into exciting and appetizing meals.

Dining is much more than just eating; it is the whole event of sitting down with friends, family, and guests at the table for good food, good drink, and pleasant hospitality. Cooks who understand and appreciate the association of pleasurable and joyful eating and sharing with friends become the greatest culinary artisans.

The science of cooking is based on centuries of trial, error, and accomplishments. From the various pots and pans that we use today to the variety of cooking ingredients available from all around the world, cooking has evolved from the very basic to the most sublime. There is a mystique to cooking, and we can begin to grasp this mystique by understanding the science behind it.

What Sarah Labensky and Dr. Fitzgerald have been able to accomplish in *The Complete Idiot's Guide to Cooking Techniques and Science* is to take those structured, scientific approaches to heat application, flavor manipulation, and food technology, and present them in a way that the average consumer can easily understand. Breaking down the components of cooking, the importance of safety and sanitation, the general principles of heat transfer and flavor construction into digestible bits of information must have been a tremendous task, but one which has been cleverly achieved.

It isn't that the science of cooking needs to be complicated. After all, it is a fact of life that we have all come to associate with grandma in the kitchen, mom at the stove, or dad at the backyard barbecue, creating family favorites out of vegetables, grains, meats, poultry, and seafood. Frying eggs and bacon in the morning, grilling chicken breasts for lunch sandwiches, or properly roasting meats for Sunday dinner can all be boiled down to basic techniques and a general understanding of the flavors, textures, and appearance of foods.

And from these basic techniques we can begin to understand the work of great chefs in fine restaurants and maybe start to emulate them. Sarah Labensky and Jim Fitzgerald have accomplished this transformation of science into wonderful eating with straightforward narratives and clear and appropriate examples we can all associate with. The book is also infused with the humor that's always appropriate in any human activity. It simply reinforces that while cooking is a practical science, it's also fun; when done well, it results in food that is a pleasure to consume.

You may not be able to master all there is to cooking by reading this book, but when you know the whys of cooking techniques, you'll be a better home chef and enjoy your time in the kitchen even more.

Michael Baskette

Michael Baskette is Director of Operations for the American Culinary Federation—America's leading organization for professional cooks and chefs with more than a 70-year history developing quality standards for professional food service. He is a Certified Executive Chef, Certified Culinary Educator, and member of the Academy of Chefs.

Introduction

Most cookbooks are really just recipe collections. And that's okay because dinnertime would get pretty boring without other people's recipes to tempt and inspire us. While recipes are important, too often cookbook authors don't really explain *why* the cook should do this or that, or what can happen if you don't abide by certain recipe rules, or what to do to fix a problem. That's where this book comes in.

We've divided the subject into sections based on the type of food you might be preparing: meats, salad dressings, baked goods, sauces, and so on. Each chapter covers a specific food or category of ingredients, with miscellaneous ramblings and digressions on related scientific principles.

You'll quickly see that we included very few recipes. Those you'll find were put here in order to illustrate some specific technique or scientific principle. While they are good, workable recipes, you should think of them as simply a foundation or starting point for your culinary education. Once you master our basic recipes, you'll better understand much of the science that underlies cooking. And then you'll be able to create your own dishes and modify other people's recipes with more confidence.

So, now it's time to get into your kitchen laboratory and get busy. No matter what happens—short of needing a trip to the ER—always remember that food is fun. It's comforting, sensual, and physically and emotionally nourishing. Besides, even if worse *does* come to worse, you probably aren't cooking anyone's last meal.

In **Part 1, "Cooking in the Raw: Past, Present, and Future Basics,"** you learn that the science of food is simply about a few raw ingredients, water being basic to the entire process. And because all food is or was alive, preparing it safely is a must.

In **Part 2, "Eat Your Veggies ... and Other Stuff,"** you discover how plants epitomize the concept of healthy, living food. How you handle and cook these foods can either maximize or minimize those qualities. While this section won't turn you into a food chemist, a little practical knowledge of plant starches, proteins, and fats just might make you appreciate your veggies a bit more.

In **Part 3, "Muscle Mania—The Handling and Cooking of Meat,"** you get a leg up on portable protein—meat. Wild game and domestic livestock play a major role in the human diet and the grocery budget. So, understanding the fundamentals of meat and muscle just might improve your dinner and protect your investment in these proteins.

Part 4, "The Aquatic Cook," explains how fish has jumped to new levels of nutritional respectability recently. This section tells you why, and explains how to keep seafood good, and good for you.

Part 5, "Beautiful Baking" dispels the concept of sugar-plum fairies and cream puffs; it's a disciplined world in the bakery. The science of weights and measures reigns supreme there, and understanding why will make you a better baker.

Part 6, "Hitting the Sauce," describes how nothing adorns a plate of food as nicely as a well-made sauce. It's where the art and science of cooking meet. Sauces can be simple or complex, sweet or savory, animal or vegetable. And this section looks at them all.

Special Features

In addition to the regular text, this book contains five extra features designed to help you learn about food science and culinary techniques.

Food for Thought

These sidebars provide extra information to supplement material in the text. You may choose to skip these sidebars, especially if you're in a hurry, but the material found there is fun, informative, or just plain interesting.

Lab Project

These are recipes from the text, written in a clear, direct form with measurements. Recipes in the body of the text are usually interspersed with step-by-step explanations and alternative techniques. When you want a quick guide to a recipe, look for a Lab Project.

Chef Sez

These boxes define culinary or scientific terms used in the text. Understanding the typical vocabulary and jargon of the kitchen helps you to understand recipe instructions here and in other cookbooks. Knowing some scientific terminology will help make the general subject clearer when you encounter these terms in another context.

Too Hot to Handle

These boxes present warnings or guidance designed to prevent injury, illness, or wasted time.

Now You're Cooking

These sidebars offer helpful hints to make your kitchen experiences easier, or to supplement information in the text.

Acknowledgments

We first wish to thank John Woods of CWL Publishing Enterprises, who asked us to write this book, and shepherded the project through to completion. Thanks also to Senior Editor Renee Wilmeth of Alpha Books for her patience and persistence. Special thanks, however, goes to our students. As any teacher knows, it is our students' questions, insights, and curiosity that force us to keep learning and growing ourselves. And to SAS, wherever you are now, eternal thanks for your inspiration that counting pots, pans, and whisks instead of sheep at night really is okay, for it turned a life-long dream into a labor of love.

In addition, we would like to acknowledge Harold McGee, author of the highly acclaimed books *On Food and Cooking* and *The Curious Cook*. Thanks to him, professional chefs and home cooks began to understand the relationship between science and food. Although many wonderful writers are now working in this field, it was McGee who first established that a scientist lurks inside every great cook. His work continues to prove that cooks aren't idiots, and for that we are extremely grateful.

Trademarks

All terms mentioned in this book that are known to be or are suspected of being trademarks or service marks have been appropriately capitalized. Alpha Books and Pearson Education, Inc., cannot attest to the accuracy of this information. Use of a term in this book should not be regarded as affecting the validity of any trademark or service mark.

Part 1

Cooking in the Raw: Past, Present, and Future Food Basics

No, it's not what you think. Cooking in the nude didn't inspire this chapter. The naked truth is simply that food science is no more complicated than understanding a few basics. Just as reading, writing, and arithmetic in elementary school prepared you for mastering Shakespeare or calculus, the basic languages of cooking and science can take you from boiling water to making a meal.

And the most important key is water. Food is mostly water, and learning its ins and outs in cooking is as basic as it gets. Going beyond water, we'll show you how food ingredients are naturally packaged. Genes, cells, and molecules can be food, and because you are dealing with something that is or was alive, preparing food safely is a must. Food is enticing to you, but also to a host of other organisms that are not always user-friendly. Learning how to handle and preserve food has been a basic task for chefs since the first cook evolved. So, through gadgets, gizmos, experimentation, and chutzpah, you will gain confidence and understand that cooking isn't rocket science after all.

Chapter 1

The Science of Food

In This Chapter

- The curiosity of cooking
- Learning to deal with water
- From pots and pans to gadgets and gizmos
- Getting to the point: knife skills

Food used to be simple. There were farms, crops, animals, and grocers. Most people lived out of town, or wanted to. Science was people like Mr. Wizard in white lab coats who made the mysterious sound easy. Science was about gravity, or about drugs to make us well, but never about food.

Nowadays crops aren't just farmed, they are engineered. Most people live in the city or suburbs, but still yearn for the country life. And food is science, health, disease; it has become either good or bad. A line now exists between food as fun or simply fuel, and food as a drug to make us well or ill.

We are concerned more about our food partly because we are not as close to it anymore. Backyard gardens, Julia Child, and grandma's comfort food are all but gone, replaced by austere chefs and cooking as a spectator sport. It is bizarre diet books, invisible particles, numbers, and measures most times beyond our comprehension. Yet, food is not more complicated … we are.

As our understanding of science and food increases, it all seems much more confusing. But it need not be this way; food can be simply understood again. When we get down to the basics of science and food, it isn't all that difficult to tackle. And when you understand some scientific basics, your cooking will actually improve and become simpler. Recipes will be less intimidating and you'll realize Grandma was probably a great scientist, even if she didn't wear a lab coat.

All of this is what this chapter is about: understanding why your food does what it does when you prepare dinner.

From Salmon to Science

We have a theory that the first cook was really the founder of science. Why? Well, science is based upon curiosity. So is cooking. Science is based upon methods. So is cooking. Science is based upon biological and physical principles of sugars, fats, proteins, cells, water, and energy. So is food.

It is likely that one of our ancestors, let's call him Mr. Cro, was walking through the forest one day and saw a salmon migrating in a stream. Having endured living on raw roots, stems, and bark long enough, he wondered if perhaps the fish would taste good. So, he caught it and took it home to his wife, Mag. As fate would have it, Cro and Mag were having friends over that evening. They proudly displayed the raw salmon as part of their buffet. It was not a big hit; it was a challenging food to most guests. Of course, all were invited to take home the leftovers, and Mr. Non took most of the salmon.

Unperturbed by his first encounter with fish, Mr. Non was determined to try the salmon once again. As it happened, it was a chilly night and Non left the salmon by the fire. When he arose the next day, hot coals had blown atop the fish, charring the salmon. It smelled good. He tried it. He liked it. And so was born the art of cooking on open coals. Non's friends flocked to his place every Friday for salmon night. And the rest, as they say, is history.

> **Food for Thought**
> Food is other living things or their parts and products that we eat. Spinach is food for a rabbit, and both the rabbit and the spinach can be food for us. An egg is the product of a chicken. It can be food for us, or the egg yolk can be food for a developing chick, which can, in turn, be food for us.

The Importance of Water

I grew up with the impression that water was pretty important in life. How many movies or TV shows did I see where, whenever someone was about to have a baby, someone else was always told to go boil water. My sisters were always admonished to be able to at least boil water as a prelude to cooking, so that they could catch a man. I figured when I was six years old that babies, life, and the food on our table came from hot water somehow. So, it was not too mysterious to me that when I finally became an educated food scientist, and began to cook for myself, that I understood the principle importance of water in life and in the kitchen.

Cooking with Polarity and Molecules

No, you don't need a degree in physics to be a great cook, but as you will see, cooking really is scientific. Most of the food we eat is made up of water. Carrots and potatoes are virtually 95 percent water. Even the T-bone steak you eat with the veggies is about 50 percent water; the animal it came from is 60 percent water. Mom was correct when she admonished that cooking is no harder than boiling water. When we cook, we are really learning to handle the science of water. When you think about it, how difficult can that really be?

Because water is the primary component of all food, everything in the food has to navigate in water to go from point A to point B. Water's *polarity* keeps other charged molecules in suspended animation because they are soluble and mixable in water. For example, take a teaspoon of salt and a glass of water. You can see each substance clearly. Now mix the salt into the water. As you stir, the salt seems to disappear. It is still there, floating as molecules in the water, yet we don't see it. We can taste the salt, so we know it's there; it has simply changed form. If you heat the glass of salted water in a small pan until all of the water disappears, the salt reappears. Water is special.

> **Food for Thought**
> Water is a tasteless, odorless, colorless liquid; each water molecule consists of two hydrogen atoms and one oxygen atom, which scientists abbreviate as H_2O.

> **Chef Sez**
> **Polarity** is the electrical charge that things carry. Water is a molecule that can exist happily with other charged substances because it has a polarity of positive and negative force fields about it. Beam me up, Scotty.

Food molecules consist of four basic types: water, protein, fat, and carbohydrates (starches and sugars). Throw in some minerals, salts, and metals, and we pretty much can design any food product we want. And that pretty much designs us, too.

For the most part, proteins, and nearly all sugars are mixable with water because they share similar polar charges. Fats, on the other hand, do not mix with water readily. Fats aren't charged up a lot; they are more neutral. This means they lack sufficient polarity to mix with water. Fats just break up into smaller and smaller droplets, never dissolving or merging with the water. This is actually a good thing for food molecules because fats in the cell membrane give the cell structure, and keep the water and other mixable parts divided into their own little neighborhoods, keeping chaos at bay.

The "Bag Cell" Theory

Think of a resealable bag filled with water, proteins, and sugars. The bag itself is the fat membrane that locks all the other stuff in a neat package; you have a basic cell here. Now, if you take a bunch of these "bag cells" and hook them all together, you start building animal and plant tissue. It's like a jigsaw puzzle. The pieces can be made from the same material: our four food molecules, some salt, and some minerals, but how they all fit together is what gives each food puzzle a unique look.

Have you ever wondered why your cutting board and table gets wet when you chop an onion? You are breaking down the basics of food into its component parts, changing its form. You are changing the phases that the food appears to have. You are releasing water. So, when you cut, chop, and slice through the cells of food, you release water and the contents of some of the cells. Kind of like poking a hole in that resealable plastic bag and letting everything run out.

It's Just a Phase

When food is fresh and alive, the bag cells contain a mixture or *dispersion* of proteins, fats, and sugars in a unique form. When we prepare food to cook or just to eat raw, we are opening the bag, and affecting the cell contents. Take a carrot, for example. When we eat a fresh, raw carrot it has a unique flavor, texture, and feel in our mouth. When we bite into it, all those dispersed contents within the carrot cells are broken down in our mouth as we chew and grind. When we chop or grate the carrot before we eat it, we change its texture and form and a little of its perceived flavor. When we cook it we do more to the contents of the carrot cells; it looks different and tastes different.

> **Chef Sez** _____
> A **phase** is an area bordered by a closed surface. There are continuous phases, like a glass of fresh water. There are discontinuous phases, like the salt particles within the water. A **dispersion** is a collection of particles in a continuous phase, such as the fat in whipping cream.

Dispersions of food can exist as solids like our carrot, or as liquids, or gases, or various combinations of *phases* in liquid, gas, or solid form. Heavy cream is a liquid. Whipped cream is a foam. Both are merely cream. But we change the dispersion of heavy cream by beating air into it. We change its form, function, taste, and appearance. Sugar is a solid. When we heat it in a pan, it turns into a liquid. When we heat it to a dark color, it changes into a liquid with a decidedly different flavor. We will discuss the aspects of the change in foods as we proceed through this book.

The science of cooking is, in part, the process of changing food from one dispersed phase to another. It is the process of handling water. When we handle a food's water, we handle the contents of the food, because the water is the river that holds all the other molecules in place. So, if you can boil water, then you can learn to cook and to understand the science of cooking techniques. It's just a matter of degrees, not degrees from some noble institution of higher learning. Though the latter achievements can't hurt.

Understanding the Fundamentals of Lab Equipment

Changing food from one dispersed type to another—cooking—requires some hardware. And the kind of hardware really depends on the kinds of cooking and food processing you plan to do. They say there's a proper tool for every job. And there are also basic principles that apply in most cooking situations. Once you understand the fundamentals, you can decide what and how much hardware is right for you.

Metallurgy: Pots and Pans

No doubt our friends Cro, Mag, and Non all applied the most fundamental hardware as they began to experiment with cooking. Prior to the invention of metals, our ancestors were pretty much limited to open-flame cooking over hot coals. Of course, if you have ever visited the many steam geysers in Yellowstone Park, you can imagine how steaming food on rocks was also a poplar option for early restaurateurs. Yet, it was the perfection of modern metallurgy that changed the way we cook, and changed our cooking applications.

You should consider three things in selecting your kitchen lab equipment: price, durability, and care. While price and durability might give you a calculation of value, you should also factor in how much you intend to use any piece of equipment. After all, something that is very expensive and will last a long time may not be a good purchase if it never leaves your kitchen drawer.

Basic cookware is made from a variety of substances, each of which has different properties, different benefits, and different problems. Cast iron, stainless steel, copper, aluminum, and ceramics are the most common substances for home lab equipment.

Cast iron probably conjures the vision of grandma cooking in the kitchen. Comfort food and slow cooking were made for cast iron. It's also the best thing in the world for making genuine southern fried chicken. Cast iron is heavy and durable but does take some special care. It is moderately priced, and even old pieces picked up at a garage sale should still work beautifully. You don't just use cast iron straight out of the box, however. It requires seasoning, which blackens the surface and helps seal the pores of the metal so that food won't stick. Cast iron is susceptible to oxidation, also called rust. Seasoning with oil can prevent this.

Now You're Cooking

Seasoning is the process of curing your cast iron pan before you use it. First, wash the pan in warm soapy water and dry it well. Then rub a thin coating of vegetable or olive oil into the surface. You can't see it, but cast iron has tiny little pores just like your skin. The oil seals these pores, which keeps oxygen from rusting the pan and keeps food from sticking. After oiling the pan, preheat your oven to 250°F put the pan in, and one hour later turn the oven off. Leave the pan in the oven overnight. The next day, apply another coating of oil, and repeat the heating process. When the pan cools, it is ready to use. When you want to clean it after use, take some kosher salt and a dry paper towel and rub away all the cooked food particles. Kosher salt works better than table salt because the salt crystals are larger and more abrasive. As you rub them across the surface, they lift away the cooked-on food—no soap and water necessary. Oil the pan after cleaning it with the salt. You and the cast iron have now bonded and will have a nice, long, happy cooking life together.

Food for Thought

Anodized aluminum is made by a process of coating the aluminum surface with a dark, non-reactive layer that creates an inert seal between the metal and the food contact surface. It does not provide a nonstick coating, however. Anodized aluminum pots and pans are recommended for those who want the advantages of aluminum without the disadvantage of reactivity and discoloration of food.

Stainless steel cookware is also made from iron, but chrome and nickel are added into the process to create a very versatile and durable cooking metal. Two advantages of stainless steel are that it doesn't rust and it doesn't react to acidic foods. It is also pretty lightweight, so you needn't be Popeye to wield these pots and pans around. Stainless steel is great for mixing bowls and food-storage containers, but plain stainless steel tends to develop hot spots and cooks unevenly.

Aluminum is the lowest-priced metal for cookware. It is also the lightest weight and the second-best conductor of heat after copper.

Unfortunately, aluminum is less durable than cast iron or stainless steel. Because aluminum reacts with certain acids in food and with certain cooking procedures, the metal can leech into the food. Not only does this cause discoloration, but if consumed in large amounts, aluminum can be toxic.

Copper is the top option for cookware. Gleaming and shiny, it gives a real flare to a kitchen. It's a heavy metal that conducts heat extremely well and evenly. Yet, the price and the need for special care pose serious drawbacks for most cooks. Copper will react to acidic foods, and copper toxicity is a problem. To avoid these problems, copper cookware is usually lined with tin or stainless steel. Tin needs special care, but a stainless-steel lining combines the best of both … at a price, of course. Uncoated copper cookware, like cast iron, is susceptible to oxidation and discoloration and needs frequent cleaning and care.

Ceramics are a cooking medium unto their own. Ceramics contain some metals like aluminum but are mostly composed of earthy things like sand and clay. High heat is used to bond the materials into a solid, durable surface. Because ceramics contain less metal, heat is transferred slowly. Ceramic surfaces are slow to heat and slow to lose heat; they function as good insulators, which is terrific when you want to hold something hot, but less advantageous for quick heating. Durability, as you might expect, poses some problems. Ceramics are heavy and glasslike and can crack and peel. If you tend to abuse cookware, this might not be your best choice.

Food for Thought

Enamelware is a type of cookware combining the versatility of steel or aluminum with the unique properties of ceramics. A nonreactive ceramic coating is often applied over cast iron or aluminum to combine the advantages of both. Coatings such as Teflon and Silverstone are also silicon-based surfaces annealed to metal pans to create stick-resistant surfaces. Both ceramic-coated and Teflon-coated pans require special care. Metal spatulas are a definite no-no.

Whatever type of metal cookware you choose, and in most cases you will own several kinds, remember that size does matter. It's a good idea to stock your kitchen lab with saucepans ranging from 1 to 5 quarts. A larger stockpot or soup pot is also recommended. Pans that can fry and sauté come in small, medium, or large sizes. It's a good idea to have variety in your repertoire. A roasting pan and various baking pans round out your cooking equipment. Of course, mixing bowls of various sizes are essential. We recommend stainless steel bowls because of their versatility and durability.

Sauce pot

Sauté pan with sloped sides

Cast-iron skillet

Sauté pan with straight sides

Saucepan

If you are a newcomer to cooking, start collecting equipment based on the things you really need to do, and then acquire new tools as your technique improves.

Gadgets and Gizmos

Next to various methods for cutting food by hand, mixing and transferring food takes on prime importance. A supply of spatulas, spoons, ladles, and measuring cups are essential to the scientific kitchen. Throw in a good whisk for special mixing jobs. And for picking up food from hot surfaces, a pair of tongs (not thongs; save those for really special cooking occasions) are handy.

Another gadget that can be very handy in your kitchen lab is a food mill. Though mechanical blenders and food processors are a good addition to any kitchen, the simple food mill helps keep food flavor intact by gently grinding rather than pulverizing. Of course, if you really need food blasted to a very smooth consistency, nothing beats a mechanical food processor.

Food Mill

When a technique requires you to separate or sift, various sizes of strainers are handy. The finest—literally and figuratively—strainer is the chinois. This is a very fine-mesh conical strainer on a handle. This strainer is essential for making some of the classic sauces smooth and unctuous (which means pleasurably greasy in texture or appearance).

Chinois

Building an arsenal of kitchenware is not the objective, however. Start with the basics. Learn to use one thing well, and then go shopping for the next new gadget or gizmo.

Knives

The most important gadget or gizmo you need, whether a novice cook or a full-time professional, is a good set of knives. Taking food from its raw to processed state in your home kitchen involves more cutting, slicing, dicing, or peeling than just about

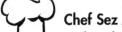

Chef Sez _____

High carbon stainless **steel** knives are forged to give maximum strength, durability, and sharpness to the blade surface. This type of knife material resists corrosion and yet is soft enough to take on a razor-sharp edge.

any other process. Purchasing a *high carbon stainless steel* chef's (a.k.a French) knife (there are numerous sizes) that fits the contour of your hand is as important as buying the correct shoes to fit your feet. You won't buy shoes without trying them on, and you shouldn't buy knives without checking for fit and comfort, either. And unlike shoes, good-quality knives can last a lifetime with proper care. You can fatigue your hand and yourself with ill-fitting cutlery. So, take some time to go to a good store and consult a competent blade smith when purchasing your first good-quality knives.

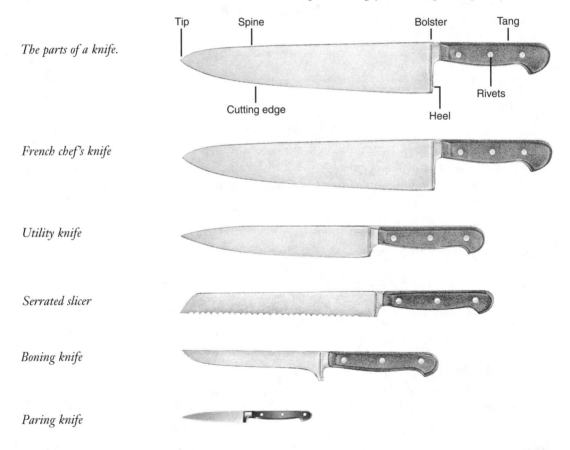

The parts of a knife.

Tip   Spine   Bolster   Tang
Cutting edge   Heel   Rivets

French chef's knife

Utility knife

Serrated slicer

Boning knife

Paring knife

Why bother with sharp knives when working with food? For one thing, sharp knives cut rather than crush. Remember that fresh food is built from tight, neat little packages of proteins, fats, sugars, and water. The contents of those packages—cells— is what you want to transfer to your pan and eventually to your stomach. Nothing is more wasteful than crushing food under the pressure of a dull knife. Do you really want to spill all of the good stuff found in fresh food on your cutting board? Remember, it's all about water and the food molecules that water contains. Slice, don't crush.

Another reason to have sharp cutlery is because the French built kitchen science upon the slice and the dice. Professional culinary students spend six weeks in boot camp training to practice knife skills before they get a whiff of a real kitchen.

Knife Skills

So, you've always wanted to go to cooking school, huh? Well, get that sharp knife out and grab some raw carrots and onions, and practice those knife skills. Your hard work won't go to waste, either. You can use your perfectly worked veggies (and the inevitable scraps) to make the stocks that we'll talk about in Chapter 23.

Too Hot to Handle
Dull knives are actually hazardous to your health. Knives that have a dull edge or fit poorly in your hand can slip on wet, juicy food. And because you have to exert more pressure to use a dull knife, any cut that results can be catastrophic. So, remember, sharp knives are better for you and your food.

Onionology 101

The first thing to do is learn the proper way to dice an onion. Take a medium yellow onion and remove the peel.

Slice it in half by cutting from end to end, right through the roots. Leave the root ends attached to each half. This will hold the onion together while you finish cutting it.

Now, with the root end facing away from you, and the half of the onion lying with its flat side down, make parallel slices about $1/2$-inch wide from one side of the half onion to the other. If you are right-handed, hold the onion with your left hand, fingertips tucked under, using your thumb to stabilize the onion. As you slice from top to bottom, while moving right to left across the onion, your left-hand fingers act as a guide, moving ahead of the blade each time. Let your knuckles gently touch the side of the knife, so that they can act as a guide as you move along. Never cut through the root tip, just up to it. Now, turn the onion 90 degrees so that the root tip is on the left. With your left hand flat on top of the onion to steady it, make a cut perpendicular to the slices by drawing your knife from right to left in the middle of the onion. Now make a series of slices, moving right to left, proceeding toward the root tip. You should now have successfully diced the onion. You discard the root-tip piece. This entire process is one of the most basic cuts to master in Onionology 101. Congratulations.

Use a paring knife to remove the stem end, but leave the root end intact. Peel away the outer skin, being careful not to remove and waste too much of the onion.

Cut the onion in half from end to end.

Cut parallel slices of the desired thickness from the root toward the stem end. Do not cut completely through the root.

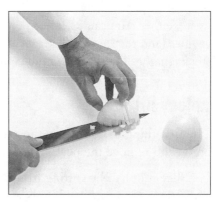

Make a couple of horizontal cuts through the onion, again without cutting through the root end.

Finally, cut slices perpendicular to the first slices in order to produce diced onion.

Preparing to Cut, Slice, and Dice

The other cuts with funny names take a bit more effort. You can practice all of them with a nice large carrot. Peel it with your paring knife or vegetable peeler. Now, cut the carrot into 2-inch-long pieces. You usually end up with 3 of these from an average carrot.

Take the piece from the biggest blunt side of the carrot. You will see that it is rounded and not at all flat sided. Because you want to practice making slices with flat sides, you need to take care of this problem, so create a rectangle with flat sides by trimming the carrot. To do that, point one tip of your piece of carrot away from you. Then carefully slice off the side on the right, cutting away about $1/8$ inch. Now you have a flat surface on one side. Lay this flat-side down. Repeat the cut. Now you have two flat sides. Repeat by laying the most recent flat side down and making another slice. And finally, repeat one more time. Now you have a 4-sided, flat, 2-inch hunk of carrot. Trim each tip end flat and you should have something that looks like a rectangle. So far, so good.

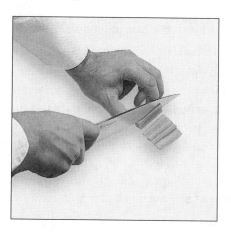

Square the item and trim it to the desired length. Cut even slices of the proper thickness.

Cut the slices into sticks of the same thickness.

Batonnet Cut

Now we are going to do what is called a batonnet cut. What we will end up with is a 2-inch-long piece of carrot with $1/4$-inch sides, which looks somewhat like a matchstick. Because you already have a 2-inch-long hunk of rectangle-shaped carrot, the 2-inch part of the work is already done. So, to make the strips, just measure in $1/4$ inch on one side and make a slice. Continue to do this $1/4$-inch slice all the way across the rectangle of carrot. You should now have a series of 2-inch-wide by $\frac{1}{4}$-inch-thick strips. Next, lay each strip down flat, and cut $\frac{1}{4}$-inch pieces, working from right to left again. When you get really good, you can stack the strips and cut your $\frac{1}{4}$-inch pieces all at once. The end point is that you have $\frac{1}{4}$-inch by $\frac{1}{4}$-inch by 2-inch long strips of carrot.

Julienne

Once you have mastered the batonnet cut, move on to the julienne, also sometimes called the allumette. The only difference between this one and the batonnet from the previous section is the size of the finished pieces. First, make your flat-sided 2-inch-long pieces just like before. Next, cut $\frac{1}{8}$-inch slices rather than $\frac{1}{4}$-inch slices. Then lay the broad strips down, and cut $\frac{1}{8}$-inch pieces from them. All the other steps are the same as for the batonnet.

Fine Julienne

Hungry for another challenge? Okay, move on to the fine julienne. It's the same technique, but now the slices are only $\frac{1}{16}$-inch thick.

If you have been a busy beaver and end up with $\frac{1}{4}$-, $\frac{1}{8}$-, and $\frac{1}{16}$-inch batonnet, julienne, and fine julienne respectively, you can turn them into nice, perfect little cubes we call dice. You know what dice are—the little cubes used to play a gambling game. Well, vegetable dice are cubes we use to make dinner with; you don't roll them, you cook them. So, to make a $\frac{1}{4}$-inch dice, select your $\frac{1}{4}$-inch batonnet and begin to cut them into $\frac{1}{4}$-inch cubes from right to left. Line up the batonnet like little soldiers in groups of three or four, measure $\frac{1}{4}$ inch, and cut them. You now have perfect little cubes of a $\frac{1}{4}$-inch dice. You can see how quick it is to make a bunch of $\frac{1}{4}$-inch diced carrots.

Brunoise

If you use the $\frac{1}{8}$-inch julienne strips, and cut them into $\frac{1}{8}$-inch cubes, you now have what is called a brunoise. And, of course, a fine brunoise is your $\frac{1}{16}$-inch cubes.

You can get crazy and create $\frac{3}{4}$-inch, $\frac{1}{3}$-inch, or 1-inch pieces by just making these from your 2-inch hunk of carrot, or potato, or celery, jicama, or whatever. The sky's the limit. Mastering these basic cuts will help you to cook better. And once you have proceeded through this basic training, you'll have an appreciation for food and the beauty than can be created very simply.

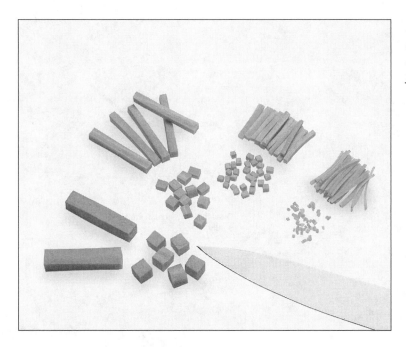

Batonnet and julienne sticks and the large, medium, small, and brunoise dice cut from them.

Keeping It Sharp and Sweet

All of the traditional French cuts, from julienne to brunoise to large dice, were not meant to create busy work for fledgling cooks and apprentices. Food cut into uniform shapes not only looks better; it also cooks more evenly, maintains its character better, and lets you utilize what nature intended. A sharp knife lets you make accurate cuts. This preserves the appearance, taste, and texture of food. You can have your knives sharpened by a professional service or cutlery store, but if you really want to cook like the pros, we highly recommend adding a *sharpening stone* and *steel* to your gadget collection and doing it yourself.

Finally, cutting requires a good surface. We recommend wood or plastic cutting boards. They not only create a neat, organized work area for you, but they also help you keep your knives sharp by extending their life. Nothing dulls a knife quicker than cutting against a hard metal or nonporous surface such as marble or glass.

Chef Sez

A **sharpening stone** is a porous sandstone rock surface that, when oiled, is used to smooth the nicks and damage that occurs to the edge of knives as they are used. A **sharpening steel** is a diamond surface rod that is used to hone or create the alignment of the steel metal into a fine, smooth cutting surface.

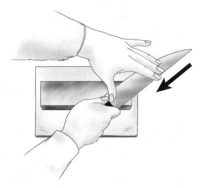

Use four fingers of the guiding
hand to maintain constant pressure.

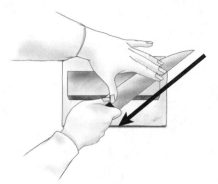

Draw the knife across the stone
gently.

Finish with the knife by drawing it all the way
through to the tip.

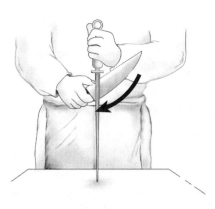

Repeat the action with the blade against the
steel's other side.

Hold the steel in a near-vertical position with the
tip resting on a nonslippery surface. Start with the
heel of the knife against one side of the steel.

Maintain light pressure and use an arm action,
not a wrist action, to draw the knife down the
shaft of the steel.

Finish with the knife by drawing it all the way
through to the tip.

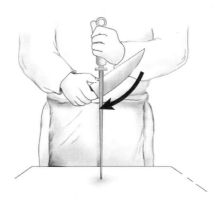

Repeat the action with the blade against the
steel's other side.

The Least You Need to Know

◆ Food is mostly water. The science of cooking is learning to deal with it.

◆ Price, durability, and intended use affect the types of cooking pots and pans
you'll choose for your kitchen.

◆ Beginning cooks should first acquire the basic items needed to execute a few
cooking fundamentals, and then add kitchenware as skill and ability increase.

◆ Stirring, measuring, flipping, whisking, puréeing, and straining are common
techniques all requiring some basic kitchen utensils.

◆ Sharp knives are safer for you and treat food with respect; buy a sharpening
stone and steel and learn to use them properly … you won't regret it.

◆ Classical French cutting techniques preserve food flavor, encourage even cooking, determine food texture, and enhance the appearance of the food.

Good Food Gone Bad

In This Chapter

- ◆ America's most wanted
- ◆ What you can do to defend yourself
- ◆ The best defense is a good offense

We have the FBI, the CIA, the FDA, the USDA, and the EPA to help protect us. We have ingredient labels and nutrition labels. We have diet doctors, diet columns, and medical solutions for everything from impotence to wrinkled skin. Yet, when handling food, the plain and simple fact is that we are our own worst enemy. And the danger to your health is more alarming than just about anything else in the food world.

Even on your healthiest day, your body is teaming with harmful microorganisms. These tiny, invisible creatures are opportunists, just waiting for the chance to multiply and colonize. And they really love human food. To these bugs, your dinner ingredients are just as inviting to them as a trip to some tropical beach is to you; a nice warm place, plenty of moisture, great dining, and a chance to kick back and get it on after dark. Understanding food safety problems, and how to prevent these risky situations, is as important as any cooking class you can take.

America's Most Wanted

Maybe if our post office walls had pictures of the real most dangerous culprits we would have better luck dealing with *food-borne illness*. Most of what makes us ill from contaminated food is due to good old basic biology. You can get sick from *chemical* contamination of food such as insecticides or things you use to clean your house. You can also become ill from *physical* contaminants that might end up in your food, such as pieces of glass or metal.

> **Chef Sez**
> A **food-borne illness** is an infection or an intoxication caused by ingesting contaminated food. **Bacteria** are single-celled organisms, some of which are responsible for food-borne illness. They are tiny little bugs. If the tip of your dinner fork was contaminated with them, about 500 might be perched on just one tine ready for the ride to your inner sanctum.

But chemical and physical contaminants comprise less than 5 percent of all food-borne illnesses. You, the food itself, and other living things are the real culprits for 95 percent of all food-borne illnesses. *Bacteria*, mold, yeast, viruses, other single-celled bugs called protozoa, and even worms can make us sick when they turn up in food. Whew, a long list for sure; but for the most part, it is the presence of various bacteria that causes most food-borne illnesses. Oddly enough, you cannot necessarily see, smell, or taste these dangerous microorganisms. For example, the critters that make food smell bad are not always the ones that make us sick. In fact, many of the worst offenders only make themselves known via your gastrointestinal track, some 12 to 24 hours after consumption.

Important Organisms That Can Cause Food-Borne Illness

Culprit	Type of Organism	Common Food Source	Symptoms of Illness
Staphylococcus aureus	Bacteria w/toxins	Eggs, custard, stuffing, potato salad, and warmed leftovers	Nausea, cramps, diarrhea, vomiting
Salmonella	Bacteria	Eggs, poultry, shellfish, meat, soup, and gravies	Headache, nausea, cramps, diarrhea, fever
Campylobacter	Bacteria	Poultry, eggs, meat, and dairy foods	Severe abdominal pain and bloody diarrhea
Clostridium perfingens	Bacteria w/toxins	Home-canned food, low-acid foods, and improperly smoked food	Vomiting, sore throat, and blurred vision

Culprit	Type of Organism	Common Food Source	Symptoms of Illness
Ergot poisons	Molds	Wheat and rye grains	Hallucinations and convulsions
Listeria	Bacteria	Lunch meat; hot dogs; and soft, fresh cheeses	Fever, diarrhea, and vomiting
E. coli 0157:H7	Bacteria w/toxins	Ground meat, sprouts, and unpasteurized juice	Severe cramps, bloody diarrhea, and vomiting

You can see from this table that a bunch of organisms can make us ill, but how do they do it? How can something as small as a microorganism (so-called because we need a microscope to even see them), hurt big people like us?

We can either become intoxicated or infected by ingesting pathogenic critters. If you imbibe in alcohol, no doubt at least once in your life you had a few too many; you became intoxicated. Alcohol is a toxin that can poison you if it reaches too high a level in your blood. Likewise, *food-borne intoxication* occurs if bacteria grow on our food and produce some toxic stuff that we eat. It's the toxins that make us sick, not the bacteria themselves.

Certain bugs are notorious for such toxic secretions, especially ones called *Staphylococcus aureus*, or Staph for short. Lots of us carry these little beggars around in our nose, or on our hands. You might think that Staph is pretty harmless because it lives on us all the time, but they are a form of bacteria that pack a punch when they take up residency in the wrong places, such as yesterday's rice pudding or mishandled salad greens. And the worse thing about Staph is that, when they live on your food, they produce a toxic waste dump worth of byproducts. Even if you then heat the food enough to kill the organisms, you will still get sick from the toxins they've left behind. The toxins are resistant to heat short of incineration. And most of us don't like our food that well done. So, with Staphylococcus, the big emphasis is on prevention through safe food-handling techniques.

Now, if you can avoid food intoxication, you still need to watch out for bacteria that can cause *food infections*. Unlike food intoxication where the toxin is the thing that makes us sick, an infection occurs when we actually ingest living organisms. And when these bugs get inside us, they do their dirty deeds. You see, bugs that can infect us are just happy to hang out on our food, passing the day away, waiting for us to eat them. *Salmonella* is one of these; you know the type: cunning, sly, and unassuming until you get them in your stomach. Then they do a personality switch, causing you to wish you had been more careful with last night's leftover chicken and rice.

Survival of the Fittest

So, how in the world did humans ever evolve, given the dangers posed by the bacterial world? Why are bacteria, and not we, at the height of the food chain? When you realize the thin line between a healthy dish and one that can kill you, it seems a miracle that we're still here.

Well, humans have actually been rather ingenious in combating food-borne illness for a very long time. Food ingredients and techniques that are antibacterial include spices, peppers, salting, drying, pickling, and smoking. The way different cultures have approached this problem is rather intriguing, and involves fundamental food science.

Take, for instance, spices and spicy food. Some food scholars believe that spices evolved to not only flavor food but also, in an indirect way, make it safe for us to consume. Various herbs and spices actually are anti-microbial. Those who used them likely were around long enough to pass on their biological and cultural genes because they lessened the chance of dying from a food-borne illness. So, the next time you enjoy sage, or a hot tamale, thank your ancestors for cultural recipes passed on through the ages.

Other cultures resorted to various preservation methods to make food taste good and make it safer to eat. Salting or pickling, as well as dry curing and smoking (which we talk about in Chapter 5) were used for centuries to preserve food from one harvest to the next. Survival of the fittest is likely attributed to our running a food race against the bugs of the world for supremacy. So far, we are just a tad bit ahead.

Not All Relationships Are Bad

All bacteria or microorganism are not bad for us. If this were the case, you would never enjoy the pleasures of cheese, wine, beer, aged meats, leavened bread, yogurt, or a bunch of other good stuff. The secret is pretty simple. Create an environment on the food that favors the good bugs over the bad ones. It's simple population control.

A basic rule in biology is that two organisms cannot inhabit the exact same niche at the same time; something has to give. We only violate this basic tenet once in a while, and that usually occurs when mothers-in-law move in. But normally, in the real world of food microbiology, we cultivate good bacteria, yeasts, and molds to outgrow their bad counterparts. The good bugs then do work for us. They secrete acids and all kinds of products by using the food we let them grow on as a nutrient. We, in turn, use them and the tasty secretions they give to the food as a great source of nourishment. The whole process is called a commensal relationship. So, the bottom line is, don't start spraying your disinfectants everywhere and try to rid the world of all bugs. It would be a really boring food world out there if you did.

The Story of Life

The goal of every living creature is to be born and to grow, mature, reproduce, and pass along its genetic material. We do it, and bugs do it. Understanding more about where and why bacteria like to live really is the first step to understanding the problem of food-borne illnesses. Understanding and responding to that knowledge is the first step in keeping bacteria in check.

Moisture

If food is so dangerous, why is it okay to keep some items in the cupboard without refrigeration? Why aren't bags of dried pasta or boxes of crackers a problem? Well, it's all about water. We may sound like a broken record, but water is essential for bacterial life.

There are lots of moisture-laden foods hanging around your kitchen. Unless you are a vegetarian, you have an ample supply of meat on a daily basis in your kitchen. Fresh meats like beef, poultry, and seafood have very high moisture content. Next on the scale are cheeses, especially fresh or soft higher-moisture types, and, of course, milk. Then you might have a fridge full of processed deli meats. Most deli meats are only partially cooked, so they are really appetizing to the bug world. In fact, all this good stuff is fair game for bacterial infiltration.

Now, what about the plant world? Most fresh fruits and vegetables serve as a potential smorgasbord for roving bands of bugs. And since many vegetables are raised with organic fertilizers like manure, they are potentially teaming with a variety of organisms from worms to *E. coli* bacteria. Just remember, you may be eating "natural," but natural includes a whole army of potentially dangerous organisms. What could be more natural than *E. coli*? Think about that the next time you're munching on organic beans sprouts and tofu. Remember, too, that plants are about 95 percent water and are very good at satisfying a bug's thirst. Throw in a pan of cooked rice or maybe last night's mashed potatoes, and you have some good things in your kitchen that, if improperly handled, can make you very ill.

> **Food for Thought**
> Water makes up 70 percent to 95 percent of what constitutes food. So, moisture is the first element in considering what and where bacteria, molds, or yeasts do it. They like it wet, and they can make it rather wild.

So, the first thing you need to know is that microorganisms like to invade those high-moisture foods and set up some command centers. Dry foods can be relatively safe, however. Stuff such as corn flakes, sugar, dried beans, crackers, and dried milk powder is inhospitable to bacteria. If you can store dried goods away from vermin such as mice and creepy crawly bugs, your chances of contracting a food-borne illness from these foods are pretty low.

Energy Source

Like us, no bug wants to set up shop without having a handy food store close by for those midnight cravings. Bacteria need an energy source. They like protein just as we like protein. They like a touch of sugar just as we like a touch of sugar. So, the bottom line is that if it has water and some good nutrients such as protein and sugar, it will be good food for the bugs. Their mission is to eat and enjoy it before you do. Nature favors an opportunist.

Safe Environment

Another thing that germs appreciate is a nice safe, neutral environment. We don't like to always eat foods that are very bitter or very sour. We prefer the lower acid and lower basic stratosphere, more commonly called the neutral food world. It should come as no surprise to learn that bacteria also prefer the neutral zone. Unfortunately, it just so happens that most foods are neutral, with a *pH* between 4.0 and 7.0. Seafood, meats, potatoes, corn, milk, carrots, rice, and pasta products all are considered dangerous foods because their pH fits this range of values. Find a food with a neutral pH, high-water content, and protein or starch nutrients, and you have something that bacteria can really sink their teeth into. And once they sink their teeth into your food, they'll soon be sinking their teeth into you.

> **Chef Sez**
>
> **pH** is the abbreviation for "potential of hydrogen," a fancy way of measuring the amount of acid in a substance. On a scale of 1 to 14, 7.0 is the neutral midpoint, 1 is very acidic, and 14 is very basic or alkaline. Distilled and purified water is the neutral standard bearer at pH 7.0. Most foods are neutral to slightly acidic in nature.

Time

Bacteria are not speed freaks, however. Even under the best of conditions, they need time to reproduce enough (or produce enough toxin) to cause us problems. In the heat of the night, that rice casserole left sitting on the dinner table all evening becomes an orgy of bacterial ecstasy. By the time you get around to wrapping it and putting it in the refrigerator, the damage is done. And of course, what do we do—we have these inappropriately handled leftovers, for dinner the next evening. Definitely not a good idea.

The Best Defense Is a Good Offense

So, what are we to do? We have teams of bacteria living on us, just waiting to strike terror into our homemade potato salad. And if bugs live on us, they surely live on the animals that provide our meat, and in the garden soil that produces our vegetables. And to top it all off, the air is also filled with all kinds of mold, yeasts, bacteria, and heavens-knows what else. It's a jungle out there. So, to lessen our chances of a food-borne illness, we need to get them before they get us.

Modern health agencies and progressive restaurants are doing what is called Hazard Analysis of Critical Control Points (*HACCP* for short) as the best offensive weapon against food-borne illness. It can work for you in the home as well. HACCP is a system to preempt the growth of bad microorganisms and keep these little beggars in check.

Chef Sez

HAACP is a plan for food safety based upon understanding the dangers in handling any food or recipe, devising ways to circumvent the hazardous steps, and then periodically checking to make sure we are on target with our plan. Food can be essentially sterilized by **irradiation**. Irradiated food is exposed to ionizing energy that literally blows up all the bacteria. You can also sterilize things using a pressure chamber and high heat that zaps the bugs. This is called an **autoclave**. Doctors and dentists do that to their surgical instruments but you probably won't do it much to your hot dogs or sausages at home.

The success of an HAACP program, or any food-safety program you apply in your kitchen laboratory, is to think about what we just talked about: What makes bacteria happy?

Clean Yourself

First, we need to understand that bugs exist on our food from day one. Nothing that we handle is sterile. After all, unless we have *autoclaved* every bit of our food-handling equipment, or have *irradiated* all food during processing, we could never approach a bacteria-free food source. So, we first live with the fact that all foods are potential targets for bacterial growth and that all food has bugs. We can handle a few microorganisms on our food. Our job is to keep them from growing out of control.

Second, if the food has germs and we have germs on us, then we have the classic case of 1+1=2. When we touch and handle food, we are transferring germs from us to the food and vice versa. So, our first line of HAACP defense is to go on the offensive to limit the transfer of bacteria from us to the food and back again. The first and foremost way to do this is to wash us and wash the food. Need we say, it's all about water here, too?

Nice hot water with soap is the best first step to safer food handling. Soaps need not contain any disinfectants to be effective. Plain old soap is a natural agent that strips the bacteria of its outer cell coat. A naked bacteria is an unhappy bacteria. So, the first thing you need to do when you enter your kitchen laboratory is to wash your hands. I like to sing the Happy Birthday jingle when washing my hands. Singing this twice as you wash gives you sufficient time to really scrub well. Besides, it makes you feel good even if it's not your birthday. So, no matter what other steps you take to combat food-borne illnesses in your kitchen, hand-washing is the first and the most important.

Hand-washing also means doing it more than once. In other words, if you are working with food and you brush back your hair or scratch your face, you've now contaminated your hand again. So, wash up those hands frequently when working in the kitchen. We are not requiring a full-body wash here; just use some common sense when scratching your nose or fixing your hair or taking a smoke. And need we mention the hand-washing procedure following a bathroom break? I didn't think so.

A hat also helps. Chefs didn't invent the toque, that large stove-pipe appendage, for its sartorial splendor. A hat keeps hair out of your food. Actually, a baseball cap does a better job and stays on more easily, but whatever type of head gear juices your lemon, wear something. Gloves, you ask? Well, in some states they are mandatory where food is handled for public consumption. But gloves can easily become contaminated themselves and give a false sense of security. Frequent washing is a better alternative unless, of course, you are working with something that might hurt your skin. Then by all means, glove up. Once you are clean, it's time to clean the food.

Clean Your Food

Fresh vegetables are easy to clean. The chlorine content of most domestic water sources is sufficient to help kill surface organisms. Don't use soap on food! Why, you ask? For one reason, soaps are not edible foods. The residues can make you sick. If restaurants cannot use soap on food because it is not an approved practice by FDA, then you should also refrain. Brushes that can be used to scrub off surface dirt are also recommended for some root vegetables. We can rinse veggies under the water tap or, if we have lots of loose pieces like mushrooms or fresh spinach, float them in a sink of fresh water. By dunking them a time or two and then letting the debris settle to the bottom of the sink, we can scoop out the clean loose veggies from the top of the water and drain off the water.

Now You're Cooking
First things first though. Make sure your sink is clean before you start to clean the veggies. It's always a good idea to start out in a nice clean working environment; after all, you wouldn't want to take a bath in somebody else's bath water now would you? So neither do those living, breathing vegetables.

Freshly washed salad greens can be spun dry in a salad spinner. This nice little gizmo is hand cranked and uses centrifugal force and a series of screens to do a good job of drying off your greens. And, as you'll learn later, it's really important to dry your greens before dressing them.

Special rules apply whenever you handle meat. To be safe, you should just assume that the surface of all meats, especially poultry, is contaminated with some *Salmonella* or *E. coli* bacteria during slaughter and processing. Salmonella is a class of rod-shaped bacteria naturally found with common foods like eggs, poultry, pork, and seafood. Because some types of Salmonella are found in the soil, many foods can come into contact with these bacteria. E. coli is also a diverse group of bacteria. Some species naturally live in our intestinal tract, so not all E. coli are harmful. In fact, good E. coli actually helps keep its bad bacterial relatives in check. One of the bad E. coli, called O157:H7, can make us very sick. Conditions that lead to possible contamination by E. coli 0157:H7 are any instances during processing when the food is exposed to potential fecal contamination. These include during slaughter and meat cutting, preparation of wild game, and any contact with manure such as organic gardening.

To prevent these bad boys from spreading around your kitchen, meat products should always be handled separately from other food. Blood and packaging material should be disposed of quickly and cleanly; knives, cutting boards, and other surfaces must be cleaned thoroughly after coming in contact with such foods. And, you might ask, should we wash meat? The answer is no. Studies actually show that washing meat spreads more bacteria than it destroys, leading to a greater level of contamination. Remember, you are going to cook all meat to a safe temperature. So, just handle it safely through each preparation step.

Always clean the cutting board and all of your knives when you move from one job to another. That knife you just used to cut up a chicken is now coated with bacteria. If you don't wash them off before you slice onions, you will just transfer the germs from one food to another. And if you happen to be using the onion raw in a salad, you can have real food safety problems.

Chef Sez

Cross contamination is the transfer of biological, physical, or chemical contaminants from one food to another, usually during processing, cooking, or serving. For example, if bacteria from one food item contaminate a cutting board, then when a second food touches that cutting board it will also become contaminated.

Cross contamination can happen, too, if other critters are running across your food or have invaded your kitchen. The worst culprit is the common housefly. They are simply flying germ-warfare agents carrying bacterial contamination to everything they contact. And if flies don't get you in trouble, insects like cockroaches will. The best defense you have against these vermin is to eradicate the living conditions they crave. Keep your countertops and cupboards clean, avoid standing water and open packages of food, and call in a real pest-control pro as needed.

Check Your Temperature

So, now we have clean hands, cleaner food, and we are working to avoid cross contamination. We have not eliminated all the bacteria, but we have succeeded in keeping them at bay. We aren't "bubble people," so we have to devise our HAACP plans to reduce bug growth. We know bacteria like things moist, not too acidic, and high in nutrients. The next area to be concerned about is temperature. Just as food has a danger zone for pH, food also has a danger zone for temperature. Controlling food pH is not always easy or desirable. Most of us prefer not to eat food that is always pickled, smoked, or brined. If we did, we would all live in Scandinavia. So, that leaves us with no alternative but to control the temperature of food as we prepare it.

Bacteria like to live in a range of temperatures from about 40 to 140°F. Not surprisingly then, we set our refrigerator temperature to be somewhere between 36 and 39°F so that it will be too cool for bacteria to reproduce. And when we heat food above 144°F for at least 30 minutes, we have effectively *pasteurized* it, killing the critters that can potentially cause problems. Given that food has germs on its surface, when we let food stay within the bug comfort zone for more than four hours, these little beggars skyrocket in population. So, your best bet is to keep food out of the temperature danger zone. Temperature control is effective birth control for bacteria.

Chef Sez

Pasteurization is the process of heating foods above the danger zone for bacterial growth to reduce contamination. Foods must be heated to an internal temperature of 144°F for 30 minutes or 160°F for 15 seconds.

Ready for some yummy leftover clam chowder? Let's say you did a good job of covering and refrigerating the soup immediately after lunch. Unfortunately, you did not cool it down first; you just put it back in the refrigerator in a rather deep pot. Well, the outside of the soup might get cool, but if the pot is big, the center of the soup in that pot may take five hours or longer to cool down below 40°F. And as long as the internal temperature is in the danger zone, bacteria are reproducing like crazy; you've created a ticking time bomb in the center of that soup.

So, here's the scene at dinner. You take that soup out of the fridge and give it a good stir, mixing all those germs and their toxins throughout the soup. But, you say, I did heat the soup again, so that should have killed the bad bugs, right? Well, yes, you probably torched some of the bugs that might cause an infection, but you may not have gotten all of them. Even more important, while the *Staphylococcus* was sitting in the middle of that nice warm soup, it churned out bunches of toxins, which cannot be destroyed by mere heat. Toxins are proteins that do not completely break down under normal cooking temperatures when we heat food. As little as 1 microgram of a toxin can make you sick. To give you an idea of how small that is, that's the equivalent of $1/5{,}000{,}000$ of a teaspoon of sugar. So, once the toxins are in the soup, you will be eating a wonderfully contaminated elixir. And though you may be rather intoxicating to your dinner date, whom you've invited over for some chowder and a movie, she/he may not appreciate just how "intoxicated" they felt by morning.

To avoid these deadly scenarios, keep cold food cold and hot food hot. This means below 40°F or above 140°F. And, most important, when you store leftovers, cool them down before storing them in the refrigerator. Transferring food from larger to smaller containers, and letting them sit in the sink or a large bowl in an ice bath does a good job of cooling the food quickly.

And never, ever leave leftovers like rice, potatoes, casseroles, or egg dishes at room temperature for more than two hours. Improper storage of cooked leftovers is second only to lack of hand-washing as the leading cause of food-borne illness for the home cook. If you can eliminate these two sources of food handling errors, you are well on your way to healthier eating.

The Least You Need to Know

- ◆ Foods harbor organisms that have the potential to make you sick. You cannot necessarily see, smell, or taste these microorganisms.
- ◆ Foods with the greatest potential to make you sick are those proteins and starches with a neutral pH and significant water content.

- Frequent, thorough hand-washing is your best defense against a food-borne illness.

- Keep tools and work surfaces clean, and work with meats separately from other foods.

- Keep hot foods hot and cold foods cold.

- Always cool leftovers quickly before storing them in the refrigerator. This is best done by transferring the food to a clean container, and then cooling the container in an ice bath.

Raw vs. Cooked: Principles of Heating and Cooling

In This Chapter

- ◆ Cooking is transferring heat
- ◆ The moist-heat method
- ◆ "But it's the dry heat"
- ◆ Combo methods: stewing and braising

Our teeth and digestive system pretty much dictate the types of food we eat and what suits us best. We have small canine teeth, good for ripping and shredding, so meat is a part of our diet, just like it is for a lion. But a lion has much bigger, and sharper, canine teeth, which can be useful if all of your meat is consumed raw. We also have some grinders, our molars, so we can handle raw foods with fiber. In a way we are like cattle, but unlike our four-stomached bovine friends, we have only one stomach. So, cattle are a bit more competitive at grazing than us. Besides, they carry around a lot more bugs in their digestive tract and can handle all of that fresh grass. We humans prefer our grass in a much different form.

So, we fit somewhere in between carnivores and herbivores. Our bodies can handle both meat and vegetables. Somewhere along the way, call it serendipity, humans learned that cooked meat and veggies tasted better than raw. Applying heat to food does make it easier to chew, swallow, and digest. Heat kills bacteria and inactivates toxins that might harm us, making foods safer to eat. Learning the correct methods of heating and how those methods apply to certain foods is the *art* of cooking; understanding why they're correct is the *science* of cooking.

Conduction, Convection, and Radiation

The transfer of heat to and then through food is what cooks it. How that heat is transferred determines the basis for classifying cooking methods and techniques. The simplest method is conduction, which is the direct transfer of energy from point A to

Food for Thought

Heat is the energy of motion we measure by temperature. Energy is applied to create heat, which cooks our food; as energy is removed, the food cools. In other words, cool food just has less energy being applied to it.

point B. If I hand you a bucket of water an arm's length away, and you hand it to another person by simply reaching out, and that person, in turn, does the same thing, we have made a transfer through direct contact. This is the basis of conduction. In cooking, when a steak hits a sizzling pan, heat is transferred directly from the flame to the pan and from the pan to the steak's exterior surface. Eventually that heat moves from the outside surface to the center of the steak by conduction.

Arrows indicate patterns of heat flow during conduction, convection, and radiation.

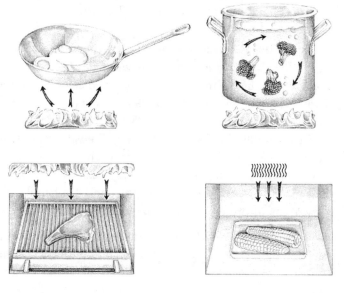

Now, let's say that I hand you a bucket, but I need to walk across the room to deliver it. You, in turn, have to walk some distance to the next person, who walks upstairs to deliver it once again. This is more than just direct contact; there is more flow required. Convection is heat transfer in a liquid (such as water, stock, or fat) or gas (air) as the energy flows from point A to point B. You know the old adage, "hot air rises?" Well, that's exactly what convection is. Hot air or hot water rises toward the top of an oven or a saucepot, forcing cooler air or liquid down to where the heat source is located. This creates rolling, swirling movements of heat known as convection currents.

A loaf of bread placed on the middle shelf of an oven is about six inches above the oven's heat source. Heat energy flows through the air in the oven before it comes in contact with the bread. Once the oven shelf heats up, the baking pan will also heat up from conduction, and then there is a direct transfer of energy from the pan to the bread. A potato rolling around in boiling water is another example of convection. Rolling, swirling currents of heat surround the potato.

The heat energy used for cooking can be generated by a gas range or electric burners, an outdoor charcoal grill or by rubbing two sticks together. The source of the energy isn't really that important; it just depends on how your home lab—you know, your kitchen—is equipped. Once the necessary heat is available, conduction and convection both require some contact along the way to move the energy from point A to point B. Radiation, another form of energy transfer, does not require such contact. Radiation is the pure movement of heat or light through microwave or infrared energy. When we talk about microwave cooking in Chapter 4, we will discuss the use of radiation more fully.

Food for Thought
Cooking is the application of energy, usually in the form of heat, to food. This energy alters the food's molecular structure, changing its texture, flavor, aroma, and appearance.

Principles of conduction, convection, and radiation are best applied to cooking when we consider the food itself. You may not have thought much about this, but every food has surfaces. Food has edges, boundaries, exteriors, and interiors. Food has depth. Some food is naturally thick in shape or texture, while other food is thin as a solid or runny as a liquid. We can make food take the shape we want. We peel, we slice, and we dice, all in order to get food into more manageable shapes. We can thin something that is thick, or thicken something that is thin. We can increase or decrease its volume. We want to manage and do all of these things to food before it is cooked, because the bottom line is that we need to be able to apply energy—cook it—evenly.

Cooking Methods One, Two, Three

All cooking methods fall into three general categories: moist-heat cooking methods, dry-heat cooking methods, and methods using a combination of both. How tonight's dinner turns out is pretty much a result of which method you choose to use.

Moist Heat

Moist-heat cooking methods are those techniques that use water to transfer heat. When you *simmer*, boil, *poach*, or *steam* you are using moist-heat cooking techniques. The food is being cooked in a water-based liquid such as wine, stock, or water itself.

> **Chef Sez**
>
> **Steaming** is a moist-heat cooking method in which food is cooked by direct contact with the hot steam rising off of a boiling liquid; the food is placed in a basket or rack above the liquid in a covered pan. **Poaching** is a moist-heat cooking method that uses convection to transfer heat from a 160–180°F liquid to a food submerged in it. **Simmering** refers to maintaining the temperature of a cooking liquid just below the boiling point at approximately 185–205°F.

When we boil water, we can be pretty certain that it is only going to be 212°F or maybe a tad less, depending upon where we live. The important thing is that this is a constant, and no matter how we might try, nothing in our kitchen lab can ever get water to boil at, say, 250°F. That's because, once it reaches that 212°F, it doesn't stay in liquid form—it becomes that gas we call steam.

> **Now You're Cooking**
>
> The boiling point of water is 212°F (100°C) at sea level, but this temperature decreases by about one degree for every 500 feet of elevation. So, in mile-high Denver, water actually boils at a mere 205°F. The result is that a boiled food, such as potatoes or pasta, will take longer to cook in Denver than in Miami. And if you find yourself cooking on the moon, better stick to dry-heat methods.

The beauty of water as a cooking medium is its constant temperature. If you are poaching something, the water should be between 160 and 180°F, while simmering water should be in the range of 180 to 205°F. And our constant friend boiling water is 212°F, no more. When we use steam to cook something, the temperature is a bit higher than 212°F because some energy is carried into the steam to change it from a liquid to a gas. But all in all, water is just ol' Mr. Reliable as far as temperature is concerned.

Dry Heat

Dry heat means cooking without water. When we eliminate water as a heat transfer medium, we are drastically changing the way heat moves and affects our food. And this is all because of the properties of water.

When we cook with dry heat, we are using one of the following techniques: roasting, baking, broiling, grilling, *sautéing*, *pan-frying*, or deep-frying. While that might seem like we are covering a lot of territory, all of those techniques share common principles of heat transfer. They all give the food a unique look, and most of all, a certain flavor because of the manner and temperature of heat transfer.

When we cook by dry-heat methods, heat is transferred directly by conduction, and in some cases, by convection and radiation. When a steak sizzles on a grill, heat is transferred directly from the hot grates to the surface of the meat. When we broil, which is grilling with the heat source above the meat, radiant energy is transferred from the top, through the air and onto the meat's surface. The broiler also has a hot surface that the food rests on, so heat moves directly to the steak by conduction once that surface gets hot. When we bake or roast, hot-air currents in the oven carry heat by convection onto the surface of the food. The heat of the oven rack and the baking pan transfer heat directly by conduction to the food. The heat energy then travels through the interior of the food, through conduction.

> **Chef Sez**
>
> **Sauté** means to cook in a pan over very high heat using a very small amount of oil or fat as the cooking medium. **Pan-frying** uses a similar process but the food is cooked in slightly more fat. **Smoke point** is the temperature at which fats burn or ignite. It is a measure of the break-down point of any fat.

We sometimes use fat in dry-heat cooking to lubricate the food and keep it from sticking to the pan. Of course, fat also tastes good and adds flavor. Fats heat more quickly than water, retain heat without changing form, and transfer heat at very high temperatures. Fat acts as a sort of conductor of heat between the cooking surface and the food. The low specific-heat quality of fat and its high boiling point enables us to reach temperatures of 350° to 400°F at which foods can brown. Yet, we cannot apply too much heat to fat without some danger. Fats burn because they are composed of high amounts of carbon. When you cook with any fat, you should be familiar with its *smoke point* and the temperature at which you can safely cook without burning.

We use a variety of fats and oils in cooking. Each is unique in composition, so each has a unique smoke point. Animal fats such as whole butter burn at relatively nperatures, from 250 to 300°F. The process of clarifying butter, described in

r 24, removes some of the solids in the butter and elevates the smoke point by

ᴗᴗ to 75 degrees. Lard can be heated to about 375°F before it will begin to smoke and break down. Solid vegetable shortenings burn at approximately 325°F. Some oils such as peanut or soybean, or commercial deep-fryer fats, smoke at much higher temperatures, ranging from 440 to 495°F. Every time a fat is used, however, its smoke point decreases. If fat is reused, it can break down and smoke at even lower temperatures than expected. This is because the used fats have already started to decompose, and any contact with salt, water, or the food you fried speeds up the break-down of the cooking oil. For safety's sake, never heat cooking oils beyond the first sign of ripples on the surface. Once this occurs, the food should be added and the temperature reduced for cooking.

Too Hot to Handle

Hot fat is, literally, too hot to handle. Because of the high temperatures reached by fat, it can cause serious burns if spilled, splashed, or splattered on delicate human skin. Be very careful when cooking with even a small amount of hot fat, and never leave a pan containing hot fat unattended in your lab, not even for a moment.

When we cook food using a waterless dry-heat method, the temperatures we use can reach well above 212°F. The temperature of our sauté pan can be 300°F, or the temperature of the deep-fryer fat can be 390F°. When food is exposed to those high temperatures, it reacts differently than it would in contact with the much-cooler boiling water. Fats and cooking oils add flavor, color, and nutrition to food, but must always be used with care and respect in the kitchen.

If you plan to do large amounts of deep-fat frying, get yourself a thermometer that can accurately measure fat temperatures. If you don't yet have a thermometer, you can gauge the temperature of cooking oil by how quickly a small cube of bread browns. When you fry a small piece of fresh white bread (a 1-inch square piece) and it changes to a golden brown in less than 20 seconds, then the temperature of the oil is approximately 400°F. If it takes one minute to brown, then the temperature is about 350°F. Remember that when you add food to the fat, the temperature will drop, so don't crowd or overfill the pan.

Combination Methods

The combination cooking methods are stewing and braising. This third category combines techniques of both dry- and moist-heat transfer.

No doubt you have had a stew, maybe at grandmas. If it was a beef or lamb stew, the meat was cut into nice, small pieces. You may not have realized this, but first the stew meat was *seared* to give it more flavor. Using a very hot pan, the outside surface of the meat was browned as a first step in cooking. The stew was completed by adding enough liquid to cover the meat, and then adding some garden vegetables and simmering the whole thing in a covered pot until it was all nice and tender. Notice the combination of dry and moist cooking methods; first searing to cook the outside of the food and to add flavor, and then simmering to slowly and gently finish cooking the dish.

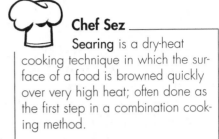

Chef Sez _____
Searing is a dry-heat cooking technique in which the surface of a food is browned quickly over very high heat; often done as the first step in a combination cooking method.

Braising is a very similar technique. A large piece of meat, or sometimes vegetables, is first seared (dry heat), and then simmered (moist heat) with liquid in a covered container. If this sounds a lot like Mom's pot roast, that's because it is. Braising differs from stewing in the size of the pieces of meat being cooked and how the dish is finished for service. When we discuss cooking meats and vegetables in later chapters, we will cover specific directions and tips more thoroughly for all of these cooking methods. What's important now is to realize that moist, dry, and combination methods of heat transfer give you flexibility in cooking. You choose the cooking method based on the result you desire.

When Heat Hits

So, now you get the picture that heat can be transferred through water or air by convection, or it can be transferred directly through conduction or radiation. The real issue, though, is the effect of that heat transfer on your dinner. There is a big difference in appearance, flavor, texture, and application between dry-, moist-, and combination-cooking methods.

Food that is cooked in water by moist heat can never be exposed to temperatures much greater than 212°F. Food that is cooked by a dry-heat method can be exposed to temperatures that really are infinite. Of course, we don't recommend eating a hamburger that has been grilled at 5000°F, but have it your way. Learning how to control heat transfer with time limits is really the art of cooking.

The basic molecules found in food, including water, react to various cooking temperatures differently. After all, sitting in a dry sauna makes you feel one way; sitting in a steam bath is another story altogether. Sugars, fats, and proteins cook as heat is applied to them, but they feel different, too, depending on whether they are in a dry sauna or a steam bath.

Let's say you're cooking chicken for dinner tonight. Boiling a chicken will give you a distinct look, texture, and flavor, while frying it gives another, and roasting the bird produces a third result. It's all a matter of heat transfer and water. You know from experience that when you boil or poach a bird, the meat becomes a rather tepid beige color, and the fat barely changes; it just gets a bit firmer. Compare this to a crisp-skinned, golden brown, aromatic bird roasted in the oven. Compare both with deep-fried chicken from the local take-out joint. You can clearly see the difference. Dry-heat cooking, because of the high temperatures possible, cooks proteins, sugars, and fats in a different way than moist-heat cooking does. Because water's temperature never goes above 212°F, you can poach that bird all day but it will never turn brown or crisp.

Chef Sez

Caramelization is a browning process caused when sugar reacts to very high temperatures. A specific type of caramelization is called the *Maillard reaction*, in which protein and fat react with sugars to aid in the browning process.

One cooking method isn't better or worse than another, it's just that sometimes we want deep, *caramelized* flavors such as those in our roasted bird. Sometimes we don't. The type of food, the menu, and your taste preferences determine which method to apply. Knowing why things happen the way they do in your kitchen lab makes it easier for you to achieve the result you prefer.

The Least You Need to Know

- Cooking is transferring heat into food by conduction, convection, or radiation.
- Moist-heat cooking methods use water to transfer heat to food and are limited by the maximum temperature that water can achieve, which is 212°F.
- Dry-heat cooking methods use high temperatures to cook foods without the use of water.
- Combination cooking methods use dry heat to initially cook the exterior of the food, and moist heat to finish the interior cooking process.
- Choosing the type of cooking method to use depends on the end result that you wish to achieve.

4

Your Microwave: Legal Things You Can Do

In This Chapter

- How microwaves really work
- What not to do
- Living in a microwave force field

Microwave ovens have been used for cooking for over five decades now. Somehow it's not surprising that popcorn was the first real food used in experiments that tested whether microwaves worked. Just visit your local supermarket and observe the number of microwaveable popcorn products; clearly this continues to be a popular choice for microwave cookery. Chalk up another one for the scientists.

The Microwave: In the Beginning Was Energy

One explanation for early humans' control of fire for heating purposes suggests that it was the harnessing of lightning. Bolts from the heavens started many a forest and grassland fire in our early evolution, as they still do today. It seems logical that someone figured out how to harness the burning bushes for useful applications, like heating and cooking, and then passed this gift from above on to successive generations. Lightening is dramatically used as the life-giving force behind many Hollywood Frankenstein monsters. Heck, even Ben Franklin experimented with lightning in his quest for electricity.

Another theory suggests that the application of fire and heat was just a fortuitous result of striking flint stones (not Fred or Wilma, just rocks made of flint) together while making weapons. Someone likely started a fire and burned down the whole village. The perpetrator probably made amends with clan elders by harnessing fire to open the first burger joint with central heating.

A third theory suggests that someone was rubbing two sticks together to kill time, when the sparks accidentally caused a flameout in the surrounding savannah grass. Fortunately, he or she survived and later did a slightly more controlled burn, demonstrating the benefits of smoking grass to everyone in the clan.

We can dispense with the first two myths relatively quickly when it comes to creating heat energy for microwave cookery. There is no noticeable fire or burner inside your microwave oven. Oddly enough, however, the third theory is related to the modern-day microwave oven, in principle at least. No, your unit doesn't have a monkey in the back, rubbing two sticks together, but microwave ovens do employ the principle of friction to cook food. But the friction isn't macro, which is a nice way to say it isn't big enough for you to see, like a flame. Rather, the friction is micro; it occurs at the molecular level.

Food for Thought

The first commercial microwave ovens appeared in 1947. They were behemoths, standing over 5 feet tall and weighing more than 700 pounds. They were also cooled by water to keep the energy unit from breaking up. Tappan Corporation introduced the first home model in 1952. It cost $1,200. By 1965, Amana, a division of Rayathon, which patented the original microwave oven, introduced a $500 model that fit on the home kitchen counter. By 1975, sales of microwave ovens exceeded those of gas ranges. Today, it is probably rare to find a home or office without one.

Saturday Night Fever, Baby

It's hard to imagine a simple glass of water vibrating and rotating at the molecular level. Yet, if you could take a trip into the molecular interior of that water, things might not seem so passive. Perhaps it would be like a visit to a disco in the 70s. You know that environment—flashing strobe lights, lots of motion and commotion, and loud, very loud, music. If you were standing outside the disco, it's doubtful you would hear or see anything, however. But go inside and it was energy to the max. So, it should not be surprising that, as you peer at a glass of water, things appear calm, but under the surface, on the molecular level, it's a different story.

Despite the vibration and shaking that is going on at the molecular level in water, things are still pretty stable. And to take that logic further, the donut you might have at your desk every morning isn't exploding or bursting into flames, even though the water inside it is moving and shaking, too. Molecular vibrations and rotations are occurring under controlled conditions. That is, until we throw cooking into the mix. Heat water on the top of your stove and you start to see some changes. Now you're adding some extra energy into the molecular mix, which begins to challenge the molecular status quo. If you add enough energy, you can watch that water change from a liquid into steam.

You've already learned that heat transfer can occur through basic conduction and convection. It makes sense; we can see it and feel it. After all, you are just moving heat from the outside of the food to the inside, using a pan, or an oven, or a grill equipped with a flame or burner. Once heat makes that initial foray onto the surface of a food, it creates the domino effect, as the heat energy bumps its way toward the center. The longer you leave the food on the heat, the more energy gets transferred, and your diner goes from rare to well done.

Even when you broil a steak, you can feel the heat energy flowing from the broiler element. It glows white hot, producing visible radiant energy. Those heat waves radiate out and strike the surface of the meat and, through conduction, move inside toward the center of the steak.

The bottom line is that once the heat energy contacts the food *molecules*, it virtually lights up the vibrations and rotations of the ingredients. Things begin to cook. Molecules of proteins, fat, sugar, and water (the most abundant molecule in food) start to respond to the heat. This sounds all well and good for conventional cooking, but there is more to this story.

Chef Sez

A **molecule** is the smallest particle of any compound that has all the chemical attributes of that compound. Elements such as hydrogen, oxygen, carbon, and nitrogen, are bound together into molecules because of their negative and positive magnetic-like charges.

Up Close and Personal

This brings us to the microwave. Microwaves don't have a hot surface. There is no visible heat source creating energy. And when you cook something in a microwave, you don't preheat the oven. In fact, as you've no doubt noticed, the interior of a microwave doesn't even heat up. The only heat you might feel is what's given off by the hot food.

So, even though you can't see or feel the energy, something did contact the food enough to shake it up, or you would not have hot cooked food, right? That something is the microwave.

Invisible energy is pretty common. When you listen to the radio, you don't see the sound waves, but you know something is there. And you know something is going on in that microwave oven, or it wouldn't pop your corn. Microwaves are a close relative to sound waves. They just move a bit faster. And the speed at which energy goes from point A to point B is measured as a frequency.

Speed Freaks

Microwaves are a form of *radiation*. The word radiation brings to mind something harmful, maybe even something radioactive. But microwaves are a form of radiant energy that is classified as nonionizing. It all comes down to a matter of speed. Waves of energy are measured on a scale called the frequency spectrum, which measures how quickly a wave passes from one point to another.

On the low end of the scale are radio and sound waves. Notches up from these are microwaves and visible light. All of these are nonionizing. Once you cross the threshold above visible light, however, you are trekking into *ionizing* terrain. Now you are into a zone where the frequency has been kicked up millions of times faster than nonionizing radiation.

Chef Sez

Radiation is the transfer of energy by electromagnetic waves. **Ionizing radiation** is very high frequency waves (millions or trillions of cycles per second); ultraviolet and X-rays are examples. Nonionizing radiation uses a much lower frequency of energy waves (around 2,500 million cycles per second); microwaves and radio waves are examples.

These ionizing waves include ultraviolet light, X-rays, and gamma rays. So, here's the rub: Waves of ionizing radiation can damage cells and molecules. The energy and power they contain is enough to break down tissue; they can directly affect your DNA or the DNA in a piece of beef. This is what happens in severe sunburn. On the other hand, nonionizing radiation affects cells by causing charged molecules (water!) to vibrate. The nonionizing radiation in cooking is heat, and it is no different than the heat caused by a grill or an oven in its effect on food. So, don't worry, food cooked in a microwave oven is not tainted or radiated.

Microwaves don't move only in a straight line. Because they are waves, they oscillate. They move up and down at right angles while going forward. You can see a wave oscillate just by standing on a beach, watching the ocean. Ocean waves are coming forward toward you. They are also moving up and down. If food had eyes (apologies to the potato), it would see a microwave moving toward it, much the same way that you see the wave coming on the seashore. The big difference is the speed and number of waves crashing into the potato in a very short period of time. This makes a difference because frequency matters.

Now, even though microwaves oscillate at a faster frequency than sound waves, they oscillate at a lower frequency than visible light energy. Yet, at about 2,500 million cycles per second, microwaves move at a pretty respectable speed. Imagine you and a friend holding a jump rope between you, flipping it up and down to create a wave. I doubt that you could simulate 2,500 million up-and-down cycles on that rope without one of you being transferred into another dimension, or giving up from heat exhaustion.

Now think of microwaves oscillating like that jump rope. And further imagine that when the wave is on the upswing, it has a positive charge, and on the downswing, negative. Now imagine this up-and-down force field in the vicinity of food inside your microwave, let's say popcorn. The waves strike the outside of the kernel and head to the interior. Microwaves penetrate the food. Microwaves go uniformly from the outside toward the inside.

> **Food for Thought**
>
> It's important to keep the inside of your microwave clean because the microwave doesn't heat its own surfaces. If the surface doesn't get hot enough to burn off food, when you spill something, it stays there. And food left at room temperature in that oven grows bacteria that can be transferred to your clean food.

This means that for most foods in your standard-size microwave, the wave hits the exterior and slightly inside the piece of food at virtually the same time. So, in the case of a tiny kernel of popcorn, there's virtually no difference in the force field outside and inside the kernel. And as long as you have the microwave oven on, the kernel is bathed in microwave energy from top to bottom, stem to stern.

Don't forget, too, that as the wave travels, it changes from positive to negative at 2,500 million cycles each second. So, in the course of going an infinitely small distance, the waves have created a field of utter confusion around the molecules of the corn kernel. Remember that 70s disco, where everyone was talking at once and the band was playing loudly, and the sounds just seemed to envelope you? Well, you get the picture. That little popcorn kernel and all of its molecules are in a similar microwave mayhem.

Waves on Water

The most influential molecule that the microwave affects inside that popcorn kernel is water. Why? Well, recall that water molecules were vibrating back and forth before the microwave even arrived on the scene. And water has polarity, which means it has a charge to it, kind of like a battery, it has its own little force field around it. Water was content to be cycling between positive and negative bliss; just happy to be hanging out inside the corn kernel.

Now, just imagine a single water molecule immersed in that microwave force field, where the wave arrives and is oscillating from positive to negative at such an astronomical rate. By the time water even thinks about being positive so that it can accommodate the negative field of the wave, suddenly the wave changes back to negative.

> **Food for Thought**
> Cooking vegetables in the microwave is a form of moist-heat cooking, basically like steaming. Vegetables should be cleaned, trimmed, or sliced as desired and placed in a microwaveable dish. Seasonings and oils or broths can be added. Cover the dish with a lid or plastic wrap. Poke a couple of holes in the plastic to release some of the steam.

So, water tries to change back to positive but, you guessed it, the wave has changed back to positive itself. Water gets very confused. It's like you trying to play patty cake with Superman, but his hands move at the speed of light. The water molecule can't decide what charge it should have. It speeds up and up and up, trying to respond to the microwave's opposite sign, but it cannot possibly match the microwaves frequency. The water molecule then literally starts to spin, like a top out of control.

Now take it one step further. Instead of one molecule of water being utterly confused and spinning out of control, imagine 100 million water molecules acting this way in a small closed space, inside that popcorn kernel. Can you imagine the bumping and grinding going on as water molecules crash into one another? This creates friction. And, just like rubbing two sticks together to create heat, molecular friction creates an internal combustion engine. You've created the food science equivalent of the disco; lots of hot bodies gyrating out of control in closed space, sharing each other's body heat. Something's gotta give under those conditions.

And in the case of popcorn, once the heat from friction boils the water and the vapor pressure becomes so great, you get corn popping, and starch gelatinizing, and proteins unwinding. You are microwave cooking, baby! When you take the popcorn out of the microwave oven and open the bag, you see that, in fact, there was tremendous heat created. Enough steam heat to cause you a painful burn. And you got all this energy by causing good old water to do the bump and grind with microwaves.

Yet, the story is not over. Touch the inside walls of your microwave oven; it's nearly cool. So, unlike the hot broiler that continues to give off heat even after you turn off the power, the microwave oven's energy is instantaneous; it is on and off at the flick of a switch, and you cannot even tell the difference.

Too Hot to Handle

Though today's microwave ovens are safe and convenient, there are some recommendations to make the use and operation of the ovens go smoothly. Never run your unit empty; never run the unit with the door open (the door should close properly, otherwise it is a malfunction); never disconnect the safety features or fuses that are intended to keep you from running the machine in any other way than as the manufacturer intended. And keep at least one arm's length away from the unit while it is running.

Hot Spots

You may have experienced the effects of uneven cooking in a microwave oven. This is a result of the delivery of the electromagnetic energy to the food. As the waves bounce back and forth inside the oven, they don't always contact every square inch of the food evenly. Sometimes a wave will cancel out another wave, and each oven has a profile where you can get hot and cold zones. The result is that food may have hot and cold spots. This is why some microwaves use turntables to rotate the food. It's simply applying the law of averages. You are bound to even out the cooking more than by just letting the food sit in one spot.

It is somewhat of a myth that microwaves cook from the inside of the food out. What is true is that conventional cooking methods—the dry, moist, and combination methods discussed in Chapter 3—cook from the exterior of the food to the interior.

This is just a matter of the laws of heat transfer. If your heat source is a conventional oven, a pot of water, a grill, a broiler, a steamer, a rotisserie, or any other cooking device, the heat energy will be delivered only to the exterior of the food. And if the food is relatively thick, the time it takes to conduct heat from the surface to the interior can be considerable. Think about the time to roast a 10-pound turkey compared with roasting a slice of turkey breast. Size and shape of the food are

Food for Thought

Soup and similar liquid-based dishes are also very good heated or reheated in the microwave. Units that have a turntable increase the heat distribution as the food cooks. It is also a good idea to stop the unit and stir the food after five or six minutes to help even out heat distribution.

key elements in cooking food conventionally. The only way to alter this generalization would be to have a probe inside the food to deliver heat inside as fast as the process of conduction brought in heat from the outside. Can you see the lack of practicality here? So, we just deal with the laws of conduction and convection in learning to cook efficiently.

Things are different for microwave cooking. With microwaves, the electromagnetic energy is literally transferred from the exterior of the food to its interior instantaneously. So, outside and inside, each and every polar food molecule is exposed to this energy simultaneously. That is why microwaves cook faster. The inside heats almost as fast as the outside. But the inside does not heat faster than the outside. What does happen is that you have conduction from the inside out, right at the beginning of cooking. So, unlike conventional cooking, where the interior is at the mercy of conduction of heat from the outside in, you do not have this impediment in microwave cookery.

It's cookery with a bi-directional heat flow. Because of heat flow, you also get carryover cooking. Foods can continue to conduct heat and cook even after the oven has been turned off. Liquids such as soups should be allowed to rest for a minute after removing them from the oven, before stirring. This will prevent the food from boiling over the edge of its container. This is particularly important for foods given to young children. What may appear cold on the surface can suddenly become steaming hot.

Food for Thought

The nutritional value of food heated in a microwave is no different than your conventional method of cooking food. Heat is heat. So, those steamed green beans from the microwave are the same composition as those you made with your ancient Chinese bamboo steamer.

Microwave Lab Experiment

Here's a tasty, yet informative exercise that will prove how microwaves heat food differently than a conventional stove. You'll explore what does and what does not heat in a microwave, and why. First, gather your supplies. For this lab experiment, you will need your favorite brand of microwave popcorn, $1/2$ cup kosher salt, 4 tablespoons of butter, 2 microwaveable bowls and a small fry pan. You also need a food thermometer. Every food lab should have one of these, so this might be a good excuse to purchase one if you haven't already done so.

Now, put half of the salt in one microwaveable bowl and the other half in the fry pan. Place the bowl in the microwave. Run the oven at its highest setting for two minutes. While that is happening, place the fry pan of salt on the stove top and heat it for two minutes. When your time is up for each, carefully measure the temperature of the salt from the fry pan, and then from the microwave. You may need to pile up the salt a bit to insert the thermometer. Carefully touch each sample of salt with the tip of your finger to also get an indication of temperature. You can now combine all the salt and reserve it for later. Was there any difference?

Now put half of the butter in the fry pan and the other half in a microwaveable bowl. Microwave the bowl of butter on high for 30 seconds. Heat the fry pan of butter on high for 30 seconds. Compare the butter in each container at the end of 30 seconds. Is there any difference?

Now make the popcorn according to the manufacturer's directions. When it's done, add some melted butter from your experiment and sprinkle on a bit of salt. While you are enjoying the fruits of your labor, reflect back on the experiment.

When you examined the salt from the microwave, it was still room temperature, no different than before you ran it through the microwave. The salt heated on the stove top should have been warmer than when you started. You should also have observed that the microwaved butter melted much more quickly, and was much hotter than the stove-top butter.

Putting this all together, you might conclude that foods that contain water absorb heat in the microwave, but foods without moisture do not. That is why the dry salt was cold from the microwave but the watery butter was hot. Microwaves heat the water, in other words.

The dry salt can still be heated by conduction on the stove top, however. So, you might conclude that conventional cooking methods work on foods that are dry or moist, but that microwave cooking only works on items that contain water. The second thing you should have noticed is that microwaves are very fast compared to the stove top. While the butter melted in both the fry pan and the microwave, its temperature and consistency was much different. The efficiency of heat transfer in the microwave is much greater than on the stove. In fact, stoves are only about 10 percent efficient in transferring heat from the burner to the food. Microwaves are 60 percent efficient in transferring electricity into electromagnetic radiation. How's the popcorn, by the way?

Appearance Isn't Everything

Microwaves cook water. The water cooks the food. Like we've said before, it's all about water. So, all this is analogous to conventional moist-heating cooking methods. Recall that water can only approach 212°F, never reaching the high heat of 340°F necessary to initiate the browning reaction. And because the interior of the oven in a microwave never heats up at all, except for the heat escaping from the food as it cooks, those nice hot temperatures that give fresh bread a brown crust will never occur.

Hot oven air is necessary to drive water from the exterior of the food by evaporation. Additionally, water moves from the inside of the food to the outside as you microwave it. The outer layer stays moist, or can even get soggy, but never crisp. The net effect of all this is that no browning products are formed. Without the browning reaction, foods cooked in a microwave are lighter in color than conventional dry and combination cooking methods. So, don't expect golden brown or crispy foods when you choose to use a microwave for general cooking techniques.

Never say never, however. You no doubt have purchased convenience foods that do brown and crisp somewhat. This ingenious addition to microwave cooking is due to a pocket insert that contacts the food surface. The insert is called a susceptor. It is a very thin, flat, smooth piece of aluminum foil. Since the foil is thin and smooth (not jagged), it doesn't spark or catch on fire. But it does conduct the electromagnetic waves and, thereby, it literally reaches temperatures high enough to simulate a frying pan; it gets mighty hot, in other words. And as the food contacts the susceptor, it can reach a browning temperature. This nifty invention is an exception rather than the rule. Your homemade foods that are not prepared commercially for browning will never achieve the depth of color or crispness of conventional dry or moist techniques.

The Least You Need to Know

- Microwave ovens produce high-frequency, nonionizing waves of energy, similar to radio waves.
- When microwaves strike food, heat energy is created because of internal friction within the food's water molecules. The heat energy created by these vibrating water molecules cooks the food.
- Most foods will not brown in a microwave oven.
- Never operate a microwave oven with the door open or the unit empty.
- Microwave ovens work best to cook high-moisture foods such as vegetables, where the frictional heat from water creates steam.
- Stirring foods during cooking will improve heat distribution.
- There is carryover cooking and heat conduction in microwave cooking. This means that foods continue to cook after they are removed from the oven.

Beyond Smoking Joints

In This Chapter

◆ What can you smoke?

◆ Flavor rubs

◆ The briny deep

◆ Chemicals to live with

Contrary to popular opinion, the first joints to be smoked were not in the crowd at a Grateful Dead concert, nor in 1960s San Francisco. We humans developed a taste for smoke long before then. Smoking joints—of meat, that is—likely first occurred when one of our ancestors accidentally placed some food near a fire and charred the outside, creating such an attractive aroma during the cooking process that this new food just had to be sampled.

We still smoke food today when we grill or barbecue. But most people purchase their smoked foods pre-packaged or from a restaurant. And that's too bad. Smoking is not beyond the realm of possibility for mere mortals like us. After all, if our ancestors were successful in smoking food, we should have the confidence to give it a whirl, too. We're more educated, have more free time, and enjoy the pleasures of food more than we ever have. C'mon now, understanding the smoking process is not that difficult.

The Smoking Section

It's easy to understand the smoking process without even entering a kitchen. If you live anywhere except California, go to your nearest neighborhood pub at happy hour. Belly up to the bar and order some fries. Have a pleasant conversation with your friends. After about two hours, go home. When you take off your clothes, smell them. We're not kinky here, just doing an experiment. Without a doubt, you, and mostly your clothes, will smell of smoke. Now, this is obviously tobacco smoke, which gives you a distinctive scent. If you live in California where all forms of the art of smoking in public are now banned, or if you live in, say, Benton, Illinois, and just want to stay home, then light up the barbecue grill. Make sure you stand downwind as the thing lights. You are sure to get steeped in smoke, and it soaks in giving you a nice surface aroma.

Smoke is a solid dissolved in a gas; it likes to attach itself to things. Whether it is you and your clothes, a piece of meat, fish, vegetables, cheese, nuts, fruits, or grains, smoke is an equal-opportunity aroma. In Chapter 1 we talked about the phases of food. A phase has a continuous boundary and a discontinuous one. This means that something small is dispersed in something big. You can have a solid in a liquid, like cornstarch in H_2O, or you can trap air in cream and call it whipped. The liquid cream is continuous, and the air is discontinuous. And we are all familiar with carbonated beverages in which gas in trapped in liquid. The liquid is continuous, and the gas is discontinuous. Champagne has bubbles of CO_2 trapped in all that nice fermented grape juice, for example.

Well, smoke is one more example of a phase. We create smoke when we burn or ignite some carbon-based life form. Food smokes when it burns. You've no doubt burned food somewhere along the way when cooking. (If you haven't even burned toast, then you need to do so just to prove it's not the end of the world.)

Chef Sez

Smoke point is the temperature at which a fat burns. Saturated animal fats tend to smoke at lower temperatures than vegetable oils.

Food burns because it is carbon based. Proteins, fats, and sugars have carbon in their basic molecular structure. Thank goodness that water, the most important food molecule, doesn't smoke or combust; we would all have burned up long ago. Maybe nature realized that something had to be around to put out fires if people were going to be smoking things. Fats, by the way, especially animal fats, are particularly good at producing smoke.

Bonded by Smell

When food smokes, it has a "smell signature." Women can recognize their infants by smell. Lovers bond by aroma. So, it should not be surprising that food, and especially smoked food, bonds to us, too. It's one of the food-aroma fingerprints. Close your eyes and think "burnt toast." You can almost literally smell something that distinctive. Now think about the fryer-grease aroma from a fast-food joint. That's their oil smoking, or reaching the smoke point, and it's a good indication that it's time to change the oil. Not all smell fingerprints are pleasant.

Because smoke has a smell fingerprint, we can use this property to flavor food. The smell signature is because smoke has hundreds of different chemicals in its makeup. These chemicals are released during the burning process. If you burn hickory wood in your barbecue, it will create a different aroma than apple or mesquite smoke. That's because of the different chemical profiles.

Smoky aromas can happen in situations where smoke combustion never even occurred. We might talk about a smoky wine, for example. The wine was not on fire. It simply shares bunches of the chemicals that exist in real smoke. A good pinot noir wine, for example, might be described as smelling like a tobacco pouch, with a bit of smoke to it.

Nature tends to be conservative in the number of things it uses. There are only a certain number of building blocks, with carbon being a very important one. So, putting these structures together often results in the same or very similar substances being formed, even though the process to construct them can be entirely different. So, a grape can hold the building blocks that eventually turn into smoky tones. This is another reason why food chemists are so clever. Once they know the chemical formula of "smoke flavor," for example, they can build it from scratch, without ever having to light a match.

We can take advantage of smoke's large variety of signatures to give our food excitement. There are correct ways to proceed, however. Smoking food isn't difficult to master, and the techniques are based upon tried and true cooking science.

Doing It Fast

Let's face it, we live at a time when we want or expect things to move fast. Fast food and fast cars are probably here to stay. The fear that cooking, and especially smoked food preparation, is laborious just isn't true. We can do it fast if you prefer.

When we want to smoke something quickly, we do what is called *hot smoking*. This technique kills two birds with one stone. We cook the food (meat, vegetables, and fish, for example) as we are applying the aromas from smoke.

Chef Sez

Hot smoking is the process of smoking food at temperatures above 180°F. This heat cooks the food at the same time that it smokes it.

Now, some things should become intuitive to you as a budding food scientist. Because hot smoking uses relatively high temperatures (at least 180°F or above), not all foods are suitable for this technique. A nice mozzarella cheese, for instance, can be smoked, but unless you want to be scraping cheese off your oven, reserve these soft, less-forgiving foods for cold smoking, which we'll discuss later.

Foods that work well with hot smoking are foods that can stand up to the higher heat used during this cooking process without drying out, dissolving, or melting away. Larger pieces of meat, whole fish, or even stout vegetables can be roasted by dry heat for periods of time to absorb the smoke. So, choose the food wisely and with common sense.

Next, choose the type of wood for smoking. Hard woods such as apple, hickory, or cherry work well for smoking. Soft woods such as pine have too much resin and will make the food acrid and your cooker sticky. Green woods won't work too well, either. In other words, in order for wood to provide the most attractive smoke, it should be hard, aged, and dry. Dry wood chips are available commercially, so please don't chop down your neighbor's cherry tree if you find yourself hooked on smoking.

Then, the wood chips need to be soaked before adding them to your smoking apparatus. This prevents the chips from burning too quickly. You want the chips to burn slowly to extend their smoky properties. A good rule of thumb is to use a handful of chips as the source of fuel. Of course, if your hands are the size of The Incredible Hulk, then maybe a third of a handful will suffice. Use the intuitive side of your brain here. Place the chips in a small bowl and add enough water to cover them. Allow them to soak for at least 20 minutes, and then drain off the water.

Finally, you need to rig up an arrangement of food, wood chips, and a covered environment for the cooking process. A roasting pan and a wire mesh rack works well. If you don't have a rack, poke some holes in a piece of aluminum foil and lay it over the soaked, smoking wood chips. The food can rest above the foil and not make contact with the chips directly. Seal the entire pan with a cover of aluminum foil to keep the smoke inside. Now, place the covered pan on a heat source.

The chips will begin to smolder and give off smoke. Since heat rises, the smoke will pass upward to and through the food as it cooks. You could also use the two-rack oven system. Place the wood chips in a pan on the bottom rack of your oven, and place the food above it in a pan on the middle rack. Of course, be prepared to spend a long time getting the smoky aroma out of your oven afterward.

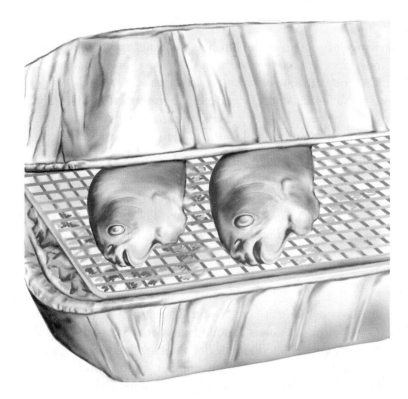

A baking pan, cookie rack, and aluminum foil can be used to create a stove top smoker.

Hot smoked foods are always finished to the temperature desired for doneness. Large pieces of meat take longer to cook than, say, vegetables. If you prefer less smoke flavor, smoke only for a portion of the total cooking time. If you only want 20 minutes' worth of smoke, but the food will take an hour to cook, just smoke it for the first 20 minutes, and then transfer the food to another pan or your oven (without chips) to finish the cooking process.

Ventilation is a very important consideration when smoking food. Ventilation fans available with some top-of-the-line home ranges can handle moderate stove top or oven smoking. But perhaps the best hot smoking can be efficiently combined with grilling. This is especially useful as an outdoor patio event in good, clean, fresh air, which handles the ventilation problem nicely. When you smoke using a barbecue grill, wet wood chips can be placed on the hot coals to infuse the food with these flavors as it grills. Food is offset on the colder side of the grill with the cover of the unit closed.

If you have some sort of duel-burner gas grill, you can create your smoke fire box by simply placing soaked chips in a container on one side and grilling on the other.

Doing It Slow

Slow dancing is a nice change of pace from the hip-hop and rap scene, sometimes. So, once in awhile, let long, slow *cold smoking* add some spice to your life. Cold-smoking techniques infuse food with smoky flavors and aromas at a very low temperature. Unlike hot smoking, the food is not fully cooked. This means that you must fully cook cold-smoked items before consuming them, or risk frequent visits to the restroom. Only pre-cooked foods that are smoked to add flavor after cooking need not follow this rule.

Chef Sez

Cold smoking is the process of smoking food at temperatures below 100°F. The food is not cooked during this process.

Cold smoking is a good technique for fragile foods. Cheese that would melt during hot smoking does nicely in cold smoking. Foods that are already cooked but that you want to accent with smoke can also be cold smoked. Fruits, delicate vegetables, or even nuts can be cold smoked to add just a touch more flavor.

The difficulty in doing cold smoking at home is the difficulty of controlling temperatures below 100°F. One logical solution is a modification of the hot-smoking procedure. Using the same pan set-up described for hot smoking, heat the chips first on the stove top, oven, or grill to create a smoky environment, and then turn off the heat source and add the food. Cover the pan again and allow the food to steep in the smoke for a short period of time. This works well for small or thin pieces of food that can readily absorb the smoky aromas. This technique adds just a light touch of smoke without cooking the food.

Too Hot to Handle

How long cold-smoked food will be safe to consume depends on many factors. Commercial or artisan smoking of country hams may take upward of three to six weeks following brining. The final product may last well over a year and still be quite moist and safe to eat. Food cold smoked briefly at home should be fully cooked, and then consumed within a week to 10 days, however.

A barbecue grill can also be used in a similar fashion to cold smoke food. Wood chips can be added to coals to create smoke and then the food added to the covered grill as the coals cool. The residual heat is usually enough to infuse the food with smoky flavors and aromas. How long to cold smoke depends on the food you are smoking and your personal preference for the taste of smoke. Larger pieces of meat usually need at least two hours for the smoke to penetrate. If, however, you simply want the essence of smoke, or if the product is more delicate, such as fish or shellfish, you may cold smoke only for only 30 minutes or less.

So, why did smoking evolve as a practice? Besides the serendipity of invention and the fact that we like smoky flavors, a major reason was for food preservation. Foods that are smoked can be preserved longer. In earlier times, when refrigeration was problematic, smoked foods could be stored for extended periods at room temperature. Smoke and its myriad of chemicals are antibacterial.

Raw food, especially seafood, poultry, and meat, which is held at 100°F during cold smoking, is susceptible to bacterial contamination. This is especially true for foods held in this temperature danger zone for two hours or more. Smoking, whether hot or cold, is typically done in conjunction with curing of the food.

Dry and wet cures, including marinades, increase the safety zone so that foods can be smoked at lower temperatures. The term "smoke curing" is generally used to describe the procedure of both curing and smoking a food. Not only does *curing* help in preservation, it improves the uptake of smoke flavors. Curing also improves the flavors and enhances the appearance of the food. Basically, there are two ways to cure food prior to smoking.

Chef Sez
Curing is a process of treating a food to preserve it. Salting, brining (pickling), and drying (dehydrating) are all forms of curing. Smoking can be added to enhance flavors and to aid in the curing process.

Now You're Cooking
Jerk is a type of dry rub made from aromatic spices characteristic of the Caribbean, particularly Jamaica. It is applied directly to raw meat, fish, or poultry as a flavor enhancer and cure.

Flavor Enhancers

The first way to cure food, especially meats, is with the application of a dry rub. The primary ingredient of a dry rub is salt. A good rule of thumb is to use about $1/3$ ounce (2 teaspoons) of salt for every pound of meat being cured. While plain salt will help to do the job of curing the food, usually you'll want to add a spice mixture along with the salt to enhance the food's flavor. Salt mixed with brown sugar and spices such as cumin, coriander, dried ginger, cinnamon, cloves, nutmeg, and various ground black and white peppercorns works well.

Applying a thick, even coating of dry rub to beef.

The salt and spice mixture is massaged into the food. If this is a piece of meat such as a pork shoulder, the surface should be well covered with the cure. As you already know, meats are susceptible to surface bacteria, but these bacteria can be neutralized by the cure mixture. Usually you leave the cure on for 24 hours, keeping the food in the refrigerator in a covered container. The next day, rinse the seasonings off with plenty of fresh cool water. Dry the surface well by patting it with paper towels or a clean, lint-free cloth.

The curing process did a couple of important things. First, one goal of curing is to partially dehydrate the food. Because the heavily salted exterior is now much saltier than the interior of the food, water from inside is drawn to the surface. It is a biological fact that water will move in the direction of the highest salt content. It flows downhill, so to speak. Because of this, you will notice a puddle of moisture in the container that held the food as it cured. As water was drawn away from the food's interior, it dissolved some of the surface cure and flowed into the pan. You have succeeded in your mission.

The second thing you did was to dehydrate any bacteria that happened to be living on the food you were curing. Heavy salts and spices also draw water out of these bugs. Without water, these bugs are DOA. By using a dry cure, you have succeeded in making your food, especially meat, safer for smoking. Now when you do smoke the food, which is another antibacterial method, you are starting with a relatively clean food surface. Bottom line? Food will be safer and better tasting if you cure it first, and then smoke it.

Once the food is dry cured and washed of the excess salt, it must be refrigerated again, this time totally uncovered, for another 24 hours. This step is important in order to further dehydrate the surface of the food. The food surface takes on a shiny or leather-like appearance, and is referred to as a *pellicle*. The drier surface absorbs smoke better and also delays the growth of any remaining bacteria.

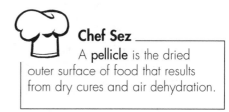

Chef Sez
A **pellicle** is the dried outer surface of food that results from dry cures and air dehydration.

The Briny Deep

Going dry is one way to cure food. Going wet and wild is another. Saltwater brines, like dry cures, help to move water out of the food. Unlike dry-cured food, though, a brined food may appear moister when you eat it. This is because while water is drawn out of the food when it is immersed in the salty brine (remember that water inside the food flows to the heavily salted exterior), salt also can flow into the food from the brine. In brining, water- and salt-flow can be a two-way street. So, when we brine, more salt and water are retained inside the food than in dry curing. Brined foods then tend to stay moister during the smoking process.

Some foods lend themselves to brining. Freshwater trout is one of these. Brining can keep the trout moist and less susceptible to drying out during the smoking process. To brine trout for smoking, make a solution that contains at least 2 parts salt for every 8 parts of water; in other words, mix 2 pounds of salt in 8 pounds of water. This is equivalent to a 20 percent solution of saltwater. A 20 percent solution is minimal brine that is needed to help draw moisture out of the food. Good brine is more than just saltwater, however. You can add brown sugar, honey, or molasses for sweetness. (A ballpark figure is to add sugar at about 25 percent of the weight of your salt. So, for the 2 pounds (32 ounces) of salt in our example, you would add about 8 ounces of sugar.) You can also add a commercial pickling spice, garlic powder, cloves, or any spices that you want to flavor the food.

Brines can also be injected directly into larger pieces of meat. Many supermarkets now carry large brining syringes and needles (don't want to put one of those in your arm!), and there are commercial sources for curing supplies. You can also purchase pre-mixed or powdered brine solutions, though it might be more fun to invent your own flavorful combinations.

As with the dry cure, the brine-soaked food must be rinsed well and patted dry. The food is left uncovered in the refrigerator overnight to form the pellicle. Now it's ready for smoking.

Nitrates and Nitrites

Go to any grocery and buy a processed smoked-meat product. Examine its color. Compared with other meats, these products are always an appealing color. This is no accident. It occurs during the smoking process because of a chemical reaction with salt additives. It is done not only for visual appeal, but also to improve food safety.

During your great grandfather's days, salt curing was done with a substance called saltpeter. Saltpeter is potassium nitrate (KNO_3). It was found naturally in rocks and soil, and was used as a fertilizer for plants. Call it serendipity, but someone rubbed saltpeter on his meat and noticed that it kept the color in and also preserved it better when it was smoked. Saltpeter thus became the salt of choice for dry-curing smoked hams and sausages.

Fast-forward to the early twentieth century when some brilliant chemists discovered that bacteria residing on the surface of meat consumed saltpeter and then excreted it as sodium nitrite, ($NaNO_2$). This nitrite did some remarkable things. First, it combined with the natural pigments in meat to keep the meat a brighter, more attractive pink color. As a salt containing sodium, it tickled our taste buds, giving that salty, sweet flavor we crave in cured meats. The nitrite prevented oxidation of fats, which is another way of saying it kept rancidity in check. But maybe most important, nitrite was toxic to *Clostridium botulinum*. This dreaded bacteria is the cause of botulism, and is the scourge of sausage makers and home canners alike. Once science proved that nitrites were the active form of the salt, which was important for flavor and safety in cured meats, it became the chemical of choice over saltpeter, and has been used for curing ever since.

TCM to the Rescue

Tinted curing mix (TCM) is today's commercial form of sodium nitrite. It consists of 94 percent salt with only about 6 percent sodium nitrite. It can be purchased most easily through the Internet from vendors who sell supplies for making homemade sausage. A little TCM goes a long way; use only 1 part TCM for every 400 parts of curing salts in your brine or dry cure. How do you calculate and use such small quantities in real life? Luckily, experienced butchers and sausage makers have already worked out these details based on the amount of meat you are curing. For every 10 pounds of meat to be cured, you need to add only about $4/_{10}$ of an ounce (0.4 ounce) of TCM to your dry rub or brining solution. In other words, add about $2^1/_2$ teaspoons TCM to your dry-cure mixture or brine for every 10 pounds of meat being cured. If you are curing more or less than 10 pounds of meat, then you'll just have to do the math yourself.

Better Living Through Science

Finally, it's worth mentioning the concerns recently in the media about consuming too much processed meat. Most of these focus on the nitrite used in the preservation process. Studies have shown that excess nitrite may lead to a predisposition for certain cancers. What has been less well published, however, is the fact that most of the nitrite found in the human body is derived naturally from normal metabolism of nitrates found in other foods, such as vegetables.

Plants readily take up nitrate that is found in the soil or used in fertilizers. When we eat these nitrates, the bacteria living in our gut can convert it to nitrite. So, the amount of nitrite consumed in a sensible diet containing smoked meat may not be very significant. Nitrite also has a good benefit in smoke-cured meat products. It virtually eliminates the chance of botulism toxicity in these foods. So, the removal of the nitrite for less-than-logical reasons may create a health problem that is worse than the cure. Smart science and intelligent cooking suggest that a better approach is to continue to eat smart but not forego the cured food products that have been part of our diet for centuries.

The Least You Need to Know

- Different woods impart unique flavor characteristics to food because of differences in smoke chemicals. Hardwood chips work best for adding flavor and aroma to smoked foods.
- Wood chips should be soaked in water for 20 minutes and squeezed of excess water (before heating) to generate smoke.
- Hot smoking cooks the food at the same time that it is infused with the scent of the smoke.
- Cold smoking is done at low temperatures so that food is flavored but uncooked. Cold-smoked foods need to be fully cooked before being consumed.
- Some foods, especially meat, should be cured before smoking, to enhance their flavor and especially to guard against bacterial growth.
- After brining or dry-curing, meat needs to be air-dried under refrigeration. This improves smoke absorption and increases food safety.
- Although optional, the addition of a very small amount of tinted curing mix (TCM) aids in color retention and improves food safety of smoked meats.

6

It's Alive! It's Alive!

In This Chapter

- ◆ Biotechnology and food
- ◆ The right stuff in the twenty-first century
- ◆ Organic methods

There's an old saying is that absence makes the heart grow fonder. This may be true for love. But for agriculture and food there is some doubt. Your great-grandmother, and maybe even granny, lived at a time when most people were raised on a farm next to food. They communed with it. Today, most of us commune with our food at a large chain grocery store. At one time in the United States, 90 percent of the population was rural and grew food, a lot of it commercially. Today, less than 1.5 percent of our population grows all of our food and the food that we export throughout the world. The food-producing community is decidedly smaller and far more commercial.

Now we get high on asparagus by watching TV chefs slice, dice, and sauté it. We expect all sorts of fruits and vegetables to be available in our local supercenter regardless of the season, and children can't relate a hamburger to Bossy the cow. Food has become entertainment, and we sometimes rely on the entertainment industry to inform us about the good, the bad, and the ugly of the food world. You might even say that, as a nation, we have been absent from our food for a long time now. And since you've been absent, shouldn't you be growing fonder of food? Well, apparently not always. And certainly not with regard to the words "biotech food." Perhaps your communing with food needs to take a slightly different turn?

We've Come a Long Way, Baby

Biotechnology did not just start last year, even though it seems to be in the news more each day. People have been mucking around with genetics for a long time. Farmers have been developing new and different strains of livestock and plants for centuries. Corn was a small, almost grass-like weed once, but underwent monumental genetic changes by selection. Farmers selectively breed plants or animals with certain traits.

> **Chef Sez**
>
> **Biotechnology** is the manipulation of living cells and their components. Food biotechnology is the application of techniques, such as genetic engineering, to modify foods or processes. A **gene** is the portion of a chromosome that makes a particular protein. The genome is the entire blueprint of genes located in chromosomes.

They kept the traits they wanted, and eliminated those they didn't want, by choosing parents. The adults were mated and the offspring again selected. It takes many years and many generations to make this kind of genetic selection. All the *genes* are recombined each time mating occurs. It's like shuffling a deck of cards, always looking for the royal flush. And if you play poker, you know the odds of getting that perfect hand.

To understand biotechnology, you need to know a little bit about genetics. And to understand genetics, you need to understand something about life. Living organisms are made up of cells and molecules and genes and enzymes; and, guess what, so is food.

Beyond the Birds and Bees

Sex is heady stuff. It is very powerful because the endpoint is a new living being, an offspring from the mating. Sex is the recombination of chromosomes from two different parents. Chromosomes contain the organism's genetic blueprint. They contain genes—hundreds of thousands of genes, actually. The genome is the entire blueprint necessary to make another you, or another pig, or another stalk of asparagus.

If you have kids, it's easy to see the miracle of genetic recombination. Take a gander at your kids, or your neighbor's kids sometime. They share qualities of both parents. That's because they share half of each parent's genome. You may even spot a bit of grandma or grandpa in them. They are truly precious biological miracles.

But recombination of genes can occur with mistakes, too. Genetic errors happen. Imagine making a copy of a book that has over a million pages. And further imagine that you had to transcribe or write each page by hand and make absolutely no errors in each copy. Monks used to do this as they transcribed the Bible. Is it possible that maybe this could be why there are variations in different versions of even that sacred document?

When the sacred genome is copied with errors during sexual reproduction, the result may not be good. Sometimes the errors result in diseases. There are now techniques to identify where and what chromosomes carry these translation errors.

Transcribing genes also leads to genetic diversity. You recombine traits to see if you can reproduce some particularly desirable quality in the offspring. So, now we are back to the farmers again. They have been practicing low-powered genetic selection and *genetic engineering* using whole plants and animals for many years. And farmers have been assisted by a bunch of scientists located at agricultural experiment stations and state universities. Scientific knowledge is now interwoven into the production of your food, as it has been for over 150 years.

Chef Sez

Genetic engineering is a technique of modifying, moving, or adding genes to living organisms, usually adding a trait that people believe is desirable. It is also called gene splicing, recombinant DNA technology (rDNA), or genetic modification (GM).

The Power and Limits of Science

When it comes to scientific subjects, it is easy to become intimidated or even confused. There are always big words and big concepts and big issues associated with understanding food biotechnology. Scientists today have more and better tools with which they can peer into the cellular and molecular realm of life. The scientists aren't smarter today than those who worked before them; it's just that science is a process of discovery. It is based on observing, asking "what if," testing under controlled conditions, analyzing results, and making new observations. The process has not changed. But what science is looking at certainly has.

When scientists were racing to get to the moon a generation ago, this was exciting stuff. It was a race that involved nations. You could grasp the goal and its importance. That science was okay. Or when Dr. Salk developed a polio vaccine, it was pretty easy to see the advantages and consequences of his work. Today, science is working on your food. And though farmers and agricultural researchers have been doing science on food for generations, what is taking place now is much different. It goes beyond sexual reproduction, breeding, and traditional methods of selection of plants and animals. Now sex is the genome, and mating is taking on a new and confusing meaning. But maybe even more important to you and some scientists, the pace of science sometimes seems to be outrunning our ability to cope with it.

And this newfound knowledge can be power, and power can be frightening. Do you remember the very first time you got behind the wheel of a car when you were learning to drive? You suddenly had power and freedom, and maybe you were a bit in awe of it. But if you were smart, you also knew you had a responsibility to use that power and freedom wisely. Likewise, you ask scientists who work with your food to exercise their power wisely.

The concerns that you and the science community share is that genetic engineering of food produces something that you want, you need, and that is as wholesome and useful as food always has been. The debate over biotechnology is debate not only about this powerful scientific approach to food production, but also about political, moral, and social values, too. And in a strange way, the history of science and discovery has been like that for generations.

Wearing Your Genes, Inside and Out

Animal and plant breeding has made major genetic progress in your food choices. Though you may not know it, that pig raised on a farm today does not look like a pig did 50 years ago. The level of fat in most animals now raised for food is, in fact, a small percentage of what it once was. The farmer didn't allow his really fat pigs to breed, so future generations became leaner and leaner.

Chef Sez _____

An organism that has been changed using techniques of genetic engineering is called a **genetic modified organism,** or GMO. **DNA** (Deoxyribonucleic Acid) is the genetic material that passes information from one generation to the next. It works with cell RNA to make the proteins that become the parts of every living organism.

You benefit nutritionally from this genetic science because, as a consumer, that is what you wanted: less fat. Pigs are bred for leaner loins, which means that they give you leaner pork chops, a most valuable cut. Pigs with leaner loin muscle were allowed to breed, but fatter pigs just weren't allowed to have a date on Saturday night. Through many generations of selection, which might take 10 to 20 years, you had more leaner loin cuts to select from at the grocery store.

On the big macroscopic scale of life then, food has been changing genetically for millennia. And you have been part of that change by selecting or discarding various options along the way.

But, like life itself, there have been big bangs and defining events that shaped food and biotechnology. The discovery of what DNA actually looked like occurred only 50 years ago. It was a defining period in food biotechnology, though not many people realized it at the time. How things have changed since then. But think about this: The microwave oven was patented about the same time that we learned that DNA is a double helix. And now look at the changes in just this one simple appliance. It's been accepted. Most people have one. Yet, still people have just a little skepticism about whether it is safe to use and whether food cooked in a microwave oven is safe to eat. That fear existed 50 years ago, and still exists today. So, if we have food fears from using a microwave today, it shouldn't surprise you that we still have some fears about DNA and our food. Questions are good; they keep you honest.

Another leap in food biotechnology occurred when scientists learned that DNA could be manipulated. It could be handled, it could be massaged, and it could be moved—and moved without sex or breeding. While this is a decided disadvantage to the pleasure of the cow or the bull, it revolutionized the speed with which genetic progress could be accomplished. Not only DNA, which may have millions of genes in the genomic blueprint, but a single, individual gene could be moved. Maybe you only want the individual gene that's responsible for height, fat production, or resistance to drought. Hey, no problem.

Like many people, you probably want to know what this biotech food stuff is and whether it's safe to eat. Will it hurt me? Will it hurt our planet? What's in it for me, anyway; why should I even want the stuff? Why can't we just leave well enough alone? And maybe you want to know which foods have biotech ingredients, and which do not. Should we label it? Those are pretty logical questions and concerns. Such questions are the who, what, when, where, and how of science.

Future Shock

All this stuff has different names. You might hear genetically modified organism, or GMO for short. You might hear genetic engineered food. How about recombinant DNA or gene splicing or genetic modification? The lingo might be confusing and perhaps a little intimidating. Especially when people start suggesting that such unknowns are built into the salad dressing that you had for lunch.

But it pretty much gets down to a simple concept. Cellular DNA makes cellular RNA. The cellular RNA makes protein. And the type of protein in the cell makes you, or it makes asparagus, or corn, or tomatoes, or a cow. It's the assembly line of life. And all of your food was, at some point, alive.

So, you might be asking, where are the other food molecules? Isn't there fat, sugar, and water? And isn't it all about water? Well, water is the absolutely essential food mixologist. It's the bartender stirring the drink. All chemical reactions that make food molecules that eventually form into food cells need water. So, the whole process cannot begin without water.

But it's the proteins that are made by the DNA and RNA that are the key building blocks for food molecules. Some proteins are structural elements that give food shape. These are like the 2×4s that hold your house together. These cell-building structures also allow the food to hold and capture water.

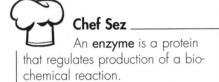

Chef Sez

An **enzyme** is a protein that regulates production of a biochemical reaction.

The other proteins are the key *enzymes*. Enzymes are like traffic cops. They regulate the flow of food-molecule traffic. They determine how fast things go and when things stop. They are switches. They control the making of the other food molecules, the sugar and fats. So, you might say that proteins and enzymes eventually make a bean a bean and a corn kernel a corn kernel.

Food biotechnology really starts at the beginning of this assembly line—the genome. Let's imagine just one gene as an example, though there are thousands. Maybe you are going to select a gene to make corn kernels sweeter. At the beginning of your assembly line, then, is the gene contained in the DNA that controls sweetness. The sweetness gene instructs and gives directions to the RNA.

RNA is the second major part of the genetic flow apparatus. The RNA copies the information from the sweetness gene to itself. It transcribes it. It is just like those monks who transcribed the Bible, making copy after copy. The transcribed RNA then passes its information to another messenger. This messenger RNA is another transfer station on the assembly line. The messenger RNA then passes on the instructions to eventually make the proteins. And the protein switches control the process. The proteins are so intelligent that they report back through the assembly line process and let the entire system know when to stop. It is a nice little self-contained system.

So, all the lingo you get about genes, and modifications and splicing and recombination all refer to that small area of the cell that is the DNA/RNA assembly line. What makes the task daunting and maybe a bit fearful is that there are millions of signals and protein switches to deal with, some routine, some not so routine. The process of food biotechnology has been built upon finding the key regulators. The key traffic cops affect an outcome, outcomes such as fruit ripening, or cheese making, or corn growing.

When you get right down to it, the only thing that makes biotechnology different from simple genetic selection is specificity and speed. Traditional selection is slow. The offspring are a mixture of the parents. It takes time to breed and to collect the results. If, however, you zero in on one key gene, which you know controls only one event, and you propagate or delete it, you've hit the target smack-dab in the center.

Whether it takes place through traditional breeding or by gene splicing, the end result is the same—genes are moved. The GMO route is simply quicker and more accurate.

Blessed Are the Cheese Makers

Biotechnology of sorts has been done since 1800 B.C.E. It involved the earliest cheese makers. Living bacteria found a happy home in milk, souring it into what might be similar to today's yogurt. You can still do this today, with attention, of course, to growing only the good bacteria, not the harmful ones.

You can make a fresh cheese that is very similar to ricotta, at home by two different methods. One method uses an enzyme that you can purchase at the grocery store, called rennet or junket. The other uses acid and heat to make the curd. For the enzyme method, you need a gallon of whole milk, $1/2$ cup of buttermilk, and about $1/3$ of a junket tablet.

To make the cheese, dissolve the junket in a tablespoon of water. Stir this mixture into the buttermilk. Warm the gallon of whole milk to just about 75°F. Measure the temperature with a thermometer so you don't overheat the milk. Add the buttermilk-rennet mixture to the warm milk. Cover the pan and leave in the refrigerator until the next day. The next day, you should find the milk has clotted. Line a big colander with cheesecloth, and spoon the cheese into the colander. Make sure you have the colander over a large bowl or pot. The liquid that drains off is whey. Let the cheese drain for a few hours, and then gather up the ends of the cheesecloth and pull them together. Squeeze out any additional whey. Fold some freshly chopped herbs into your soft cheese. Because the cheese is fresh, consume it in two to three days for best flavor.

If you cannot find rennet, then add 2 cups of buttermilk to your milk. Bring the milk to a gentle boil and add the juice from two lemons. Boil this for five minutes. The heat and acid from the lemon causes the curd to form. Ladle the hot milk into your cheesecloth-lined colander. Gather the ends of the cloth together, just like before, and form a ball. Let this rest for about an hour to drain some more. You then should have a nice fresh cheese.

Though no one knows for sure, it is likely that harder cheeses first resulted from someone carrying milk around in goat or lamb stomachs. These handy little bags were a perfect environment for cheese making. Why? Well, the stomach lining of lamb, goat, or calf produces a substance called rennet. Though folks did not know it at the time, rennet causes proteins in milk to coagulate into a curd. Coagulation by rennet is an actual biochemical process. It is a protein enzyme that hooks up with milk proteins. With rennet now clinging around them, the milk proteins can no longer float freely around in the milk. These proteins fall out of the milk water and settle on the bottom of the liquid. The settled-out solid proteins are the curd, and the curd is fashioned into cheese. So, any time milk was sloshing around in a bio-canteen, it likely would have reacted to the calf stomach cells, forming some curds.

Now, if you move from the time of the birth of the cheese-making process until circa 1984, you move into the modern biotechnology era of cheese. Scientists discovered what the active part of rennet was that caused milk to form a curd. (You are right if you concluded that science did not move swiftly to resolve this question.) That substance was another protein called chymosin. It was the smoking gun that shot proteins out of the milk to form curd.

Chymosin is so powerful that only 1 part of it in about 5 million parts of milk can cause curds to form. This was 1000 times more potent than rennet.

Food for Thought

You need a driver's license, a marriage license, and numerous permits to be legal. Bioengineered food also needs permits. In the U.S., three federal agencies are involved. The Food and Drug Administration (FDA) regulates food products. It evaluates the food from a nutritional standpoint. For example, does it differ from the nonengineered food in composition? Does the food contain allergens? Is the food generally recognized as safe? The United States Department of Agriculture (USDA) regulates field-testing of crops. What is the impact of the GMO on neighboring weed populations, for instance? Is there a danger of developing super weeds? Finally, the Environmental Protection Agency (EPA) oversees pesticide tolerance in the environment.

A GMO First

It isn't just the development of chymosin that is important to you; what's really significant is the way chymosin is manufactured. Back in 1990, chymosin became the first genetically modified product approved for use in the food industry. Today, most commercial cheese makers use chymosin manufactured through biotechnology. And it has been accepted not only in the U.S. but also in Europe, which has tended to ban most other GMO-derived products.

So, why is chymosin a biotech product? Well, cells in a calf stomach contained the gene that directed the production of rennet. The active form of the rennet is chymosin. Once the gene was located, it could be literally plucked off the DNA, like picking a single grape from a whole cluster of grapes.

Once scientists had the gene that makes the protein chymosin, they had to find an easy way to get it to work outside its usual cell machinery. The technique generally used in biotechnology is to take the gene and put it into a microorganism, such as a bacteria or yeast. These microorganisms grow tremendously fast, are easy to reproduce, and can provide a bio-factory of the gene product wanted. Once the gene is transferred, these little single-cell organisms then think the gene is their own; and if the process is successful, the gene does what genes do: They make the RNA and eventually the protein; in this case, they make chymosin. The assembly line process is turned on.

So, once yeast cells are churning out chymosin, the next step is to grow millions of these cells. If you make yeast bread, you will understand how to grow yeast pretty efficiently. Once billions of cells churn out chymosin, the rest is relatively simple. Just isolate the chymosin and, voila, you have a biotech product.

The advantage of producing chymosin this way is that you do not have to grind up millions of pounds of stomach tissue to get it (or some mushrooms where it is also, curiously, found). This is good for the calf, good for cheese making, and, ultimately, good for you the consumer.

One Tomato, Two Tomatoes

Tomatoes quickly joined cheese as a biotech food. In 1994, a product called the Flavr Savr tomato was marketed in the United States. Tomatoes, like all fruits, need to ripen. But almost as soon as a tomato reaches the perfectly ripe state, it starts to deteriorate. So, the goal was to engineer a tomato to delay ripening. This would allow firm tomatoes to be shipped, and extend their shelf life.

Genes that control tomato ripening were discovered and, you guessed it, once the switch was found, it was possible to turn off the ripening gene. This type of GMO differs from bioengineering of chymosin. The ability to turn off the gene for tomato ripening was actually functioning in the cell of the tomato. It became part and parcel of what was eaten. In cheese making, chymosin is engineered as a separate product, which then is used as an ingredient that causes cheese curds to form. So, in the case of chymosin, you have a genetically modified product, but the tomato was a whole food genetically modified organism.

The Flavr Savr tomato actually had within its cells a genetically modified part. The gene to turn off ripening was added to the cell and so, too, was a marker gene that made it easy to identify which tomato plants were keepers. In other words, scientists had to know which plants that were genetically engineered actually were successful transfers of the ripening gene. The bottom line was that the tomato you ate had genetically modified parts. And the modified parts did not come through traditional breeding methods; they came through genetic engineering.

Flavr Savr tomatoes were removed from the market in 1996 for economic, not health, reasons. This goes to show that not all bioengineering efforts are always successful. What the biotech tomato did do, however, was to usher in a cascade of other processes based on its technology.

Bye-Bye Bugs

Most of the GMO products marketed to date have been developed to make production methods easier or more efficient for farmers. You know how hard it is to keep weeds out of your own garden. Soybeans, corn, rapeseed (canola), and cotton all have been produced using assembly-line methods of bioengineering. The gene engineering focused on how to make a crop resistant to an herbicide. Then, when the weed killer was sprayed around the plant, it would survive but the weed wouldn't. The advantage is that rather than having to sprinkle on five different herbicides to kill five different weeds, a general all-purpose herbicide could be used. This technology caught on with farmers. They can now plant more acres of these crops and use less herbicide. This is good for the land, for the plants, and, ultimately, for you.

Food for Thought _____

Corn has been genetically modified with a natural toxin derived from a bacterial organism called *Bacillus thuringiensis* (Bt). Actually, 50 different natural insecticides have been isolated. These natural insecticides have been used for decades in organic agriculture. Biotechnology has succeeded in placing the gene that produces the insecticide directly into the corn plant's cells. Tomatoes and potatoes have also been successfully engineered with Bt. In 1995, the Russet potato became the first such insect-resistant crop to be approved through the federal regulatory process. Because the GMO-derived potato plant produces the insecticide naturally at all times, it has been a very effective tool for pest management. Today, sweet corn engineered with Bt needs 12 fewer chemical insecticides throughout its growing cycle than does nonengineered corn.

But weeds aren't the only thing that you battle in growing food. Another focus of bioengineering is to develop GMOs that are resistant to insect predators. For instance, genes placed inside a corn plant can produce a toxin that kills a particular bug that comes chewing on it. Again, the intent is to reduce the need for chemical pesticides.

Food as Pharmacy

It is anticipated that the next frontier for GMO crops will be to provide nutrient enhancements for grains and animals in order to benefit you more directly. You know that you can go to a pharmacy and buy vitamins, supplements, and medicines. It will be possible in the future to have a plant cell or animal cell churn out these supplements and give you the added benefit of getting your daily dose with your lunch. Along the same line of reasoning, plants that are engineered to have reduced levels of allergens may someday become part of your meal selections.

Organics Among Us

You might conclude that if conventional agriculture, which relies on herbicides and pesticides and now increasingly on biotechnology for producing food, is one form of farming, then *organic* agriculture would be just the opposite. And you'd be more or less correct.

Organic farming is a multi-billion-dollar part of agricultural production. Organic foods are produced according to a set of standards, whether grown in the United States or imported. Those standards require that the food be produced without using most conventional pesticides, petroleum-based fertilizers, sewage sludge-based fertilizers, hormones, bioengineering, or ionizing radiation. Producers cannot label an item "organic" unless the farm where the food is grown has been subject to inspection, to make sure the farmer is following all the rules necessary to meet USDA organic standards. All companies handling or processing organic food before it reaches your local supermarket or restaurant must be certified, also. Proponents argue that organic products are better for you, better for farm workers, and better for the environment.

> **Chef Sez**
> **Organic** refers to the process of growing food, both plants and animals, using no chemical herbicides or pesticides or GMOs.

Nothing New Here

Organic agriculture and farming methods didn't just sprout up recently. Over 40 years ago, the explosion in concern over DDT, a pesticide that killed songbirds and spread widely through the environment to other species, was a lightening rod that fueled an entire environmental consciousness. Recently, with the debate over GMOs as another mirror for reflection, organic farming again has become a popular alternative agricultural practice. Organic agricultural is now certified by the USDA. This means that federal and state governments, in conjunction with organic growers, regulate labeling of all organic products.

Organic agriculture offers some very sound approaches to farming and, in combination with some of the best conventional farming practices, needs to be a part of the whole of agriculture. Replenishing the soil with natural fertilizers like manures and reducing herbicides and pesticides is sound practice when done appropriately. Helping to make food-production methods sustainable so that key resources are not totally spent before they can regenerate is part of a healthy ecosystem. Practicing a healthy conservation is good from a scientific as well as a social perspective.

Risky Eating

You might get the impression that organic food, which some call natural, is somehow superior to food produced by conventional means, or through biotechnology. But there is no scientific evidence that any bioengineered food has caused illness, or differs in nutritional quality from organic food. Some people simply choose to eat organic for political or social reasons.

And you really should not be surprised to learn that "natural food" still contains toxins. Plants produce toxic substances in their seeds, stems, and leaves. These toxins are natural deterrents to pests. They are the defensive shield of plant crops such as soybeans, rapeseeds, barley, and rye, all of which produce toxic substances naturally.

An interesting study done over 10 years ago looked at exposure to toxins naturally found in foods. These natural toxins were compared with the intake of man-made herbicides. You might be surprised to know the results. The intake of commonly occurring toxins naturally found in plants is much greater than any known man-made chemicals. Natural exposure to such things as caffeic acid in lettuce, potatoes, carrots, and plums, and d-limonene in orange juice and black pepper occur routinely if you eat these foods. In fact, more than 99 percent of the chemicals you eat are naturally occurring plant pesticides, not chemicals applied by spraying.

Now, don't run to the kitchen and throw away your lettuce or dump your orange juice. The conclusion is not that natural foods will cause cancer; far from it. The point is that stringent protections against man-made chemicals are greater than any protection from naturally occurring ones, which you consume every day. Simply put, eating is, and probably will always be, a risky business. But it's better than the alternative.

The cost of your food and its long-term affordability are additional considerations in the food-production debate. If all agriculture suddenly converted to organic methods tomorrow, our ability to produce the quantity of food necessary to sustain the growing human population would be in jeopardy. Food cost is certainly another hotly debated question for scientists. Perhaps in the end it will be some marriage between organic and conventional agriculture, including biotechnology, that will be the best practice for guiding and sustaining food production through our new century.

The Least You Need to Know

- Foods that utilize bioengineering methods have been produced and consumed for a decade or more.
- Most commercially produced cheese is made with a GMO-derived ingredient.
- Adverse health or environmental effects never have been documented for GMO-type foods.
- Organic foods are those produced without intentional additives such as hormones, pesticides, or synthetic fertilizers.
- Organic foods are not toxin free, nor do they differ in nutritional quality from conventionally grown food.
- Combining organic agriculture with conventional agriculture using biotechnology is likely the best way to proceed into the new millennium of food production and sustainability.

Part 2

Eat Your Veggies ... and Other Stuff

You were always told to eat your vegetables so you would grow up to be strong. That was good advice then and it is good advice now. Plants epitomize the concept of healthy, living food. Vibrant colors, aromas, textures, and nutrients are plant food's signature. How you handle and cook these foods can either maximize or minimize those qualities.

As living food, you will examine the many parts of plants that we use as main courses or ingredients. Whether seeds, stems, roots, or leaves, there is virtually no part of the collective plant world you don't run into somewhere along your journey through the kitchen. Plant foods virtually cover the globe as the most abundant source of our food energy. You can roast or toast, bake or fry, simmer or boil parts and pieces of plants as food. Obviously, a little practical knowledge of plant starches, proteins, and fats will make you appreciate your veggies a little bit more.

The Color Purple

In This Chapter

- ◆ Keeping veggies and fruits colorful and youthful
- ◆ The carrot and the bean: texture experiments
- ◆ Just like grandma used to make

Without plants, there would be no food chain for you to be part of; in fact, there would be no you. You owe the air you breathe and the food you eat to plants. Life through plant photosynthesis is built on the color green. Funny, but, come to think of it, many of your most important symbols also are built on the color green. You use the greenback. You go on green. You are children of the green revolution. There was the greening of America. When you were young, you were green in judgment, according to Shakespeare. Even when you eat too much food, you look a little green. Or maybe you have a green thumb or are green with envy for your neighbor's vegetable garden. Green seems pretty basic to food and to life.

Of course, plants include a lot more colors than just green. This chapter will cover unique and special aspects of orange, red, yellow and even white veggies during the handling and cooking process. Nutrition, taste and appearance all depend upon how you handle the colorful vegetable palate.

A Pigment of Your Imagination

There are three basic classes of colors found in plants. All of the colors of the plant world are divided into these three categories, depending on the dominant *pigments* they contain. Most common is the green of chlorophyll. This is the pigment that is essential for *photosynthesis*. Carotenoid pigments dominate in orange, orange-red, and yellow plants, whether carrots, cantaloupes, or maple leaves in autumn. Flavonoid pigments dominate in purple, blue, and red plants, such as blueberries, cherries, and red roses. And surprisingly, flavonoid pigments also dominate in colorless or off-white plants such as cauliflower, onions, and potatoes. Just as we have different skin tones, plants are diversified by the colors that define them.

You are pretty much stuck with your skin color from birth to death, though. Oh, you may have the occasional suntan, but human skin biology is pretty much fixed naturally by the level of the pigment melanin. Plants are a bit more creative; their color changes as the plant ages and matures. While most plants start out pretty green, they might go through a range of different colors from youth to old age. Sometimes stress causes a plant to change colors during its life cycle. Of course, stress affects our pigments, too; our hair might turn prematurely gray, for instance.

> **Chef Sez**
>
> A **pigment** is a natural substance in plant or animal cells that imparts a color characteristic. Pigments are grouped into classes based upon their light-reflecting properties. **Photosynthesis** is the process by which plants use the gas CO_2 (carbon dioxide) to produce sugar, which is their food. In the process of photosynthesis, plants produce and give off oxygen.

Vegetables and fruits don't come in a vast array of colors just for fun. Color is an attractant, and plays into a plant's survival and evolution. Color attracts you and other creatures such as birds and bees. You tend to eat things that are attractive, because a healthy color indicates a high nutritional value. Being eaten by birds and bees and other beasts is actually good for the plant, because these creatures end up as plant messengers, spreading the seeds to help complete the plant's life cycle. So, you might say that plant color is important in the evolution of not only photosynthesis but also natural plant genetics.

We humans get a charge out of the color of fruits and vegetables; they attract us. They add variety to our meals, and they're good for us. So, cooking them without destroying their color and nutritional value is an important part of food science and culinary technique. Not surprising, the different color pigments found in plants react differently to acids, bases, and heat during cooking. Ever wonder why your spinach or asparagus turned mushy or olive drab? Hang on; you're about to find out.

Stable and Unstable Colors

The vast array of colorful vegetables looks quite impressive in your grocer's vegetable section, doesn't it? But sometimes they don't look so nice by the time we get them on the dinner table. Although once a vegetable is mature and ready to eat, its pigment level is mostly fixed, the pigments can be affected by how we handle the food. Peeling, slicing, dicing, and cooking all can affect the color of plant foods. Understanding the science of pigments and the changes that occur in them will help you keep the color of the food vibrant and alive as you cook.

Colors That Are Stable

The most stable pigments in plants and vegetables also happen to be the most abundant in nature. The carotenoids that you see in carrots, tomatoes, oranges, sweet potatoes, yellow squashes, pumpkins, sweet corn, and red peppers all belong to this family of pigments. The pigments in these foods are markers that you use to judge freshness and nutrition.

Carotenoids also exist in substantial amounts in green leaves, but they are hidden from you. Chlorophylls dominate, making leaves appear green. Spinach and most green vegetables have a high abundance of carotenoids that you cannot see. Carotene is a necessary substance that your body needs in order to make Vitamin A. That's one reason why spinach is so healthy for you.

Food for Thought

Carotenoids naturally come out of hiding in a glorious way each year. If you are lucky enough to have seen the northeast in the fall, you have experienced the miracle of carotenoids appearing. In the summer, tree leaves are mostly brilliant green. Come the first good frost, though, green gives way to the special array of reds, oranges, and yellows that signify the onset of autumn. Leaves undergo stress when cold weather arrives, and chlorophyll activity ceases. Now the carotenoids dominate. The change in the foods and colors of summer, typical when chlorophyll was king, give way to the crisp, cool colors and smells of autumn as the carotenoids come into full bloom. Our emotions are definitely affected by color, and seasonal cooking is cooking based on color.

Carotenoids are not just another pigment with a pretty face; they do serve a function for the plant. Carotenoids protect chlorophyll. Chlorophyll is important in generating the sugars for the plants by capturing light energy through photosynthesis.

But oxygen can act against chlorophyll, making it less active. Carotenoids keep oxygen at bay and enable chlorophyll to do its thing. Carotenoids also help plant roots grow and mature properly.

The substance beta-carotene is the most abundant carotenoid found in our food. These pigments increase in the plant as it matures and grows. Take the tomato as an example. Fried green tomatoes are a staple in the south but contain less carotenoid that those wonderfully vine-ripened tomatoes we enjoy. Even if you pick a tomato when it is green, it will continue to produce lycopene, the carotenoid that makes tomatoes red. Tomatoes go from light to very deep shades of red as lycopene levels increase.

One of the advantages of working with foods containing carotenes is that the pigments are generally sturdy and strong. This means that fruits and vegetables with plenty of these pigments are more forgiving of the abuse cooks dish out. Part of this stability is because of the structure of carotenoids. They are chains of carbon linked together with rings attached to each end of the chain. Because they exist in a fairly straight line, like a chain-linked fence, there are less nooks and crannies. Also there are less appendages hanging out. So, things such as heat, acids, or enzymes that might attack and destroy pigments have less of a chance of doing so. Acid or prolonged cooking may reduce the color intensity of carotenoid-dominated foods (think of over-cooked carrots, here) but all in all, plants in this color family are pretty stable foods.

Colors That Are Unstable

Chlorophyll and flavonoid pigments are not as stable as carotenoids. The chemical nature of these pigments presents interesting challenges when preparing vegetables such as green beans or red cabbage.

Chlorophyll's structure contains the metal magnesium in a ring-like molecule. Think of the molecular structure of chlorophyll as a bicycle tire, with magnesium firmly attached in the center where the spokes meet. The structure of chlorophyll is very important for it to be able to do its thing. And that thing is to capture enough energy from sunlight to make sugars for the plant to use as food. But because it is a ringed structure, it is less stable. Chlorophyll does not like heat. Chlorophyll also does not like acidic conditions. Both heat and acids change the position of the magnesium in the wheel of the chlorophyll molecule. And when this happens, the color of the pigment changes dramatically and quickly, right before our eyes. Those beautiful green beans can suddenly appear a drab olive brown.

Flavonoids are also ring-like pigments. Flavonoids are found in fruits and vegetables that appear blue, purple-red, or on the off-white end of the color spectrum.

Examples of foods containing flavonoids are grapes, blueberries, red cabbage, radicchio, cauliflower, or onions. There are two types of flavonoids. One is called anthocyanin, which is the pigment that gives the blue-violet shades. The other flavonoid is called anthoxanthin, which gives cauliflower and onion their yellow or off-white tones.

Unlike our friend chlorophyll, which doesn't play well with acid, flavonoids love acid. They would love to bathe in vinegar or lemon juice. Acids make them brighter and redder. But give them some baking soda, which is very alkali, and look out. The ring-like structure that was so happy taking a shower in white wine vinegar suddenly turns into a completely different creature. Your nice red cabbage turns an amazing shade of blue. Or those nice blueberries suddenly develop a greenish cast.

So, what gives? Mother Nature has put an array of colors in vegetables. Many times they exist in the same plant at the same time. Yet, we know that different pigments like different things and don't necessarily always get along. How do the pigments remain so stable in the veggie, yet when we handle or work with them in the kitchen we can change a perfectly beautiful green bean into something less than attractive? What the food looks like on your plate depends upon what you choose to do to it. And your choice ultimately depends on your knowledge of how the plant was put together in the first place.

Back to Anatomy Lessons

Plant cells are like large department stores. Different departments and compartments provide different services. Generally, the store is very coordinated and runs like a well-oiled machine; the parts and pieces provide a division of labor to improve efficiency. You usually don't buy underwear in the same aisle where you purchase pots and pans. So, plant cells don't keep pigments in the same place where they keep acids, especially if the pigments don't do well around such things.

Cell walls are the rigid structures of plants that provide the basic scaffolding to hold everything together in a plant cell. The cell wall is the outside covering that holds all the goodies inside, just as our cell baggie example described in Chapter 1. And of course, helping to glue together the millions of little cells that comprise a carrot, for example, are substances called pectin and cellulose. These plant glues function just like the sticky substance called collagens that we will discuss when we talk about meat and fish later on. Within these plant cells, floating in a sea of

Food for Thought

Plant fiber is the nondigestible part of the cell wall comprised of cellulose and pectin substances. The cell wall provides structure and rigidity for plants, just as our bones and cartilage do for us.

liquid sap and water are our compartments. Some compartments hold the chlorophyll and carotenoid pigments. Some compartments hold the starches or sugars used as food. Other centers are command units such as the nucleus, which acts as one big computer running the whole show through DNA and the making of enzymes. Some compartments hold acidic compounds that are important for plant defensive mechanisms against bugs and predators.

The names of these different plant-cell compartments are not really important for us. What is important is the understanding that different things are segregated. They are segregated so that control and communication are achieved. They are segregated so that things that don't get along together are kept apart. It's a pretty impressive arrangement in nature when you think about it. When we disrupt this arrangement during preparation and cooking, it is likely to have consequences.

When a carrot is harvested, its relationship with nature is changed. When you cut, peel, slice, and dice that carrot, you are breaking down the compartmentalization of the living cells. Where once there was organization, now there is chaos. Where once acids were stored in nice little private compartments within the cells, now acids run into pigments, which run into enzymes through the cell sap, as contents are mixed together. As cooks, we change the appearance of the food by processing it. At the same time, we want to preserve as much of the color and nutrition as possible. Understanding the cell chemistry and biology will help us to achieve both goals: serving more nutritious food, and serving it in a texture, form, and color that are appealing.

Though you might think that working with enzymes only happens when nerds in white lab coats perform experiments, you have already experienced enzymes first-hand in your own kitchen. You've likely sliced apples, or bananas, or potatoes, or an avocado, and left them to sit on the counter for some time while you were preoccupied with other chores. When you came back and looked at your food, it had turned a nasty brown, looking less than appetizing. You just experienced enzymes and the process of *oxidation* first-hand.

By cutting the food, you sliced through some cells. Before you cut into the food, the cells were happy little kingdoms, neatly packaged with all of their enzymes, acids, and pigments neatly tucked away for safe keeping. Suddenly your sharp knife exposed an interior surface, releasing some of the enzymes to the oxygen in the air. The enzyme that is the culprit for browning your food is called phenoloxidase.

Along with oxygen, phenoloxidase attacks some of the phenols in the food. Phenols are in the family of flavenoids. When the enzyme latches onto the phenol, it changes its structure. The change in the phenol molecule now appears as a brown spot. The longer the exposure, the more brown the food becomes, because the more phenol is changed by the enzyme.

> **Chef Sez**
>
> **Oxidation** is the process whereby oxygen steals part of the energy from another molecule. This energy is in the form of a charge called an electron. When oxygen steals an electron, the compound becomes less stable. For foods, this instability may manifest itself through the way it looks or tastes. Oxidation in nature is like first-degree robbery. It might decrease the shelf life of a food, or make it appear old and tired. Antioxidants are added to foods and function like guards in a bank. They deter the crime of oxidation. Many pigments serve as antioxidants. We also do things to food to reduce the chances of oxidation. These things include the magic of plastic wrap, airtight containers, freezing, and vacuum packaging.

So, do you have any recourse to prevent it and keep your food looking fresh for as long as possible? Fortunately, it is lemon juice to the rescue. Phenoloxidase does not like acid, but phenols do. So, rubbing lemon juice on the cut surface of the food blocks browning. You can also do a few other things to prevent what is called enzymatic browning, or those ugly brown spots. Covering the surface tightly with plastic wrap prevents the oxygen from contacting the cut surface. Covering and refrigerating the food works even better. Enzymes such as phenolase do not like the cold, so they work slower, and when they slow down, enzymatic browning slows down.

You can also plop the food in a bowl of water containing slices of lemon; this also prevent oxygen contact, and adds acid at the same time. Place potatoes in a pot of salted water to prevent them from browning. Or, if you don't mind the added sugar on some foods, coat the surface with some sugar syrup or jelly glaze. This also seals the surface from oxygen. Enzymatic browning does not occur in citrus fruit or tomatoes. Why? Because there is no phenoloxidase enzyme. Besides, even if there were, the fruit is so acidic that it would not be too active, anyway. So, slice and dice citrus all you want, and don't worry about browning.

Texture and Handling

So, let's recap. Vegetables are comprised of cells. Within the cells are the basic machinery that runs the biology that makes a carrot a carrot, for example. Nature has designed the carrot to carry on life so that other little baby carrots follow. The carrot has pigments, enzymes, and DNA to help it make proteins and to synthesize food such as starches and fats. Now you suddenly decide to break into a carrot. You peel it and cut it and, in so doing, make a major onslaught into its interior cells. Your knife is disrupting the machinery that once was the carrot. We are opening its tissue up to more oxidation, which can further deteriorate its color. You are slicing through compartments, releasing acids and pigments that now can intermingle. After this onslaught, what do you expect to happen?

Actually, the effects depend on the class of pigments you are working with. It's easier to explain by doing a little kitchen experiment. Let's take the carrot and its stable pigment carotene first. Or for that matter, choose any vegetable that fits into the carotenoid category. You can slice and dice them, boil them or *blanch* them. You can cook them uncovered or covered, salted or unsalted, with vinegar or without. Not much happens to the color. If anything, a quick blanch for one to two minutes actually makes them a bit brighter. This is mostly due to the fact that the heat forces oxygen out of the carrot cells, so the pigment actually reflects light better. So, you might conclude that foods that contain carotenoids are pretty forgiving. And if you want to choose a class of vegetables that keep their color from processing to plate, this is a good choice. Of course, we are not recommending that you cut carrots and leave them sitting on the counter for 32 days. They will dry out. And carotenoids do go through oxidation. But for the most part, these classes of pigments and veggies are on our "A list" for stability.

To demonstrate this for yourself go get some fresh bright green beans. *Blanch* some and reserve the rest. To blanch beans properly, bring 1 gallon of water to a boil with 2 tablespoons of kosher salt. Get another pan or bowl large enough to hold the beans and fill it halfway with cold water and ice cubes. Have a strainer handy. Cook the beans for three minutes by immersing them in the boiling water. If the water stops boiling when the beans are added, allow the water to begin boiling again before beginning your timer. When the three minutes are up, use your strainer to transfer the beans to the bowl of ice water. Notice the green color of the blanched and *shocked* beans compared with the raw ones. The blanched beans are much brighter. You can now drain the beans from the ice water and keep them refrigerated.

> **Chef Sez**
>
> **Blanching** is a technique in which fruits or vegetables are plunged into boiling water for a very short period of time. The food is then **shocked** or refreshed by immediately placing it in ice water to stop the cooking process. Blanching is used to firm texture, remove skins, or set color.

You are going to cook the remaining beans in a covered pot. Take a little water, just enough to cover half the amount of beans you have, add some salt and pepper, and put the beans in a pan with a lid. Cover and simmer (no peeking) until they are tender. This might take 15 to 20 minutes, but never remove the lid. While they are cooking, take a hot skillet and add some olive oil. Toss in the beans that you previously blanched and shocked, and cook them with some salt and pepper and, if you like, some chopped garlic. Cook uncovered for three to four minutes, or until they just soften but still have a snap. Now put them on a plate. By this time, our covered beans are done. Take off the lid and put them on a plate besides the other beans. Compare the color and notice how bright and green the blanched beans are compared to the beans cooked in plain water in a covered pot. Now think back and recall how bright the carrots remained no matter what we seemed to do to them.

From this little exercise we might conclude that carotene pigments are pretty stable but that chlorophyll in green beans can be affected by our cooking method. Chlorophyll is not bomb proof under all circumstances. Green beans blanched and then reheated in a pan with oil remained bright green. Beans simmered in a covered pot were drab olive green. This raises the eternal question, why?

Now You're Cooking

Cooking any vegetable is a process to break down the plant cells and make them more palatable. The fiber of the cell walls actually starts to melt from the heat. And when this happens, the cells begin to leak their contents. Whatever substances were neatly packaged away in the raw cells begin to react to the heat. The contents of the cells, such as acids and enzymes and starches, begin to mix together as the interior of the cell was damaged by the heat. So, just like chopping and dicing releases some of the cell's contents, which we see as water on our cutting board, cooking does the same thing. And, as the cells give up their contents, it can have a dramatic affect on the pigments.

When we blanch and partially cook green beans, we are using heat to destroy one of the enzymes that would typically be released from the cell to cause the destruction of the chlorophyll molecule. This enzyme is called chlorophyllase. We do the same thing when we heat the beans covered; the enzyme checks out, so to speak. This can actually be a good thing because, by blocking the enzyme that destroys chlorophyll, we should keep the plant a nice, bright green.

Yet, by cooking the beans in a covered container with a small amount of water, we actually are doing something more. The acids that are released from the cells of the beans as they cook cannot escape from the pot because of the lid. They percolate back into the pan and bathe the beans. So, the magnesium that was happy sitting in the center of the chlorophyll molecule when acid was neatly compartmentalized in the raw cell, now suddenly finds itself bathed in its own acid rain. In response to the acid, chlorophyll can no longer hold onto the magnesium, and releases it. As magnesium leeches out, chlorophyll changes into another substance entirely, one that is a dull olive brown.

Conversely, when we cook beans in a large amount of water without a lid, some of the acids are released into the steam. There is no acid rain. And because we have so much water and only a few beans to blanch, the remaining acids that might stick around in the water don't have a chance to get to the chlorophyll because we have diluted them with so much liquid. So, blanching green beans for a few minutes in large amounts of water with the lid off keeps the beans bright green. And when we reheat the beans later, we do so for only enough time to complete the cooking process, not long enough to destroy the chlorophyll with excess heat. The end result is that by applying our knowledge of cell chemistry and cooking, we can serve a brighter green bean for dinner.

So, you ask, is it true that adding baking soda to the pan and cooking the beans covered will keep the color bright? Well, yes, this is true. Baking soda neutralizes the beans' own acids. This is equivalent to you taking some antacids to counter acid reflux in your stomach. But there's a big trade-off. Baking soda also causes the fiber in the bean to melt much more than it normally would from heat alone. Pectin, one of the cell glues, dissolves much more in the presence of an alkali such as baking soda. This is a double whammy as far as the texture of the bean goes. The fiber melts so much from both the heat and the soda that the beans turn to mush, which isn't very palatable. So, while many old cookbooks recommend this procedure, blanching and reheating are by far the best method to keep both the green in and the texture crisp. Unless, of course, you like bright green bean mush, then by all means load up on baking soda.

Cooking Like Grandma, Sometimes

Unlike chlorophyll, flavonoids love acid. The blues, violets, and white colors in fruits and vegetables are actually maintained better with some acid around. And, as you might expect, baking soda is a big-time enemy. Making an *étuvée of* red cabbage is a great way to demonstrate the principle of acids and bases. It's a form of moist-heat cooking where vegetables are sweated in their own juices. Because the pot is covered, you create an environment where all the acids from the veggies return to the dish, helping to soften the vegetable. Your choice of vegetable to étuvée determines the outcome because of the effect on various pigments.

> **Chef Sez**
>
> **Étuvée** means to cook in a covered pot with a minimal amount of liquid. It is especially good for preparing vegetables, and is a form of moist-heat cooking similar to braising. **Render** means to cook a fat piece of meat until the fat melts out and the meat crisps. Always use low heat so the meat does not burn.

Remember that veggies with flavonoids love acid? They adore a covered pot and slow cooking. You can demonstrate this for yourself with an étuvée of red cabbage and red onion.

Find a Dutch oven or lidded pot that is large enough to hold 2 heads of shredded red cabbage comfortably. Slice 1 large red onion. Melt an ounce of butter in the pot. Add the onion and cook for two minutes. Toss in the shredded cabbage, some salt and pepper, and 3 tablespoons of cider vinegar. Some really classic versions add a dollop of red currant jelly, too. This jelly is tart yet sweet, and adds a nice contrast to the vinegar. Now cover and cook on low until the cabbage is tender, about an hour, maybe longer. You should have a beautifully melted cabbage dish with nice color and a little bite. The heat and the steam from the liquid that seeped out of the cabbage and onion cells mixed with the vinegar. These juices percolated to the top of the lid and fell back into the pot. You've succeeded in creating a nice, warm acid-rain forest, and the flavonoids kept their color.

Now, you can take our word for it or you can cook the same red cabbage dish but make a few ingredient substitutions. Instead of vinegar, dissolve a couple of tablespoons of baking soda in $1/4$ cup of water. Omit the salt and sprinkle the red onion and cabbage with the soda water. Cover and cook. You should have nice blue cabbage and onions. You've succeeded this time in creating alkaline rain. The soda now changes the flavonoids chemical structure so that it looks blue.

You can use the knowledge of acid to help keep other flavonoid-containing vegetables brighter and more natural looking. Acids such as lemon juice can keep cooked cauliflower brighter. Even potatoes, which contain the flavonoid anthoxanthin, will stay much whiter when cooked in water with a splash of lemon juice or vinegar.

The Least You Need to Know

- Fruits and vegetables change color as they ripen; preparation and cooking also affect the color of vegetables.
- Carotenoids, found in such things as carrots, red peppers, pumpkin, corn, and squash are the most abundant pigments, and are very stable to most handling and cooking techniques.
- Green vegetables contain chlorophyll and are most susceptible to damage from cooking, so blanch them in an uncovered pot of boiling water to keep colors bright.
- Cooking green vegetables with slow moist heat will soften and discolor them, but can add deep flavors. An alkali such as baking soda will turn green vegetables to mush.
- Red cabbage, red onions, cauliflower, and other vegetables containing flavonoids are most stable in acids such as lemon juice or vinegar. These vegetables do well cooked by slow moist heat.

Chapter 8

Starch: Not Just for Shirts Anymore

In This Chapter

- ◆ From French fries to baked spuds
- ◆ Potatoes aren't rice
- ◆ Keeping rice nice

You cannot possibly learn even the basics of food science without running into starch at every turn. That's because plants are pretty important in your diet; and starch is the plant's food that is important in their diet. So, if you eat plants (and who doesn't?), you have eaten starch. And if you have enjoyed grains and cereals and flours and all the good stuff made from them, then you have eaten starch. When we talk about sauce-making later, you'll find that starch is one of the prime players there as well. For now, let's examine two starchy foods considered diet staples—potatoes and rice—in detail.

It Starts with Sugar

Sugar is a relative of starch. Table sugar is composed of two *carbohydrates*, glucose and fructose. They bond together like a brother and sister, creating sucrose. A spoonful of table sugar easily dissolves in liquids. That is why it is such a good sweetener in foods and beverages. It is highly *soluble*.

___

Chef Sez

Carbohydrates are sugars. They may be single molecules (monosaccharides such as glucose), two molecules hooked up (disaccharides such as sucrose), or several molecules hooked up (oligosaccharides, which humans can't digest). When hundreds of thousands of sugars hook up, they are called polysaccharides. Starch is a polysaccharide. **Solubility** refers to the ability of one substance to dissolve into another substance. Water is usually the standard we use to determine solubility. Usually substances that are highly soluble in water are less soluble in other liquids such as oil.

___

Now take a look at cornstarch and compare it to table sugar. Cornstarch is nice and white and smooth to the touch; it even looks like powdered sugar. But there is a big difference in the carbohydrates that make up cornstarch as compared to the carbohydrates that make up table sugar. Starch is made of very long chains of glucose hooked end to end. There are not just two sugars hooked up like table sugar; there are millions linked together.

Consider this: When you have only two small substances hooked together, it is easier to fit them into a space. Think about holding hands with another person. It's fairly easy to imagine walking down the street hand in hand. Now imagine holding hands with someone who is holding hands with someone else; walking down the sidewalk becomes a bit more difficult. Next imagine that there are 1,000 people all holding hands. The task of keeping everyone aligned and hooked together is much more problematic. The sugar linkages in simple sugar are like two people holding hands, while the linkages in starch are like 1,000 people holding hands.

Starch, with its billions of tiny little sugars hooked up, creates a stable world for itself by bending and folding. It's arranged something akin to a wound-up ball of yarn tightly packed together. These wound-up balls are starch granules. The cells of starchy foods such as potatoes and rice are full of these granules. And these granules love water.

The term "hygroscopic" means "water-attracting." Starch loves water, so it is naturally very hygroscopic. Starch's water-loving property is critical in how starchy foods react when you cook them. Each granule can soak up hundreds of times its weight in moisture. Cooking potatoes or rice involves getting water into the starch grains that are packed into the cells. Potatoes are one of the most important vegetables for understanding starch food chemistry. Rice is another.

You Say Po-TAY-to; I Say Po-TAH-to

The potato is a tuber, the underground stem in which a plant stores its food for winter. That stored food is starch. Although there are many different kinds of potatoes, we sometimes get hung up on cooking one type called the Idaho or russet. Sometimes we throw in some round red or round white ones. When the potatoes are very young, we might serve up new potatoes.

Yet, potatoes need not be brown-skinned with a white interior. When the potato was first cultivated by the natives of Peru thousands of years ago, they developed many different types. The interior can range in color from blue to black to deep red. It just so happens that when the Spanish took some varieties back to Europe, the white potato caught on best. No matter what color or type of potato you might want to cook, the basic premise of cooking them is pretty much the same. The goal is to attack those starch granules. Not surprisingly, some potato varieties have more starch than other varieties. Knowing which type of potato you have, and applying the best cooking method for that type, will give you the best results from your kitchen lab.

Packed and Ready to Roll

If you take your sharp chef's knife and cut through an Idaho spud, you can peer inside and look at the starch. You can't see it as you would a bowl of cornstarch because it is packed inside all of the cells of the potato. You'll likely strike a little water and see this moisture start to ooze out from the cells you just sliced open. As you make each new cut, something should begin to happen to the potatoes as they touch your knife blade. The potato slices tend to stick to the knife.

What you are doing as you cut up potato cells is releasing starch and water. Since water loves to flow toward something dry, and starch granules are packed full of dry interwoven starch molecules, it's a natural fit. And because starch is not too soluble in water, the starch in the water from the potato has tackiness. It coats and sticks to the surface of the knife.

Let's cook some starch to see how it behaves. To do this, you need to cook the starch without any surrounding cellular material getting in the way. Cornstarch is the perfect pure starch for this purpose.

Put 4 tablespoons of raw cornstarch in a small saucepan. Add 1 cup of cold water and swirl the pan around. Put the pan over medium high heat. Swirl the pan back and forth as the starch cooks, lifting it off the burner a time or two as you swirl. You will see changes. As the starch cooks, it begins to lose its milky white appearance. The liquid clears a bit and begins to thicken after about two to three minutes. Now pour half of the liquid out onto a plate. Let it sit for 10 minutes.

Meanwhile, add about a cup of cold water to the hot pan with the remaining cooked starch. Swirl and add more water until a quarter of the pan is full. Now the suspended cooked starch is much clearer. You still have a thin layer on the bottom of the pan, but the starch became noticeably more soluble in the cold water after it was cooked. After 10 minutes, look at the cooked starch that you poured on the plate. It has set a bit and has a very soft gel-like feel. Rub your finger over it; pick some up and let it slip between your thumb and forefinger. It's slippery and smooth. Now take some raw cornstarch and sprinkle it over the cooked starch on the plate. Mix this together with your fingers. As you add more and more raw starch, the slippery, silky smooth cooked cornstarch starts to get sticky and tacky.

Chef Sez

Gelatinization is the process by which starch granules are cooked. When placed in a liquid and heated, starch will absorb moisture and then swell and soften. Gelatinization occurs at different temperatures for different starches. For most food starches it occurs between 135 and 160°F.

So, what really happened in this little series of experiments? You have just demonstrated an important event called *gelatinization*. All starches gelatinize when cooked. You suspended the starch in cold water and then added heat. Before the mixture was heated, the billions of tiny granules were suspended in the liquid like so many billiard balls. Raw starch is sticky and tacky when cold, but soft and slippery when cooked.

When you cook a spud that has cells jam-packed with starch granules, the basic process of gelatinization is the same. All potatoes are not created equal, however. While all potatoes are packed with lots of starch and have a good supply of protein, there are two basic types of potato: waxy and mealy. The difference in these two types has to do with both the starch content and the air retained after cooking.

Potato Types by Starch Content and Use

Potato Type	Starch	Varieties	Best Used In
Waxy	Low	Red, small white	Salads, stews
Mealy	High	Russet, long white	Baking, fries, mashed

When waxy potatoes cook, the cells are denser, with less separation at their cell boundaries. Mealy potatoes cook up lighter because the cells separate when heated. Mealy spuds have so much more starch that when the cells swell during gelatinization, they actually burst, creating air spaces.

From French Fries to Baked Spuds

Potatoes can be cooked by all cooking methods. You can use dry heat for French fries, hash browns, or baked potatoes; you can use moist heat to boil or simmer them for mashed potatoes or potato salad; you can braise them as part of a stew; or you can use steam by baking them wrapped in foil, or under wax paper in the microwave.

No matter which cooking method you choose, your mission is the same. You want to cook the potato through to the interior. The surface appearance depends upon the cooking method you choose to use, and the size and shape of the pieces of potato you cook.

Fry Me to the Moon

The challenge in making a French fry is to get a nice brown crust, a somewhat crisp surface, yet, at the same time, a creamy soft center. Thickness matters. It matters because of heat transfer. It simply takes longer to cook the interior of thicker pieces of potato. So, when you immerse a piece of potato chock full of starch into hot fat, you have to think about how long it will take to cook both the outside and the inside. As you might expect, the surface will cook much faster than the interior.

The outside cooks faster in a French fry because the cut surfaces are coated with starch. And since gelatinization occurs at about 140°F, plopping a wet sticky fry into 375°F fat exceeds this temperature nearly three-fold. Add in some surface protein and you get browning.

The problem of overcooking the outside of the fry while leaving the interior underdone is best solved by a double cooking process. But before you do the Texas two-step, you need to deal with your sticky wicket, the outside starch on the spud.

Food for Thought _____

If you do French fries or other vegetables a lot and want to cut them into a consistent shape, you may want to invest in another gizmo. It's called a mandoline. You can't play music with this device but it speeds up cutting and enables you to do specialty cuts that are not possible with a knife alone. The mandoline is a frame built around very sharp cutting blades. The blades can be adjusted to cut French fries, thin slices of potatoes, and smaller matchstick shapes. There are also fancier blades that can do waffle cuts good for homemade potato chips.

Cut and shape each fry consistently for even cooking. Then plop them into a pot or bowl of cold water containing 2 tablespoons of salt per gallon. Chill the potatoes for an hour or so. After soaking and chilling the fries, rinse away the salt water and drain the potatoes thoroughly in a colander, and then spread them out on some towels. Wet potatoes and hot grease do not mix.

Next, heat your fryer oil to 325°F. To be really precise, you can use a thermometer designed to measure fat and candy temperatures. If you have a fryer with a basket, you can add the potatoes to the basket and lower it into the oil. If you are using a frying pan, make sure there's an inch or two of oil, so that the fries float and don't stick to the bottom. Don't overfill your pan or fryer with potatoes; putting too many in at one time will lower the temperature of the fat and make the potatoes soggy. Cook the spuds until the outer surface just starts to brown. Do not cook them completely; just cook them lightly, about two minutes. Lift the potatoes from the fat with a slotted spoon or tongs and drain them on a wire rack or paper towels. Spread the fries out and let them cool completely. If you want, you can even cover and refrigerate them overnight, which can be a time saver for tomorrow's dinner. Next, you proceed to step two of frying.

Raise the temperature of the fryer fat to 375°F. Now, fry the blanched potatoes again, this time until the surface color reaches a nice golden brown. When nicely golden, drain the fries as before; don't stack them. Season liberally with salt, and then eat and enjoy.

Behind the Scenes

The science behind the Texas two-step process for fries enables you to slowly transfer heat from the exterior of the fry to the interior in step one. The interior has a chance to cook before the outside browns too much. Soaking the potatoes in cold salted water dilutes excess starch from the outside, reducing over browning. But never fear, because chilling converts some starch to sugar. The fries will brown more, but you have it all under control. Potatoes also lose a bit of water when given a salt bath, creating a less soggy or steamed fry inside. The potato is also firmer. You don't stack fries at the end because hot fries give off steam; steam cooks and you end up with soggy limp potatoes. Nobody likes something limp staring them in the face, right?

Oh, there is one thing you can do if you want to skip frying the second time. After blanching the fries, bake them in a 375°F oven. And give the sheet a spray of vegetable shortening to keep the fries from sticking. When the potatoes are golden brown, they are done. This technique reduces the total fat content and works well because both baking and frying in fat are dry-heat cooking methods.

A Baker's Dozen

Dry heat is not only good for making America's favorite French fry, but also is the method of choice for baking potatoes. Making the best baked potato is a simple three-step process.

Preheat your oven to 425°F. Choose a mealy Idaho russet potato and clean it well. Prick it with a fork in a few spots around its surface, set it on a baking sheet, and bake for about one hour, or less if it's a smallish spud. You can check for doneness after 45 minutes by piercing it with a paring knife. When you can slide the blade in to the center of the potato and out with ease, the starch has sufficiently gelatinized. That's another way of saying that it's done.

Needless to say, there are some variations to the above program. You may want to coat the spud with extra virgin olive oil. The fat coats the skin and helps it crisp and conducts the heat, just like oil helps transfer heat in a fry pan. If you like a crunchier surface, then use oil. You still need to pierce the skin in several places with a fork so that steam can escape. You may also want to rub some coarse kosher or sea salt on the spud after oiling it. The salt simply adds flavor and a nice salted crust.

Too Hot to Handle

Do not wrap baked potatoes in aluminum foil. Cooking a spud wrapped in foil is steaming. The foil acts like a lid on the potato. And cooking food with liquid in a covered container is steaming. The liquid just happens to come from the potato itself. Steamed potatoes do not have the fluffy texture of a real baked spud; they are softer and wetter.

To Glue or Not to Glue

Now let's tackle the boiled spud. Boiling a potato is a prerequisite for making mashed potatoes or potato salad. So, the first thing you need to decide is what type of potato to use. For mashed potatoes, go for the mealy kind (russets or Idaho), which fall apart when boiled. For salads, choose the waxy varieties (red, Yukon Gold, white, or all-purpose), which hold their shape better after cooking.

Now, to peel or not to peel? That is the question. The potato peel is a barrier; it is the vegetable's equivalent of skin. So, an unpeeled spud will not absorb quite as much water as a peeled one during cooking. So, for potato salad, this can make the chunks firmer, and the peel adds another color to your salad. You can always take off the peel from a boiled potato before you dice it. Or leave the peel on and eat more fiber. You may also want to leave the peel on when making mashed potatoes. These are often called smashed potatoes because they are coarser.

Let's just assume you peel them. You want to cut the spuds into even pieces. If the potatoes are small, just halve them. If large and long, cut them into quarters. Have a pan of cold water ready and put the potatoes into it. When they are all cut, drain away this water and rinse the potatoes well. Add fresh cold water, just enough to cover the spuds. Add 2 tablespoons of salt for every gallon of water.

Bring the spuds to a simmer and gently cook them so that they cook through but don't disintegrate from rapid boiling. Check doneness with a fork or a small paring knife. When you can pierce a piece of potato smoothly and gently with little pressure, the potatoes are done.

Immediately drain the water away. As the potatoes cook, get a small cookie sheet warm by placing it in a 200°F oven. When you drain the spuds, spread them out on this warm pan and pop the pan back into the oven for only five minutes. This step will allow excess moisture and steam to escape. When making mashed potatoes, this keeps the spuds fluffy, not watery.

Now comes a critical step—how to mash. You chose a mealy potato because you wanted one that would be fluffy after cooking. A potato ricer, which looks like a big garlic press, squeezes the potato gently through a sieve; this is good. So is a food mill. A hand whisk is the third choice. Then comes the electric stand mixer with its whisk attachment. And if you must, use a rotary hand mixer, but be gentle. It's a good idea to season the potatoes with warm milk or cream and butter as you mix them. Add just enough to produce the consistency you prefer. Season with salt and white pepper and enjoy one of life's great pleasures.

Lab Project

For mashed potatoes, peel and dice russet potatoes, placing them in a pot of cold water as you work. When you are ready to cook them, drain off the water, rinse the potatoes, and place them in a large pot with enough fresh cold water to just cover them. Add 2 tablespoons of salt for each gallon of water. Place the pot on medium-high heat and bring to a simmer. Simmer, uncovered, until the potatoes are tender. Immediately drain off the water and spread the potatoes out on a cookie sheet. Place the cookie sheet in a 200°F oven for about five minutes, to remove excess moisture from the potatoes. Mash the potatoes with a ricer, food mill, hand masher, or electric mixer. Add warm milk or cream and butter, as desired, to thin the potatoes. Season with salt and pepper and enjoy.

There are valid scientific reasons for some of the things you just did. Rinsing the potatoes before cooking takes away excess starch, so the spuds are less gummy as they cook. Always use cold water; never start the cooking process with hot water. Remember how quickly starch gelatinizes when you heat it? If you put the spuds in hot water, the outside will gelatinize and get gummy before the interior has a chance to cook. So, go slow and easy. As the spuds cook and the starches gelatinize, the potatoes soften. Salt is added to bring out the flavor.

Finally, the worst thing you can do is "smash them spuds" to smithereens with a mixer. In fact, if you went so far as to use a blender to make mashed potatoes, you could really do damage because it would blast those spuds into a glue-like paste. This should be a capital crime. So, go slow and don't over mix. You were smart to choose mealy potatoes that fluff up with air, don't beat the stuffing out of them. A potato ricer does less damage to the cells of the cooked starches than mixing with an electric mixer. So, find an old ricer, or get a food mill, or get some exercise and whisk by hand.

Potatoes Aren't Rice

Most of the world's starch is consumed as either rice or potatoes. But rice and potatoes are different, and we must approach cooking their starches differently. While potato starch is pretty much the same in all kinds of different varieties of potatoes, rice starch is not. There are many types of rice, each with its own type of starch and its own preferred use.

Different Strokes for Different Folks

Size matters in rice. The rice grains can be long, short, or medium in length. Medium-grain rice has a width and length that are about equal. Long rice has a length four to six times its width. Short-grain rice is stubby. It is wider than it is long. Now, this discussion is not meant to teach you the geometry of rice. The different types of rice grains contain different types of starch, each of which is best suited to a different cooking technique.

Amylose is one of the types of starch. It is long, unbranched chains of glucose. Amylopectin is the second type of starch. It is highly branched. All rice has more amylopectin than amylose. But short-grain rice has the most amylopectin of the three primary varieties.

Now You're Cooking
Brown rice is any rice with the bran still attached. Bran is the second layer on a grain below its husk. The bran adds fiber and gives the rice a tan color, a nutlike flavor, and a chewy texture. White or polished rice is any type of rice with the husk and bran removed. It takes longer to cook brown rice than white rice.

Now You're Cooking

Converted rice has been parboiled to remove some of the surface starch. Parboiling also forces nutrients from the bran into the grain's endosperm. So, converted rice retains more nutrients than regular milled white rice. Converted rice is not a pre-cooked or instant product; in fact, it cooks a bit slower than regular white rice.

Chef Sez

Pilaf is a cooking method in which a grain is lightly sautéed in fat before a hot liquid (usually stock) is added. The mixture is simmered until the grain absorbs the liquid. Rice pilaf is a dish named for the pilaf method of handling grain.

Okay, this sounds very nice, but so what? What does the difference in these starches mean to the cook? Well, the type and amount of starch determines the consistency of the rice when it is finally cooked. Rice can either be fluffy and easily separated with your fork, or it can be creamy and moist with grains that stick together.

It's pretty easy to tell the difference, too. Starches in long-grain rice cook up and gelatinize well, and, when totally cooked, are dry and fluffy. Long-grain rice is best suited to simple steamed rice dishes and rice *pilaf.*

Rice Cooking: Beyond the Basics

Just like cooking starch in potatoes, when cooking rice, the objective is to permeate the starch granules packed into each grain of rice with hot water. This will cause the starch to expand, gelatinize, and soften. While potatoes can be cooked with virtually any cooking method, only three general techniques are used for preparing rice, and many other grains for that matter. They are simmering, pilaf, and risotto.

In all three methods, the ratio of liquid to rice is critically important. For the simmering and pilaf methods, you will need $1^{1}/_{2}$ to 2 times as much liquid as you have rice. For 1 cup of uncooked rice you will need about 2 cups of water or stock. It's that simple. The risotto method is a bit more complex and will be explained a little later.

Chef Sez

Basmati is a very aromatic long-grain rice from the Himalayan foothills. Its sweet, delicate flavor and creamy color is widely preferred in Indian cuisine.

Should rice be washed? The normal reply is to wash all nondomestic brands. Rice produced in the United States tends to be washed and cleaned more before packaging than imported products. Aged rice such as *basmati* should always be washed well before cooking.

Simmer

For simmered rice, pour the necessary amount of liquid into a pan that is large enough to hold triple the volume of the uncooked rice. The pan also needs to have a lid. Now preheat an oven to 350°F. Bring the liquid to a boil in the pot. The liquid can be water or stock (which you'll learn to make from scratch in Chapter 23). If you're using plain water, add 1 teaspoon of salt. You can even add things like a bay leaf or other herbs or spices if you want to flavor the rice. Just remember that whatever you add must either be served with the rice or plucked out at the end, when the rice has cooked. Obviously, a bay leaf or cinnamon stick is easier to remove than chopped parsley.

Stir in the white rice. Bring the liquid back to a simmer. Cover the rice and pop it into the oven. In 18 minutes the rice will be done. Take it out of the oven. Take a peek under the lid if you are skeptical. All the moisture should be absorbed. Leave the rice covered for 10 minutes. Then uncover, and fluff it with a fork.

Of course, if your saucepot lacks an ovenproof handle, it would be best to finish cooking the simmered rice on the stove top. Just cover and reduce the heat to a low simmer. Don't peek, and in about 18 minutes your rice should be ready.

Too Hot to Handle

If your rice scorches or sticks to the bottom of the pan, it's probably because the heat was too high or there wasn't enough water to begin with. Or, perhaps you just neglected to remove the pan from the heat soon enough. Unfortunately, the nasty aroma of scorched rice permeates the entire pot and you'll have to start over. Next time, add more water or reduce the cooking temperature, and watch the process more closely. And don't worry, all great chefs and scientists learn from their mistakes.

So, what happened in that covered pot? Hot liquid cooked the starch through convection and conduction. The steaming effect of liquid percolating back into the pot was your cooking chamber. And it's the same old story again. Starch granules swell as they soak up the hot water and, at 140°F, burst loose and gelatinize. Because you can't pierce the rice grains with a paring knife to tell if it is done, you need to taste the rice when you think it has finished cooking. It should be soft but not mushy. A little resistance is good. If it is still hard, then simply cover the pot and cook it a bit longer.

Pilaf

To make long-grain rice pilaf, all you do differently is toast the rice with some fat (oil or butter) before adding the liquid. You need to have two pots. Bring the liquid to a simmer in one pot; sauté and simmer the rice in the other. First, add a bit of chopped onion and a bay leaf to the pan with the oil. Then sauté the rice, oil, and onion for about two minutes, stirring every 30 seconds or so. Don't let the rice brown; it should just become translucent. Then add the hot liquid all at once. Bring it to a simmer, cover, and pop the pilaf in the oven as before.

In addition to adding toasty flavors, the pilaf method does one other thing. Since rice grains are coated with starch, hot oil helps to gelatinize the surface starches quickly, so when the rice is done, it is less sticky and is fluffier.

Lab Project _____

For rice pilaf, heat 1 tablespoon of butter and 1 tablespoon of olive oil in an ovenproof sauté pan. Add 1/4 cup of finely diced onion and a bay leaf; sauté until tender but not brown. Stir in 1 cup of long-grain white rice. Coat the rice with the hot fat, but do not allow it to brown. Add 2 cups of hot chicken stock and a pinch of salt. Cover the pot and place it in a 350°F oven. Bake for 18 minutes or until the liquid is absorbed and the rice is fluffy and tender. Remove the bay leaf and serve.

Risotto

So, when do you use short-grain rice? Well, this type of rice cooks up moist and creamy. So, it is ideal for the dish called *risotto*. A popular medium- to short-grain variety is Arborio. This one is also a good bet for making rice pudding. The special rice used for sushi is also a sticky short-grain variety.

Chef Sez _____

Risotto is both a cooking method for grains (especially rice) and a finished dish. The grains are first lightly sautéed in fat, and then liquids are gradually added. The mixture is simmered with nearly constant stirring until the still-firm grain merges with the liquid, creating a creamy but toothsome dish.

Much mystery surrounds the making of authentic Italian risotto. Understanding some simple rules will take the mystery out of this process, however. The ratio of liquid to rice and the manner of adding the liquid are the most important parts of making good risotto. There should be about $3\frac{1}{2}$ times as much liquid as rice. The liquid can be salted water or any stock. Wine is also often added for additional flavor.

The liquid must be hot when it is added to the rice. But first, the rice is cooked in hot fat, just like in the pilaf method. Once the rice is cooked in oil for two minutes on medium high heat, the hot liquid is added gradually. As the liquid is ladled into the rice, it is stirred. The rice will absorb the liquid quickly. As soon as the first amount of liquid is absorbed, add more. Keep stirring and cooking the rice on medium heat, adding all of the liquid gradually.

Taste for doneness. Risotto should be soft but not mushy. It should still have a slight resistance. The rice should also be creamy, not dry. Once the rice is to this point, immediately remove it from the heat. It's a good idea to have a bit of extra liquid handy when making risotto. If the rice is not quite done enough, more liquid can be added to finish cooking the starch. Also, adding hot liquid to risotto just before serving adds creaminess. Flavorings such as cream, butter, cheese, and sautéed vegetables or shellfish are typical additions that will turn your side dish into a real meal.

Sauté the rice and onion in butter.

Add the stock gradually while stirring.

Stir in butter and grated cheese at the end.

Lab Project

For risotto, bring 5 cups of chicken stock to a simmer. Heat 2 tablespoons of butter in a heavy saucepan and sauté ¼ cup of diced onion without browning. Add 12 ounces (about 2 cups) of Arborio rice to the onion and butter. Stir well to coat the grains with butter, but don't allow rice to brown. Add ½ cup of dry white wine to rice and stir until it is completely absorbed. Reduce the heat to medium and add the simmering stock to the rice, about ½ cup at a time. Stir frequently and wait until the stock is absorbed before adding the next portion. After about 18 to 20 minutes, the rice should be tender and creamy. Remove the pan from the heat and stir in 2 tablespoons of butter and 2 tablespoons of grated Parmesan cheese. Serve immediately.

Arborio and other short-grain rice cooks up creamy because amylopectin, its dominant starch, is very highly branched. When the starch gelatinizes and cools, it retains its softness more than amylose, which dominates in long-grain rice. The result is a very smooth consistency. Cooking and adding liquids slowly allows the amylopectin to leech out and fully gelatinize.

The stickiness of some short-grain rice varieties makes them ideal for things like sushi or rice cakes. Sticky rice can be molded and formed into balls and rolls without drying out. The amylopectin starches also keep it soft after it cools.

Wild at Heart

Wild rice isn't really rice. It's a grass. Rice was first cultivated in Asia and India. Wild rice is native to North America and was domesticated by the Native Americans. We call it rice because the grains basically look like rice, but with an attitude.

It has a beautiful black outer layer that pops open to reveal the starches inside when the grain is cooking. Because the rice has more protective coats, it takes much longer to cook. It also requires more liquid. It takes twice the amount of water to cook wild rice as it does to cook plain white rice. You can also add an extra 20 to 30 minutes to the steaming process. Wild rice is a crunchy, elegant grain. And it's a great way to get grass into your diet legally.

The Least You Need to Know

- Always begin cooking potatoes in cold salted water; always begin cooking rice in hot liquids or oil.
- Mealy potatoes such as Idaho russets work best for mashing, baking, and French fries; waxy potatoes such as reds work best for cold salads and stews.
- French fries are best cooked with a two-stage method after soaking them in cold, salted water.
- Long-grain rice is best for the pilaf method as the grains cook drier and stay separate.

Beans: Riding Elevators Without Fear!

In This Chapter

- Planting the seeds of nature
- Beans you didn't know were beans
- Preparation techniques
- The musical fruit

Beans have been the butt of many jokes. But that is not our intention in this chapter. Rather, we intend to elevate the bean to new heights with a clean air of respectability. The bean is truly a culinary and scientific wonder. Basic knowledge of bean science doesn't obligate you to suddenly feature them in every meal, of course. But beans can and should be considered an integral part of a healthy diet. They add nutrition and are compatible with many different foods; beans work well behind the scenes. Your fear of beans is due in part to a lack of knowledge of preparation techniques, as well as excess worry about the consequences of eating them. This chapter will describe the whys and wherefores to help lessen these fears.

Nature's Seeds

Plants must have a way of making another plant. Though we do not hear about it much in the popular press, plants have sex, too.

You consume the seeds of the plant's reproductive apparatus when you eat beans. There are two ways you can enjoy your beans. You can eat beans when they are fresh. The most common ones consumed ripe and ready are green beans, fava beans, and lima beans. Fresh snow peas and crispy green sugar-snap peas are also in the bean family and eaten fresh. When you enjoy fresh green beans or some of the pea varieties, you are eating both the seed and the pod. The pod is really the fruit portion of the bean, with the seeds enclosed within it. In reproductive anatomy terms, this is equivalent to the uterus and ovary story situation.

> **Food for Thought**
> Beans are those food-plant species that have edible seeds and seed pods. For some varieties, the entire pod is eaten fresh; for others, only the seeds are eaten. Some seeds are eaten fresh, but most are dried and then rehydrated during cooking.

> **Food for Thought**
> Legumes are the seed portions of a bean found in a pod. The legumes comprise a large family that includes peas, lentils, soybeans, and peanuts. A pulse is a dried legume seed.

Though lima beans and fava beans can be eaten fresh, you don't eat their pods. The seeds when fresh are just too succulent to enjoy in the pod, which is not that palatable anyway. So, you shell them and eat them *au naturel*.

You enjoy fresh beans because they taste good and are good for you. You can also consume bean seeds in a dried form. This, in fact, is the most common way for people to eat beans in all their glory.

The bean pods are dried and the seeds shucked and dried further for storage. A dried bean is really a plant embryo waiting to be born. Nature designed the little package to be able to produce another generation of the same plant. So, if you are the seed of lima-bean plant, or a navy-bean plant, or a black-bean plant, then your sole purpose in life is to make a slightly different copy of you. You can learn a lot about these little seeds just by looking at their anatomy.

Buy a package of dried lima beans and check out the seed. It has a tough, shiny outer covering called the *seed coat*. You wear a coat to protect you from the elements. Beans wear coats, too. The seed coat protects the reproductive jewels located within the seed. Look at the bean more closely. You will notice a slight indentation on one edge of the bean. This is called the *hilum*. This is where the bean was hooked into the pod. The pod was a nice little protective carrying case for the seeds. When the seed was shucked, the attachment to its pod broke at the hilum.

If you were to look inside that dried lima bean, you might observe the nuts and bolts of the seed's reproductive machinery. Reproduction is a costly event in the life cycle of things. Nature has built food stores into the seed to get the process rolling and to provide nourishment. So, the nutritional apparatus for the new embryo makes up a good part of the interior of the dried seed.

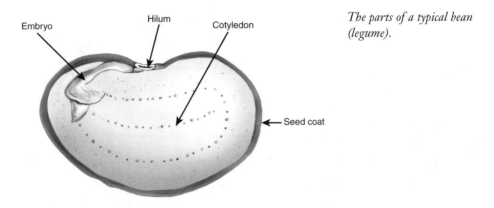

The parts of a typical bean (legume).

Looking inside a dried lima bean is not that difficult. Usually when you buy a package of lima beans, there are some broken ones. Look closely at one of these. You will see mostly a tan, smooth interior. This area is called the *cotyledon*. It really is the food factory for the bean. It's comprised of starches, proteins, enzymes, and vitamins. This starchy and protein-rich cotyledon surrounds the *embryo* proper. It's hard to see the embryo in a dried bean, but if you look really closely, you can see a small area in one corner of the bean. It is thinly outlined away from the cotyledon. The embryo is basically a root and the first pair of leaves that will develop when the seed *germinates*.

Chef Sez

Germination is the sprouting of the dry seed caused by it absorbing water.

Later on, when we talk about soaking beans, repeat the anatomy lesson by looking at the inside of a soaked bean. Now you can clearly pick out the embryo root stems and the first two leaves. Also check out the seed coats. Some of these often completely split off from a few beans and float to the surface. You want to discard them before cooking, but you will be amazed at how tough these seed coats really are.

So, that's it, a legume. Just a tiny little plant embryo sandwiched between layers of nutrients called the cotyledon, all designed to get the plant on its way after germination. Fortunately for us, we can interrupt this reproductive process and enjoy the taste of bean seeds as part of our daily nutrition.

All About Beans

It's astounding just how many beans are grown in the United States alone. Latest figures show we are tops in bean production at 1.5 million metric tons per year. We consume nearly half this amount domestically, and the remainder head out of Dodge for export to other countries.

Bean diversity is truly amazing. There are various colors, sizes, and shapes. There are varying cooking times. There are various textures and flavors to enjoy; and all of this from a simple dried seed. The following table lists only a small sampling of this very extensive family.

Beans Galore

Bean	Color	Cooking Time (hours)	Common Uses and Flavors
Pinto	Mottled beige and brown	1.5 to 2	Refried beans, and Tex-Mex; earthy flavor, powdery, texture
Navy	White ovals	1.5 to 2	Pork and beans, baked, soups, stews, and purees; earthy flavor, powdery texture
Baby Lima	Creamy white	1.0	Side dish, casseroles, and flat stews; sweet flavor, creamy texture
Black	Black oval	1.0 to 1.5	Rice and beans, thick soups; earthy, sweet, mushroom hints, powdery texture
Black-eye (pea)	Cream and black dot	0.5 to 1.0	Rice and Southern soul; savory, light, smooth
Cranberry	Creamy, burgundy highlights	1.5-2.0	Italian dishes; soups, creamy
Dark Red Kidney	Deep Red Brown	Canned	Chili, rice, and salads; full robust flavor, soft
Garbanzo (chick pea)	Beige round	1.0-1.5	Middle Eastern food, soups, and Mexican dishes; nutty flavor, firm
Large Lima	Flat, cream	1.0-1.5	Soups, casseroles, and side dishes; creamy, sweet

Bean	Color	Cooking Time (hours)	Common Uses and Flavors
Pink	Small pale pink	1.0	Chili and Old Wild West recipes; rich meaty flavor
Small Red	Dark red	1.0-1.5	Chili, Creole dishes and salads; full robust, soft
Great Northern (haricot family)	White oval	1.0	Soups, stews, and cassoulet; mild flavor, powdery texture
Light Red Kidney	Large, red	1.5-2.0	Chili, rice (Mexican), and salads; robust full flavor, soft

Beans provide plenty of nutrition. Remember that the bean's mission in life is to make another bean someday. So, they have packed away lots of protein. Most beans have 7 to 8 grams of protein and only about 100 to 120 calories per 4 ounce serving. This means that, on average, a whopping 24 to 30 percent of a bean's total calories come from protein. Add a low percentage of fat calories (less than 1 percent) and a high energy value derived from its 70 percent starch content, and you can see that nature has built a lean, clean fighting machine. And beans need not fight with your digestive system if cooked with care.

Food fiber reaches new heights in the bean world. Fiber is a complex group of starches found in the cell walls of plants. It is basically nondigestible to us because we lack the enzymes in our gut. For an animal like a cow, with loads of microorganism in the stomach, it is a key nutrient. Fiber is an amalgam of cellulose, pectin, hemicelluloses, and lignin; all of these complex starches that help give beans their firm structure. Though we don't break down fiber as energy, it forms bulk in the diet. So, beans help clean out your pipeline. Not a bad ending when you also consider all the other nutrients you grabbed from the bean along its digestive journey.

Handling and Cooking Beans

The objective in cooking plant foods is to soften them to increase their palatability and make them more digestible. Two things become pretty self-evident when you and a dried lima bean are staring at each other eye to eye. The first is that the bean is a lot harder than you are, and certainly harder than any fresh plant foods you might choose to cook. The second thing is that behind that hard exterior is all the good stuff we want to eat. So, it's going to take some work to soften it and make it easy to eat and digest.

The reason pulses (that's dried legumes, for anyone who nodded off earlier) are hard is that they have a water content of only about 10 percent. The reason we want to take a fresh bean pod, with a water content of over 90 percent, and turn it into this hard pulse is to protect it from decay. Bacteria, molds, yeasts, and insects would love to munch on our fresh beans if they could. So, you dry the seeds. The effect is to delay their decay as long as possible. The trade-off is that you now find yourself with some cooking challenges. But when you think about it, cooking up a pot of dried beans is not really rocket science. Since you know that fresh beans cook up relatively quickly and have high water content, it's logical that if you can just get the water back into the dried bean, your cooking problems will be solved.

Dry seeds are transformed into a germinating sprout. When you plant seeds in a vegetable garden, the first thing you usually do after covering them with soil is to give them a long drink of water. The water softens the seed and allows the embryo to break out of the shell, so to speak. This is germination. The water also dissolves some chemicals in the seed and activate the bean's enzymes. These enzymes begin to break down the starch into simple sugars. The sugars now serve as a source of food for the embryonic plant.

So, if water is that important in turning a tough guy bean into a softie, then it seems pretty logical to use water as a cooking medium. Moist-heat cooking methods, such as simmering and boiling, are in fact the only methods for softening and cooking beans.

Yet, all legumes were not created equal. Though all dried legumes appear to be tough as nails, some are tougher than others. This means that it will take a bit more work to soften some varieties with water. The reason is that the seed coat of beans is not the same thickness in all legumes. Beans with the thickest and toughest coats will take more soaking to allow water to penetrate the seed coat's nooks and crannies, while others can be pretty much cooked straight away with little or no soaking necessary.

Lentils and black-eyed peas are two varies that need not be soaked in water, though if you choose to do so, for very good reasons (see discussion on tales from the crypt), soaking will allow them to cook much faster. Lima beans or pintos, and just about every other variety of bean, need to be soaked in water before cooking them.

So, let's go to the lab and cook some dried pinto beans. The first thing you need to think about is quantity. Dried beans expand when they are soaked in water. In fact, they should triple in volume. So, if you start with 1 pound of beans (about 2 cups), then you will end up with about 6 cups. Considering that about a half a cup of cooked beans is a typical portion size, 1 cup of dried beans can serve about six people comfortably. Leftover beans are great, though. Most beans eaten the second or third day after cooking actually taste better. The flavors mature and meld just like changes in a fine aged wine. So, making enough to have some leftovers is a good idea. Just be sure to chill the leftovers quickly, and keep them refrigerated to avoid getting a food-borne illness.

After choosing the quantity to make, you need to clean the beans. This means sorting through the dried beans and discarding broken or discolored ones as well as stones or other foreign particles that may be lurking around. So, if you don't want to risk eating rocks, better clean your beans.

After sorting, there are two ways to soak the beans. The first is pretty simple. Get a large enough pot to hold triple your volume of beans. Add the sorted beans to the pot and cover with lots of cold water. A good rule of thumb is to use 5 cups of water for every cup of beans for soaking. This gives the beans plenty of water to drink, and guarantees that the beans won't soak all of it up and dry out. Now, cover the pot and let the beans sit overnight at room temperature.

If you are in a rush, you'll need to employ the second method of soaking, called the "quick-soak method." Cover the beans with cold water and bring them to a boil. Allow them to boil for only three minutes, and then remove the pot from the heat. Cover the pot and let the beans rest for at least one hour. If you have a bit more time, three or four hours of soaking is even better.

No matter which soaking method you choose, the following steps always apply. Discard the soaking water. Rinse the beans well with fresh water, and then add back some fresh water. Conventional cooking techniques call for cold water, but food science says it's okay to use hot water instead. In fact, starting the cooking process with hot water actually speeds up total cooking time slightly. The water should cover the beans by about an inch, but no more. You don't want to dilute all those good bean flavors and nutrients as they cook. Now bring them to a boil, and cook for 10 minutes uncovered. You will see foam and scum float to the surface. Skim it away.

After 10 minutes, reduce the heat to a simmer, partially cover the pot with a lid to allow some steam to escape, and cook until the beans are tender. Make sure that the lid does not cover the pot completely; you need to vent the steam to allow it to escape. The actual cooking time can vary from 30 minutes to two hours; use the chart in the preceding table as a general guideline. But remember, any dried product could have been dried for variable periods of time, so a standard approach may not work with each batch of beans. And with so many varieties of beans, these cooking times are, at best, only a guideline. Determine doneness by tasting the beans each time you cook a batch. Spoon out a couple, blow on them to cool them a bit, and bite into the beans.

They should be tender and smooth, but not mushy. Hard beans obviously need to cook longer. Check the beans frequently during cooking, tasting them to gauge doneness. It's also important to keep the level of liquid over the beans so that the beans on top don't dry out. If you need to add back a bit of water, do so.

Now that you have passed bean basic training, you should have some questions. What about seasonings? When should other ingredients be added? And why go through all that soaking in the first place? These questions are all important. Fine-tuning your bean cookery is the science of avoiding those dreaded bean nightmares!

Cautionary Tales from the Crypt

Let's blow the whistle on one problem right from the beginning: flatulence. Some folks hold beans at arm's length just because of this digestive phenomenon. It's not pretty but it can happen to anyone. Basic bean training took you through crucial steps that greatly reduce this problem. Let's review the steps and explain in more depth why it is important to follow the basic bean cooking procedures.

Soaking is the remedy for many of the fears of bean eaters. Soaking is not only important to start the softening process and allow for even cooking, but the water also helps draw out compounds that strike fear in our hearts, namely the flatulence gang.

Beans are high in starch, and some of the starches are called oligosaccharides (oligos for short). These are small compounds that have only four to six linked sugars (compared with the thousands of linked sugars in starch molecules). Oligos are not readily digestible by us but are really tasty for bacteria that happen to live in the human colon. So, the story is pretty simple. If you mistakenly leave a lot of the oligos in the bean when you cook them, then you are creating a feeding frenzy for the bacteria in your lower gut. Feeding these bacteria produces the dreaded consequences. Bacteria churn out methane gas as a by-product, and well, we all know what happens next. By soaking the beans, we are diluting out the oligos. And the longer we can soak the beans, the more oligos leech away. This is a good thing. It is also a good thing to further wash and rinse away all the soaking water as an extra safety measure.

Once you handle the oligo problem, we turn to cooking the beans properly. Boiling the beans for the first 10 minutes is a crucial step. It destroys some of the chemical arsenals these seeds have stored inside. The heat of cooking destroys compounds such as protease inhibitors and lectins. This is also a good thing because it effectively neutralizes a potential digestive upset. That's another reason why munching on raw beans or some varieties of raw bean sprouts, (especially lima sprouts), isn't such a great idea. Cooking helps make the bean digestible and safe to eat for you and for those around you.

And why cook with the lid off? Well, cyanogens are the culprits to deal with here. These compounds are found in many legumes. Fortunately they are *volatile*, which means they vaporize when heated. The heat converts cyanogen to hydrogen cyanide and it then can escape with the steam. So, leaving the lid partially off the pot allows this important step to occur.

So, we have handled a few of the nasty events from the crypt by proper cooking, but what about seasoning beans? Not surprisingly, seasoning legumes is a matter of food chemistry, too. Ever had hard beans that never seem to get tender, no matter how long they cook? Most likely the culprit wasn't undercooking; it was simply adding the wrong thing at the wrong time during the cooking process. Even adding a simple seasoning such as salt can ruin your beans if done at the wrong time.

Chef Sez

A **volatile** compound is one that will evaporate or vaporize rapidly at room temperatures. Culinary examples include alcohol and the flavor oils in citrus rind. Heat usually speeds the disappearance of these compounds.

Look back at the beginning steps once more. You first added water to help soften the bean's starches. The starches in the seed coat are comprised of different celluloses; some are hemicellulose, others are pectin. Collectively, the cellulose connection is called fiber. Fiber's job is to make plant cell walls sturdy, much the way Rebar or 2 by 4 studs function in a building. It just so happens that hemicellulose really gets a stiff upper lip when the cooking environment is acidic, or has certain minerals to deal with, such as calcium. So, if you happen to add tomatoes, lemon juice, vinegar, or other acidic ingredients to the cooking water, you affect hemicellulose.

In fact, the beans stiffen up so much from the chemical reaction between hemicellulose and acid that no amount of boiling helps. Adding other things like molasses, when sweetening beans for baked beans for example, is another killer. Molasses contains lots of minerals, including calcium, which stiffens the resolve of hemicellulose just as much as acids.

Interestingly, some recipes for baked beans call for molasses in order to stiffen up the beans during the early cooking stages on purpose. The rationale for hardening the beans is to help them withstand the baking process without getting too soft. Yet, this is a rare exception to most cooking techniques for legumes. Even the minerals in table salt or hard tap water will prevent beans from softening properly. So, never salt the soaking water, and avoid the temptation to salt your cooking beans too soon; wait until they have achieved the desired tenderness.

So, you are probably now thinking that if acids work against legumes softening, can't we add something to counteract the acid? Well, yes, you may see recipes that add baking soda. Baking soda will raise the pH of the cooking liquid, making fibers dissolve more rapidly. The problem with this technique is that the beans may soften too much. If you happen to be cooking the beans and pouring off the liquid, you could risk losing essential vitamins, starch, and minerals in the water. This greatly lowers the beans nutritional value. You also have to deal with the taste of the beans. Too much soda can cause the beans to taste soapy or slimy, which is not such a good thing.

So, the bottom line is that care must be exercised in adding seasonings to beans. The safest thing to do is to get the beans nearly cooked, before adding any seasonings. This ensures that the cellulose will be softened before any chemical reaction occurs to prevent softening. But safe seasoning of legumes for optimum cooking is best done near the end of the cooking process. How can you do this conveniently? Well, if your extra seasonings need cooking themselves to deepen flavors, then cook them separately. This method works well for things such as onions, chilies, tomatoes, or spices; all of them can be cooked together and added to the beans as a seasoning blend at the end.

The Least You Need to Know

- ◆ Some beans can be eaten fresh, but all dried beans need to be cooked; cooking time varies with the bean.
- ◆ Most dried beans must be soaked in fresh water to allow the bean to soften before cooking; discard the soaking water and then rinse the beans and use fresh water for cooking.
- ◆ Beans should be boiled for 10 minutes and then simmered gently until cooked to reduce the effects of various plant compounds on your digestion.
- ◆ Beans should be cooked only partially covered so that steam can escape.
- ◆ Never add acidic foods such as tomatoes, or ingredients that have calcium, to beans during the early cooking stages. Season beans with salt after they soften.
- ◆ Cool bean dishes thoroughly and quickly, and then cover and store them in the refrigerator.

Cereal Grains: Beyond Breakfast

In This Chapter

- ◆ Cookin' corn
- ◆ Other nourishing grains
- ◆ The basics of grain cookery

Like legumes, cereal grains are foods that come to us in the form of plant seeds. Throughout the world, different cultures have developed advanced agronomic practices for cereal crops, and cereal grains are the major part of many diets today. Cereals aren't just breakfast food; they are used as flours, beverages, and even sources of fuel.

To a sheep or cow, grass is caviar, but for you or me, no thanks. Until you realize that we eat some grasses every day in the form of cereal grains. Now your basic pasture grass is mostly cellulose, a fiber that our digestive enzymes aren't particularly fond of. But cereal grains such as corn, wheat, barley, rye, and rice contain food molecules that we can use. They contain the basic food molecules that you are already familiar with: starch, proteins, fats, and water. Oh, they have fiber, too, which, as we've said before, helps keep your internal plumbing in working order. But it's the starch and protein in grains that make them valuable as a versatile food source.

Corn: It's Poppin' Fresh

It's hard to imagine standing in the center of a cornfield surrounded by 6-foot high stalks, knowing that this plant is a relative of the stuff you mow in the front yard each weekend. You can thank genetics, though, for the change from a scraggly looking grass plant of 4000 years ago into the behemoth we call corn today. Corn kernels are the individual seeds of the grain. They grow on a seed pod that we refer to as an ear of corn.

Chef Sez

Hybrid corn is the off-spring of two different parents selectively bred for better qualities. Improved qualities might be yield, flavor, or resistance to diseases. **Field corn** or dent corn is the type planted for livestock feed. Sweet corn and popcorn are used for human consumption. When corn is used for planting, it is called seed corn.

Modern corn is a nutritional and food-engineering miracle. Corn kernels are arranged on an ear and covered by a soft husk. The ear forms after the stalk and leaves of the corn grow large enough to produce energy by photosynthesis. Once the corn stalk has taken root and established itself, it provides enough energy to support the growth of the ear. Astounding as it sounds, modern corn plants can grow an inch per day in the summer if the weather cooperates. If you want to wow your friends with some culinary trivia, tell them that an ear of corn has about 14 to 16 rows around the cob, and that each row supports about 40 to 50 kernels. Do the math and you can see that an average ear of corn has a minimum of about 550 seeds. That's a lot of future corn plants or plenty of food energy for you.

Kernels come in different colors; yellow and white are common, but blue, red, and black corn are also used for food. Color pigments can occur in two parts in the kernel. Pigments appear in the outer layer of the kernel called the *aleurone*. The aleurone is the seed coat also called the bran of the corn. That's where the fiber is. It gives the kernel strength and protects the seed from insects. Most of the decorative corns, reds and blues for example, have flavenoid pigments in the aleurone coat.

Color pigments also live inside of a cereal grain, in what is called the endosperm. The endosperm is made up of mostly starch and protein. But when you look at yellow and white corn, you're looking straight into the starchy endosperm containing all of those carotenoid and flavonoid compounds that you read about in Chapter 7: carotene, xanthophylls, and anthoxanthin.

Food for Thought

Sweet corn is a genetic mutation. Often we think of genetic mutations as a Frankenstein monster or something worse. But it is likely that the ancient Peruvian corn called *Chullpi* gave rise to the sugar corns we enjoy today and have selectively improved through gene modification. Sweet corn can be deep yellow or off-white, or may contain kernels of both colors. Sweetness is classified by genetic variety into standard, sugar enhanced, super sweet, and synergistic. The genes of each of these types have been selected to turn more or less of the corn's sweet sucrose into starch. The more starch, the less sweetness, and vice versa. But the sweetness comes at the price of texture. The outer seed coat of these super-sweet corns is tough and thick. Seems you can't have everything. But modern plant genetics is changing traits even as you read this, so stay tuned. There is little doubt that we will enjoy these different genes with great pleasure. And they will contribute to our nutritional well-being for a long time to come.

Not only does corn come in different colors, but corn also has different types of starch. It is the difference in the starches and sugars that determines its use as a food. You like corn and so does livestock. But you and a cow like different kinds of corn. Cows eat corn that has some very hard starchy endosperm inside. You, on the other hand, prefer the softer, sugary endosperm of sweet corn. So, what's the difference?

Starch is not just starch when it comes to corn. All corn is composed of about 80 percent starch, but how the starch is arranged in the kernel determines part of its application as food. The other thing that is important is the amount of sugar that is not part of starch molecules. In dent corn, the floury tasting starch is partially surrounded by a hard layer of protein and fiber.

When the kernel dries as it matures, the softer starch endosperm inside collapses as it loses some of its water. This creates the characteristic indention or "dent" in the corn kernel. The harder outer layers of fiber and protein literally push into the endosperm to create the dent cavity. Less than 2 percent of the endosperm is now free sugars such as sucrose. All the other sugars have hooked up into starch chains.

Sweet corn has about one third more sucrose than *field corn*, and it has less starch. That is, it has less starch when the corn is young and ready for your dining pleasure. If you let your sweet corn age too long, this sucrose changes into starch. So, the bottom line is this. Sweet corns are sweet because they contain more free sugar and less starch than dent corn. So, don't make the mistake of letting your sweet corn age too much either on the stalk or after picking, or you'll lose all those sweet sugary flavors. If you grow corn in your backyard garden, we'd suggest putting the pot of water on to boil before you pick a few ears for dinner. Now that's fresh.

There is one important exception to your normal preference for sweet corn. And that's the craving for popcorn, especially in a movie theater. Though popcorn is really buttery, soft, and luscious when the kernel pops correctly, it is among the hardest of the corn varieties un-popped. This should not be surprising to you now that you know the difference between sugary sweet corn and field corn.

All corn is made up of starch, sugars, proteins, fat, and water. But popcorn is unique because its water is located smack dab in the center of the kernel. It is totally surrounded by the endosperm and the protein cover of the kernel. Sweet corn and field corn don't have water surrounded by starches and proteins, and that is important for poppin'.

Lab Project

For a bowl of good old-fashioned popcorn made without a fancy popper or the microwave, give this a try. Find a heavy 4-quart pot with a lid. Measure out 1 cup of popcorn. In another cup, measure $1/3$ cup of peanut oil. Never use butter; the smoke point of butter is much lower than vegetable oils, so butter will scorch, smoke, and can catch on fire. Save the melted butter for seasoning at the end. Now add the oil to the pot and place on a burner set to medium high. Add a kernel or two of corn to the pot and place the lid on loosely so that steam can escape. When these two test kernels pop, remove the lid and quickly add all the rest of the kernels. Replace the lid, but make sure you let the pot vent a bit by tilting the lid off center slightly. This lets the steam escape and will help keep the popcorn tender. Shake the pot gently back and forth across the hot burner. Make sure you have a dishtowel to steady the lid and the pot so you don't get burned. When the popcorn starts to vigorously pop, remove the pan from the heat. Keep shaking gently as the hot oil now cooks the rest of the corn. Taking it off the burner prevents the popped kernels from burning on the bottom of the pot. After the popping stops, take off the lid and turn the popcorn into a clean bowl. Season as you wish with salt, grated cheese, or some nifty spices. How about Cajun salt, for example? Butter is optional. By the way, never season the corn kernels before popping them. Salt has a nasty habit of making the kernels tough as they cook. Now, enjoy the movie!

When the popcorn kernel is heated, this water literally boils. The hot water partially gelatinizes the starch, cooking and softening it slightly. This helps give the popcorn its soft smooth texture. But as the water then turns to steam, it finds that it is completely encircled by starches and proteins. Imagine a leather baseball filled with water on the inside. Then think about heating up that baseball. Do you understand that something has to give? That hot steam has to go somewhere. And in the case of the popcorn kernel, where it goes is blasting out of the sides of seed. What happens is a small explosion. But it's a good explosion because we get to eat the leftovers.

Other Nourishing Grains

Wheat, rye, oats, barley, and rice make up our other primary cereal grains. Throw into the mix some sexy grains such as amaranth and quinoa from ancient South America, or some millet from Asia and you have a veritable armada of nutrition. Rice was discussed along with potatoes in Chapter 8 because, let's face it, you're either a potato eater or a rice eater, and presenting them together just seemed to make sense from a culinary perspective.

Food for Thought

Buckwheat isn't wheat; it isn't even a cereal grain or a grass. It's actually the tiny fruit of a plant related to rhubarb. Buck-wheat kernels, known as groats, can be used like rice or milled into a flour. With a nutty flavor and distinctive tannish-gray color, it is commonly used in pancakes, blini, and soba noodles. Roasted buckwheat groats are called kasha and are popular in eastern European and Russian dishes.

Cereal Seed Anatomy 101

Wheat and rye are seeds botanically similar to corn. Both grains grow on thin grass-like plants without any leaves or husk to cover them up. Although they are somewhat naked to the world, both do have a seed coat called bran. Bran, like all good seed coats, has its share of fiber. Bran also has a fair amount of waxy fat and protein. The fiber, fat, and protein combine to help the bran covering in its role as protector of the germ and endosperm reserves inside the seed.

Wheat flour is valuable to you because of its use in breads, crackers, cakes, and virtually everything sold in your local bakery. Different types of wheat contain different types of protein, which you'll learn more about in later chapters on baking. Durum wheat is a special type of very high protein wheat used to produce semolina flour. Durum wheat endosperm is coarsely sliced into fragments that become the semolina flour. Now don't get the idea that you can go out and buy some durum *wheat berries* and slice them with your chef's knife. Leave that process to modern

Chef Sez

Whole kernels of wheat are called **wheat berries**. When the berries are broken into different size fragments, they are called cracked wheat. Bulgur is wheat berries that have the bran removed, and are then steamed, dried, and cracked into small pieces. Bulgur can be cooked like rice and is the basis for tabbouleh salad.

Food for Thought _____
Couscous looks like a grain but it's actually small spheres of high protein semolina dough that are rolled, dampened, and coated with a finer wheat flour. Couscous is a staple of North African diets.

milling plants. But you can go out and buy some semolina flour to make pasta. This flour is particularly well suited to the making of pastas that you plan to dry completely before cooking.

Oats and barley aren't naked grains; they do have a husk. Like the usual suspects in the cereal world, they also have a bran layer. The husk isn't soft and pliable like the covering on corn, but hard, much like the covering of a nut. It's mostly a tough protein matrix that gives these grains more rigidity and protection.

Getting Physical with Cereal Grains

There are two ways to use cereal grains: whole or ground. Whole grains that are cleaned of their husks (a process known as hulling) are rich sources of energy, fiber, vitamins, and minerals. Take a peek at the ways you can cook and utilize these grains in the next section of this chapter. You can also get physical with cereal seeds and extract a number of parts that make unique contributions to our cuisine.

Most often today, you aren't going to purchase many whole cereal grains and grind them yourself; though this is entirely possible, and there are mills you can add to your home lab equipment if you like. *Milling* cereal grains is necessary for people to make use of these seeds as food. The grains are ground by hand with large mortal-and-pestle-like grinders, or stone-ground using an old-fashioned miller's wheel, or are crushed and sifted with modern rollers. Each of the cereal grains has unique and diverse components that have various uses. Let's go through the catechism of cereal grain breakdown from top to bottom.

Chef Sez _____
Milling is a process in which grains are cleaned, hulled, cracked, and sifted in the process of breaking down the seed into the germ, bran, and endosperm.

The simplest way to mill a seed is to remove any tough outer husk and then just grind up all the parts. If you do this, you end up with what is called whole-grain flour. It contains the bran, the starch, and the germ. Whole grains do contain more vitamins, minerals, and good stuff because, well, they're whole.

If you don't want all the parts just mixed up into a meal, then you are faced with separating each of the component parts. The basic task for a cereal grain is separating the bran from the endosperm from the germ. While milling sounds pretty simple, modern milling techniques are quite involved and can have over 200 steps. And each grain has its own unique steps because of its anatomy and the final products desired.

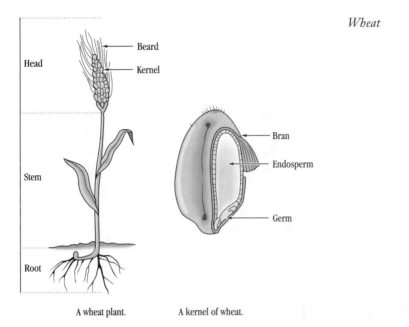

Wheat

A wheat plant.   A kernel of wheat.

In general, though, first the grain is cleaned when it comes from the farm. Then it is moistened with warm water to help soften the tough outer seed coat. The softer seeds can now be passed through a series of sophisticated rollers; think of them as high-tech rolling pins, moving in opposite directions crushing the seeds between them. Parts and pieces such as the germ, endosperm, and bran fall out onto a conveyor pan and are sifted out by size. This process is repeated several times. So, what you end up with are coarse particles and fine particles. Bran heads one way, germ another, and endosperm another.

Of course, the endosperm is the prime objective because it can be turned into flours and meals. Starchy endosperm ends up in a myriad of products, from the invaluable wheat flour, to corn starch, corn syrup, paper, and even gasoline. Anyone who likes bran breakfast cereal has experienced the edible form of the seed coat. After it is knocked off the cereal grain, the bran is flattened, rolled, and cooked into the cereal form we know. And the germ, well, the germ can be turned into oil because it has such a high fat content. And lest you think that all the other by-products such as spent germ or hulls are wasted, don't forget our livestock friends. Most of the milled particles not used in the myriad of human foods become part of the food chain for domesticated beasts.

Beer for Breakfast

That starchy endosperm of grains serves another purpose besides its use as flour, meal, or a cooked side dish. Cereal grains are the foundation of alcoholic beverages such as beer and distilled spirits. Alcohol is produced when yeasts, those little microscopic fungi that also make breads rise, come in contact with a sugary food source. And the endosperm of grains such as barley, rye, corn, and wheat is a great sugary food source. The unique combination of a grain's starch chemistry, different types of yeast, and the skill of the brew master all contribute to the various flavors and styles of alcohol beverages.

Beverages made from cereal grains include bourbon and other whiskeys, vodka, gin, and the huge number and styles of beer. And the great thing is, not only is modern science showing that grains are good for you to eat, but that alcohol consumed in moderation is a good form of grains for you to drink. Isn't science just wonderful?

Grain Cooking Basics

The simplest way to cook cereal grains is to simmer them in a liquid such as salted water. Your objective is to heat the grain to gelatinize the starch inside and soften the outer seed coat. Nothing new here; remember vegetable and bean cookery?

The secret to success is the ratio of liquid to grain. Not all grains were created equal. Their shapes are different and the chemicals that make up each grain and the fiber that protects the seeds are different. All these unique qualities mean different strokes for different folks. Fortunately, there are tried-and-true guidelines for you to follow.

Ratio of Liquid-to-Grain Guidelines

Grain	Cups of Liquid per Cup of Grain	Time and Tips
Amaranth	2½	Simmer 20 minutes. Casseroles, side dish
Barley	3	Simmer about an hour. Use like brown rice.
Bulgur	2	Steep for 10 minutes. Salads, soups, desserts
Corn meal (polenta)	4	Add slowly; then simmer 30 minutes. Great as a side dish

Grain	Cups of Liquid per Cup of Grain	Time and Tips
Corn grits (coarse)	4	Add slowly; then simmer 30 minutes. A southern classic
Couscous	2½	Steep in hot water for 10 minutes. Great side dish
Oats (whole)	4	Simmer 60 minutes.
Oats (rolled)	2	Simmer 10 minutes.
Quinoa	2	Simmer 20 minutes; use in salads, soup
Rye	2	Simmer 10 minutes; flour used in bread and baked goods

Once you've mastered the simmering routine, there are other variations you might want to add to your cooking repertoire. Remember the pilaf method for cooking rice? Actually, just about any grain can be a pilaf. All you need to do before adding your simmering liquid is to lightly toast the cereal in some hot fat. Barley can be cooked as a barley pilaf, for example. Try this technique to add a toastier flavor to cereal grains and add some zest to your cooking style. You might have heard the term pearl barley. No, this is not something you wear as a necklace. It's barley that has been hulled to remove the husk, and stripped to remove the bran. Then it's polished up a bit to clean it, and then steamed. After all that, it is, as you can imagine, more tender when cooked.

Versatility is really a virtue for some whole grains, and reaches its zenith in cooking corn. The vegetable grain corn is the major exception to the rule of just simmering grains. You not only can buy the sweet kernel in various forms, but you often love to buy the entire ear, husk and all. Some people even enjoy growing it from scratch. For most of us, this is as close to nature you can get with a cereal grain, unless you happen to be a farmer.

Corn can be roasted or grilled, in the husk or out. To do it in the husk, peel back the green layers and strip away the silk. Then gently place the green husk back over the corn. If you are not real fat conscious, you can stroke the ear

Lab Project

For barley pilaf, sauté ¼ cup of finely diced onions in 2 tablespoons of butter. Cook until they are translucent but not brown. Add 1 cup of pearled barley and a bay leaf. Sauté until the grains are well coated with the butter. Pour in 1 pint of hot stock and bring to a low simmer. Cover and continue cooking until all the liquid is absorbed and the grains are tender, about 20 to 30 minutes. Season with salt and pepper and enjoy.

with some butter and add a bit of salt and pepper before you put the husks back over the kernels. Then simply place the corn on a medium-hot grill and cook them. Some methods suggest that you soak the ears of corn in water to help keep the corn from burning or becoming dry. Others might wrap the ears in foil. Feel free to experiment until you find the technique you prefer. Turn the ears frequently to keep them from burning. After 15 to 20 minutes, the ears have steamed to perfection, and the smoky grill flavor has just scented them lightly.

If you want to dispense with the green husks, you can butter and season the naked ears and grill them directly on the hot coals. If you season with butter, remember that it can burn more quickly, so you may prefer to use oil or a combination of oil and butter. Of course, you can roast the ears naked in the oven at about 375°F. Turn the corn once in awhile to cook it evenly, and when you do, slather it with more butter to keep the ears moist. The corn roasts in about 15 to 20 minutes, or when it is just tender to the tooth. Season the corn well with your favorite spices or pepper and sea salt.

In the unlikely event that you will have leftover cooked grains, remember to handle them properly to avoid food-borne illness. All leftover grains are good sources for bacterial contamination that can lead to a food-borne illness. They offer bacteria plenty of protein and moisture, the right pH, and a nice, warm environment. So, before storing cooked grains, they should be cooled thoroughly and quickly. Then cover and keep them under refrigeration. To reheat, add back a bit of moisture and bring them to a simmer, stirring to prevent scorching or sticking. By the way, it's also important to store dried grains away from ants, bugs, and other vermin. Remember, these critters want a piece of the tasty grains before you do, and unfortunately, they leave a dirty trail behind that can contribute to food-borne illness.

The Least You Need to Know

- Cereal grains can be cooked whole or used as many different products, from flour to beverages.
- When simmering cereal grains, the ratio of liquid to quantity of grain is specific for each grain, as is cooking time.
- Grains are cooked until they soften sufficiently to be palatable to your tastes.
- Leftover grains need to be cooled quickly and then stored covered, under refrigeration, to prevent food-borne illness.
- Store dried grains in sealed containers away from ants, flies, and other critters to prevent cross-contamination.

Chapter 11

Just Nuts

In This Chapter

- ◆ Not all in the family
- ◆ Nuts about health
- ◆ Hot nuts warm hearts
- ◆ Nuts inside and out

There's a famous expression that goes, "I may not be able to define pornography, but I know it when I see it." Well, you know what a nut is when you see it, too; or do you? Nuts are an interesting family. There are nuts that belong to the clan because they are truly part of the botanical family. And then there are nuts that were put there for convenience's sake only; they're part of the extended nut family.

True Nuts and Imposters

When is a "nut" not a nut? A nut is an edible seed kernel of a fruit surrounded by a tough, hard shell. When it's contained in a pod, it belongs to the bean family. Peanuts are really legumes. The peanut plant even resembles a pea plant. But you and 99 percent of your friends likely classify the peanut as a nut, not a bean. The peanut is sort of an adopted nut. It was once called the ground pea, groundnut, or goober, the latter a derivation of the African word for the plant. Word-smithing being what it is, it is likely that groundnut and ground pea were merged to give the word peanut.

And so, a handful of salty peanuts, though not really nuts, remain the standard bearer of the nut family for most Americans. It's what you think of when you think nuts. In a way, that is not wrong. There are lots of foods that are grouped by how we use them, rather than strictly by their biology. We do it for the tomato, for example, which is a fruit used like a vegetable. So, you aren't nuts treating nuts like you do, now you're just more educated.

What this means, of course, that the nut family is truly a diverse one. Most nuts grow on trees. They are found globally and are an important source of food and nutrition. Today, many nuts are cultivated as a large part of modern agriculture.

But no matter what you call a nut, you can usually call them good and tasty. So, who cares whether you're eating a real nut or an imposter? What you care about is how to get the most out of your nuts.

Too Hot to Handle

If you are one of the unfortunate people who has an allergy to nuts, then eating them is a deadly business. You are joined by about 1.5 percent of adults and 6 percent of children with true allergic reactions to some foods. Nuts are one of the Big Three for causing allergic reactions, the others being eggs and milk. Although you may outgrow childhood allergies to eggs and milk, you probably will never outgrow an allergy to nuts. There is no way to cure a true food allergy to nuts except to avoid the food. The culprits are pieces of proteins that enter the blood from the digestive system. They switch on your immune system, leading to antibody production called an IgE; and this eventually leads to the potential shock reactions associated with the allergy. A clear sign of a food allergy to nuts is that the reaction occurs within a very short period of time, usually within minutes after ingestion. So, to protect yourself, always know if nuts are included as ingredients in any food that you may eat. That's the best way to avoid the problem.

Good Stuff in Nuts

You like nuts because they are handy, a real convenience food. You can carry them around. They are a versatile food to use in cooking. And perhaps most important, they have what we really crave with a passion: lots of mouth watering *fat*. So, to understand a nut, you first need to think about fats and oils.

Unless you just arrived from another planet, you've heard plenty about dietary fat during the last 20 years. You no doubt know that there are good fats and bad fats, that there are natural and artificial fats, that low-fat foods are either very good or very bad, and that cholesterol is the worst fat for you in your diet. Some of those statements are "value" laden. This means that you believe them to be true because everyone seems to hold them as truthful, while others of those statements are based upon scientific evidence and fact, and are proven either to be correct or false. So, which are based on fact and which are just nuts?

Chef Sez

Fat is a concentrated food-energy molecule. Fat that is made up from the sugar glycerol hooked to three fatty acids is called a triglyceride.

"Fatology" About "Nutology"

Well, to understand nut fat, you need a bit of a general primer in basic "fatology." The easiest analogy to think about what a food fat looks like is to picture a three-pronged pitchfork minus the long handle. Think of the tines and the base of the fork analogous to the sugar base, which is called glycerol. Glycerol is the basic anchor that fixes other things onto it, much like tips of your salad fork spear a piece of lettuce and hold onto it.

Now imagine a string of capital letter C's attached in a line, stretching out from each tine of the fork, kind of like this for one of the tines: ---C-C-C-C-C-C-C-C-C. Usually you can have from 12 to 18 C's in each line. Those C's are the *fatty acids*, and are composed of carbon. So, on that 3-prong fork you could have three of the same fatty acids or three different fatty acids. That difference gives each fat its character and uniqueness.

Let's focus on only one tine of the fork and begin to make a fat model. (Of course, most models don't want to be fat, but there are exceptions.) Now those fatty acids, our long line of carbon C's, are all not just lined up like naked people in a movie queue—the ticket window being the point of the tine, by the way. The C's might be clothed in hydrogen. Recall that water is made up of two hydrogen atoms hooked to a single oxygen atom (H_2O.) Hydrogen has a liking for carbons as well. Let's just call hydrogen H for short. And let's give each C some H, one on the top and one on the bottom.

```
H H H H H H H H H H H
-C-C-C-C-C-C-C-C-C-C-C
H H H H H H H H H H H
```

So, if all of our lined-up C's are fully clothed head to toe, meaning that not one of them is without a pair of "H-on's," they are called *saturated fatty acids*. If, however, everyone in the line of C's has clothes on except two individuals who happen to be half-naked and standing ninth and tenth in position from the movie ticket window, then the fatty acid is mono*unsaturated*. If everybody in the line except four has a pair of H-on's, meaning that you have four half-naked C's, our friends in line at 9 and 10 now joined by the pair at the sixth and seventh spot, then your fatty acid is *polyunsaturated*.

```
H H H H H   H   H H
-C-C-C-C-C-C=C-C-C=C-C-C
H H H H H H H H H H H H
```

And, like life, there are always a couple of wise guys who show up toward the front of the line. If, in your line-up, the naked C's are located first at position 3 and 4, followed by nakedness for our usual suspects at 6 and 7, and 9 and 10, then the fatty acid is a special one called an *omega-3 fatty acid*.

```
H H   H   H   H H
-C-C-C=C-C-C=C-C-C=C-C-C
H H H H H H H H H H H H
```

So, let's recap. If your fork has mostly saturated fatty acids across all the tines, meaning that all of your C's have their full complement of H-on's, then you have a predominately saturated fat. If all three tines are hooked up where at least two or more C's are naked in each line of C's, then your fat is polyunsaturated. And our monounsaturated fat is just what it sounds like: only one pair of C's (or "mono") being naked in each row. And lastly, if the fat has an omega-3 fatty acid stuck in there, beginning in position 3, you have our special class of fats, the omega-3 fatty acids.

Load Some Hydrogen

If you like to use vegetable shortening, or prefer vegetable margarine to butter, then you are consuming a hydrogenated fat. An unsaturated fat is oil that flows as a liquid. Fats such as lard and butter are solid at room temperature. Your scientific inquisitiveness at this point should tell you that if vegetable oils from plants and things such as nuts are fluid, yet vegetable shortening or margarine made from vegetable oils is firm and solid like butter, then something was done to the oils to make them act like butter or lard. And what was done to vegetable oils was to force-feed hydrogen onto the unsaturated carbons. This changed the oil to a solid fat.

The process is called hydrogenation. Extreme pressure and even the use of heavy metals like nickel are needed to load the hydrogen into the carbons of the unsaturated oils. Because it isn't possible to load all the carbons with hydrogen, shortening and margarine tend to have a slightly softer texture than either butter or lard. That's also why commercial brands can say that they are higher in polyunsaturated fats. And because the fats are more hydrogenated, they have a greater shelf life. The process of hydrogenation has created two useful products for cooking. The drawback is that the fat is more saturated than in the original oil. Some health benefits from hydrogenation are traded for the utility and use of the fat.

Quantity and Quality

So, why is this important to a nut, or to you, for that matter? Well, the differences between foods that have more or less of one type of fat have been implicated in a variety of health- and diet-related illnesses. Or, if you want to look at it more positively, some fats are actually better for you than others. The difference between a food containing a saturated, monounsaturated, or polyunsaturated fat is important to your health. It really gets down to the quantity that we eat in our daily diet. That is where the nut story comes back into play.

Nuts do have a high *constituent fat* content. In fact, they are a food with one of the highest fat contents. For most people, this raises the red caution flag. Weren't we taught that food fat is bad, you ask? Actually, you and nuts go well together nutritionally. Many scientific research studies are showing the benefits of consuming nuts. So, the general conclusion that all fat foods are bad for you is not really correct. Fat composition is important; and how much of any fat consumed is the real bottom line.

> **Chef Sez** _____
> Fats and oils that are separated from plant or animal cells such as lard, butter, or shortening are called *visible fat*. Fats and oils that we consume as part of a basic food such as nuts, meat, milk, or eggs are called a **constituent fats**. **Lipid** is any substance that dissolves only in solvents such as alcohol-based compounds, but not in water. All fats are lipids, but not all lipids are fats.

Cholesterol: Good or Bad?

Cholesterol gets a lot of attention these days. You are warned to watch out for it, though most of you have never seen the stuff. It has been the bad-boy poster child of fats. Well, first of all, cholesterol is not a fat. There's no glycerol on three fatty acids. Cholesterol is a *lipid* found in animal products such as butter, eggs, milk, and meat. Cholesterol never appears in plants; never has, never will. Because it's a lipid, cholesterol doesn't dissolve easily in water. Now you ask, since my blood is like water, what keeps the cholesterol in my blood from floating around like an oil slick on broken vinaigrette?

Well, there are fatty acid-protein combinations that ferry cholesterol around in your body, just like you use shopping carts to move your groceries around the supermarket. Some called HDLs are good cholesterol movers because they move the cholesterol into your liver. This is good because HDLs help keep excess cholesterol from taking up residence in and clogging small arteries in your heart. Other cholesterol movers called LDLs are bad. They are bad because they move the cholesterol back into the blood. You do need cholesterol. Cholesterol is used to make many of your hormones, without which you would not have sex, children, or even be able to control your water content. So, both HDLs and LDLs are doing what they are designed to do. The problem arises when you get too many LDLs in your blood; that's when they become bad boys. And this is where eating nuts comes into play.

Nut Movers and Shakers

Foods like walnuts, hazelnuts, and pecans reduce the LDLs. These nuts likewise favor the production of HDLs. So, you end up with a net deposit of cholesterol in the liver rather than in your arteries, with just enough left over for sex. Nuts are a major player in the so-called Mediterranean Food Pyramid, and the effects they have on the HDL/LDL ratio may help explain part of the heart-healthy nature of this diet. So, eat more nuts as part of your daily diet; it can't hurt. And it may help your love life in the long run.

Food for Thought

Cooking oils are primarily composed of mono- and polyunsaturated fats, and are liquid at room temperature. You might be most familiar with oils extracted from plants such as corn, olives, and soybeans. Yet, nuts provide another source of valuable cooking oils. Peanut oil is especially useful for frying because it is bland and has a high smoke point. This means that it is less apt to catch on fire at the higher temperatures needed to fry nice, crisp foods. Walnut and hazelnut oils provide unique flavors for salad vinaigrettes. Add in the health benefits of consuming nutritionally positive unsaturated omega-3 fats, and the use of nut oils in cooking looks even better as part of your kitchen repertoire.

Most of the fat found in nuts is unsaturated. The consumption of mono and omega-3 unsaturated fats benefits you in a number of ways, from lowering your blood cholesterol to improving heart health. And because there is no cholesterol in nuts (nuts are plants, right?), you don't have to worry about that problem. Of course, nuts are more than fat. Because they are seed fruits, they have a higher proportion of fiber than many foods. And you already know the positive benefits of fiber—it keeps your internal plumbing in good shape. Nut fiber also may protect you by helping to check your blood cholesterol level. The following table outlines some of the nutritional values of various nuts. So, as you can see, it's not all nuts to eat nuts.

Nutritional Content of Some Tree Nuts (3 oz.)

Nut	Sat	Fat (g) Mono	Poly	Omega	Grams of Protein	Sugar	Fiber
Almond	4	32	12	12	21	20	12
Cashew	9	27	8	8	15	33	3
Hazelnut	4	46	8	8	15	17	10
Macadamia	12	59	1	1	8	13	8
Pecan	6	41	22	22	9	14	10
Pistachio	4	25	14	14	21	27	10
Walnut	6	9	47	46	15	14	7

Data derived from International Tree Nut Council

But you don't have to limit yourself to eating nuts in the raw just for snacks. Sure, nuts have ample protein and sugars that provide you with quick high-energy fuel. But the ratio of fat, protein, and sugar built into a nut makes them ideal as an ingredient, especially for dishes where you want to add toasty flavor. It all gets down to delicious, savory nut chemistry.

Roasting, Toasting, and Flavors

Nuts are comprised of the four basic food molecules: fat, proteins, and carbohydrates. Throw in some moisture and some minerals and you have a pretty complete food.

But you can alter what nature has already perfected. And one way to do that is to apply heat energy to the nut. In other words, you can cook them. And when you use a dry-heat cooking method, some very interesting things happen to the nut components. Here's a pretty easy and tasty experiment to do.

Go to the market and buy some nuts. Peanuts, walnuts, or pecans work best for this little project. Don't get the dry-roasted kind. You want the raw nut, in or out of the shell. If you do get nuts in their covering, just remove it. If you buy nuts out of the shell, get them without any seasonings or salt added. Now take those naked nuts and spread them out on a cookie sheet. Save a few raw ones; you don't want to toast them all.

Then pop that pan into a preheated 350°F oven. After about five minutes, open the oven door and give the pan a shake to move the nuts around a bit. This helps them toast more evenly. Close the door and toast another three to five minutes. Watch the nuts carefully. You want them to brown but not burn. When the nut has taken on a nice suntan, take the pan out of the oven and let it cool. Now just pop a raw, untoasted nut in your mouth. It's firm to the tooth but creamy, maybe a bit earthy and a bit sweet, perhaps; or maybe there's a hint of bitterness? Now try a toasted one. A bit harder to the tooth, maybe with a little more crunch now, and drier; and it definitely has a broader sweetness to it, deeper and toastier. It fills the mouth more. Look at the difference in the colors of a raw nut and a toasted one. Note the depth of browning in the toasted version. Try adding a little salt to the raw and roasted nuts now, and repeat your taste test. The salt will accentuate the sweetness, bringing it out more. And for your toasted nut, salt really broadens and deepens the sensation of toastiness.

Roasting builds deeper, slightly sweet or sometimes even slightly bitter flavors that were not present in the raw nut. It all depends upon the nut and the base molecules you started with. In general, roasting a nut brings out round and full flavors. The aroma that permeates your kitchen from toasting nuts gives you the first clue that the sugars, fats, and proteins are undergoing some interesting changes in your oven. And as simple as it is to roast nuts, the chemistry that is happening inside that nut is anything but simple.

Nuts About Chemistry

When you roast nuts, you are creating what is called the "browning reaction." That's pretty easy to visualize, as the nuts do turn a golden shade of brown. If you like robust, deeply flavored coffee, then you like your beans roasted. In the nut, this is a special form of browning that happens when you cook foods that have lots of protein, sugar, and some fat. It is called the *Maillard* reaction.

Chef Sez

Maillard products in cooking come from foods such as meat or nuts that contain protein and sugar or fat, which react to form new substances in the presence of high heat and low moisture. They contribute to the so-called nut-like flavor.

You crave those toasted nut-like flavors of the Maillard reaction. What you are creating in your kitchen is a virtual soup of hundreds of different chemicals in the roasted nut. So, what is going on? The dry heat evaporates some moisture from the nut. This contributes to the nut's crunchier texture. And with less water around, the dry heat continues to cook the fat, protein, and sugar to a higher temperature. As the proteins and sugars cook, their chemical structures change.

These new protein and sugar by-products don't just sit still, they hook up into new forms, creating entirely different chemical mixtures. Chemicals with challenging names like pyrazine, thiophene, pyrrole, and oxazole now permeate those nuts. The fats in the nuts literally melt, too, and coat these new chemical mixtures. You can feel a bit of the fat when you pick up a warm nut; it's a bit oily. Your hot roasted nut has become a luscious chemical test tube.

Coatings, Stuffing, and Mixtures

Nuts have ideal proportions of fat and protein, along with texture, to be used in so many fundamental cooking techniques. This may not be new information to you if you have used nuts in cooking before, and it is certainly not new to the nut. They have been the cook's companion for eons.

Skins Game

Hazelnuts, sometimes also known as filberts, are produced in large quantities in the United States. In fact, over 95 percent of domestic hazelnuts are produced in the state of Oregon. You might purchase hazelnuts with the skin still attached to the kernel. The skin has a bitter taste because it has a higher concentration of tannin-like compounds, similar to those found in red wine. It's best, therefore, to skin the nuts before you use them. This doesn't mean using a very tiny pairing knife to peel off the skin, but is best done after toasting the nuts. You need a cookie sheet and a moist dish towel. Preheat the oven to 350°F and roast the nuts for about 8 to 10 minutes. Give the pan a shake once or twice to turn the nuts so that they toast more evenly.

Then, while the nuts are still hot, carefully rub small handfuls in the folded-up towel. The skins will fall off, and the cleaned nuts can be gathered into another bowl. Of course, if you prefer the taste of the skins, then skip this process. But you might find that leaving the skin on nuts used for baking doesn't add much to the recipe except brown flakes.

Nutty Condiments

Nuts were once a common thickener for sauces. Before the use of cornstarch, butter, or flour, finely ground nuts or nut pastes were used to thicken sauces. This should make sense to you if you think about. Butter can be used to thicken pan drippings because it has such a high fat content. So, nuts, with over 60 percent fat, would make a logical substitute. And the starches found in nuts behave like the starches in flour and grains to assist with thickening as well. Although nuts aren't used much to thicken contemporary sauces, fortunately the nut has not been entirely abandoned. One of the most craved nut mixtures used as a sauce today is pesto.

Pesto is really any finely ground nutmeat that you happen to like that is formed into a thick sauce. You can use pine nuts, which are pretty traditional, or walnuts, almonds, or even pistachios. To make 2 cups of pesto, choose your nuts and measure out 3 ounces. Roast them in a 350°F oven to create all those good browning products. Cool the nuts. Now measure 8 ounces of fresh basil and give it a quick rinse to clean it a bit; then drain and dry the leaves. Peel a couple of cloves of garlic, grate 4 ounces of Parmesan cheese, and measure out 4 ounces of extra-virgin olive oil. The rest is a snap.

Using your food processor, add all the ingredients except the oil. Grind to a moist paste. You may have to scrape down the sides of the bowl once or twice to mix everything well. Then empty the mixture into a clean bowl. Gradually stir in the olive oil until a smooth paste is reached. Taste it. If it needs salt, add a pinch or two, mix, and taste again. When you have the right seasoning, your pesto is done. Now, if you're a purist, and own a mortar and pestle, pesto can be made from scratch the real pesto way. Pesto means "pestle," so if you want to relive a bit of history, go for it. Now go make some pasta for your pesto.

Lab Project

For a pesto sauce, toast 3 ounces (about $1/2$ cup) of pine nuts or walnuts. Place the toasted nuts in the bowl of a food processor fitted with the metal blade. Add 8 ounces of fresh basil, 2 peeled cloves of garlic, and 4 ounces (about 1 cup) of grated Parmesan cheese. Process to form a thick paste. Remove the paste from the bowl and stir in about $1/2$ cup of extra-virgin olive oil, some freshly ground black pepper, and salt to taste. Toss this sauce into cooked pasta or refrigerate for later use.

The making of a pesto sauce relies on the chemical make-up of the nut. The fat and protein in the nuts creates binding that helps hold things together, along with a touch of oil to increase the smoothness. When you add the olive oil at the end, it's best to do so without a high-speed food processor. Olive oil contains a high proportion of monounsaturated fat, which is susceptible to oxidation. Remember that it already has lost some hydrogen and is a bit naked; this exposed fat is more apt to be affected by the air. Whizzing at too high a speed will break down and oxidize the fats even more, creating some bitter flavors. So, gentle mixing is best.

Pesto can be stored in the refrigerator but it will darken. The basil will oxidize and brown in the air from our dreaded enzymatic browning. You have pretty much chopped up and injured the basil in your processor, so it is not surprising that it, too, is susceptible to further deterioration. You can reduce this by refrigerating or even freezing it. And adding just a thin layer of oil over the top of the pesto also helps to seal out the air. Wrap your bowl tightly with plastic wrap or use an airtight container. And always remember that nuts soak up odors easily because they are a high-fat food. So, storing raw nuts, or mixtures like pesto, requires an airtight seal for keeping the best flavors in and odors out.

Nuts also make great additions to flavored butters. The nut fat permeates the fat in the butter to give you a great taste combination. And the wide range of nuts to choose from makes this a versatile technique. First toast your nuts of choice, and then grind them finely in a food processor. Next, take some softened whole butter, about 1 pound for every 3 ounces of ground nuts, and mix the nuts and butter together in a mixer or by hand. Don't melt the butter; it should be just soft enough to permit you to stir in the nuts and flavorings. Store the flavored butter in a container in the refrigerator. Or pipe the butter into rosettes on a cookie sheet if you want to be a little fancier. Nut butters also freeze well.

There, you have just succeeded in making a nut-compound butter. And it can be used wherever plain butter might be used: to thicken and flavor sauces, to finish soups, or even to top a broiled piece of fish.

Because nuts contain fat, they are also ideal to infuse into heavy cream. What this does is let the fat in the cream grab some of the fat and aromatic flavors from the nuts. Toasting the nuts first creates a deeper flavor, of course. To do this little trick, just heat some cream and add your chopped toasted nuts. Let the cream and the nuts steep (like a cup of tea) for 20 minutes. Then simply strain out the nuts and cool the cream. You can now use the cream for making ice cream, custards, or sauces, wherever you want to introduce nutty flavors.

Lab Project

For a macadamia-lime butter, lightly toast 3 ounces (about $1/2$ cup) of unsalted macadamia nuts. Allow the nuts to cool, and then grind or chop them finely. Soften 1 pound of whole butter to room temperature and place it in a mixer fitted with the paddle attachment. Add the chopped nuts, a pinch of salt, and the juice and finely grated zest from 1 fresh lime. Mix on medium-low speed until the ingredients are incorporated. Store in an airtight container in the refrigerator or freezer. Top grilled or broiled fish fillets with a spoonful of this butter; the heat of the fish will melt the butter to create an instant sauce.

Nut Coats and Stuffings

And if you are still in a nutty mood, ground nuts can be used as a *breading* for meats and fish. In fact, ground nuts make a great coating. The moisture from fat and protein helps the crumbs cling to the food. And using nuts in the standard breading proce-dure discussed in Chapter 17 will add texture, color, and, most importantly, nutrition to your food.

And if you aren't stuffed with enough information already, toasted ground nuts used in stuffing can add spice to your cooking repertoire. A stuffing is a preparation that typically uses moistened breadcrumbs as the binder. Nuts can be used to add a crunchy texture of stuffing. Nut fats also add binding properties that help keep stuffing from falling apart. This is particu-larly useful if the stuffing lacks moisture and you want to add something more than just water. And, of course, toasted nuts will deepen the flavor and often complement the food being stuffed.

> **Chef Sez**
> To **bread** food is to coat it with a fine or coarse crumb. The process is a standard technique to add flavor, protection, and crisp-ness to foods cooked on high heat.

The Least You Need to Know

- Nuts contain a good supply of healthy fats, protein, carbohydrates, and fiber, and are an energy-dense food source.
- Roasting nuts enhances and builds flavor molecules that enliven their flavors.
- When roasting nuts, watch them carefully, as they can burn quickly.
- Nuts have good binding properties and therefore are ideal in breading, stuffing, and sauce mixture.

Part  Muscle Mania–
The Handling and
Cooking of Meat

Meat is portable protein. Wild game and domestic livestock have played a large part in human eating patterns throughout history. So, understanding the fundamentals of meat and muscle biology is important in your kitchen. After all, you probably spend a fair portion of your food budget for meat. Taking a little time to study this subject just might improve how to get the most out of your investment. And, just as location is the key to buying and selling real estate, location and anatomy are really important for choosing a cooking method to apply to the meat dishes you prepare. The planning starts on the hoof and travels right into your kitchen.

Chapter 12

Anatomy 101

In This Chapter

◆ Muscles in motion

◆ Cells, fibers, and bundles of joy

◆ When heat hits meat

You can probably come up with your own idea about how and why plants were the first preferred food as human civilization evolved. One reason is clearly that plant foods were pretty easy to catch. Let's face it, if you weren't fast enough to catch berries or grains attached to plants impaled in the earth, the chances of you surviving a saber-toothed tiger breathing down your neck weren't too good. So, in order to survive, humans first domesticated plants. Then something happened. Wild ancestors of cows, sheep, pigs, and goats eventually discovered that those plots of grains and grasses growing over on Cro and Mag's land were pretty tasty. So, they started moving into the neighborhood. At first the invaders weren't easy to catch, but Cro persisted, eventually domesticating early versions of today's farm animals.

Discovering that the beasts of burden were valuable for things such as transportation, manure, and cultivation started one of the ultimate familial relationships. Animals and people became commensally related. They supported one another. The beasts provided mechanical power and ate things people couldn't; grass fiber wasn't as popular then for breakfast cereal as it is now. In exchange for services rendered, the beasts gave up a portion of their offspring as food, clothing, and fuel for their two-legged partners. And, in most cultures, it's been more or less like that ever since. So, what is it about meat, especially red meat, that humans find so appealing?

Muscles in Motion

In the carnivore food chain, muscle is a primary target. Of course, in our lingo we don't refer to muscle as food. There are no "muscle markets," "muscle courses," "muscle tenderizers," or "muscle thermometers," in food-world speak. The *muscle* that you munch on is called meat.

Muscles were designed to move organisms. Plant life doesn't have muscles. You can go out to your back lawn this evening and take a chain saw to every living tree you have and none of them is going to jump back in horror or be able to defend itself. Plants cannot take flight and flee from you. Nor can plants go and find their own food. They pretty much stand there hoping for something good, such as rain, to come along.

Animals, though, are much more animated. They can walk, run, swim, and pounce. Thanks to muscles, they possess the power of locomotion. So, the muscles'

> **Chef Sez**
> **Muscle** is contractile tissue used for locomotion and movement. It's also meat.

sole purpose in life is to contract. If contraction was just random, it would be as if a rubber band sprung out of control. No, muscles are attached to things called bones. Or if not connected to a bone, they might be connected to another piece of tissue. They are never alone. Muscles are part and parcel of the animal as a whole.

The geography of the muscle had meaning and purpose. A muscle that happened to be connected to an arm or a leg has a certain motion that it performs for the animal. It works well with the bones to give an animal posture and rigidity. This is valuable, because the force of gravity is always pulling things down. Muscle works against the forces of gravity to keep creatures upright and mobile. When muscles contract, they toughen up, and the muscle's toughness affects how you should cook it.

Special muscles work not to move the animal, but to move things along within the animal. Hearts and other muscles such as the diaphragm or reproductive muscles are equally important. Those muscles contribute survival value. Even the tongue is a muscle. Ruminant animals—sheep, cattle, water buffalo—chew a lot and grab things with their tongues. It takes the place of fingers and hands. Tongues work hard, and you will come to realize as we said before that cooking muscles that work hard is a whole different ballgame. And because muscle is so diverse in form and function, it gives rise to a very diverse group of meats. Understanding the biology of structure and anatomy are important for your best use of meat as food.

Food for Thought

In recent years, medical authorities have found links between a cattle disease called bovine spongiform encephalopathy (BSE), commonly but incorrectly called "Mad Cow Disease" and an extremely rare human disease known as new variant Creutzfeldt-Jakob Disease (nvCJD). BSE is lethal to cattle. Humans probably contract nvCJD by eating meat or other products processed from animals infected with BSE. BSE reached tragic proportions in Great Britain in 2000, when over 175,000 head of cattle were found to be infected. Cattle were probably infected with BSE from contaminated feed, but the type of organism causing BSE is still unknown. The outbreak of BSE in Great Britain resulted in 79 human deaths there, three in France, and one in Ireland. All of these cases were traced to consumption of contaminated meat. In the United States since 1990, when England's current outbreak was first reported, there have been no known cases of BSE. Nor have any Americans been diagnosed with nvCJD. Practices that allow infected ingredients to enter the human food chain probably don't occur in the United States because of differences in livestock management practices. Consistent cooperation among farmers, health professionals, and the food industry are necessary to safeguard our food supply against this and other food-borne illnesses.

Cells, Fibers, and Bundles of Joy

To repeat: Meat is food that comes from living tissues we call muscle. The basic units of all living things are cells, and cells are made up of other stuff—proteins, fats, and water. Doesn't this sound familiar?

Most muscles are divided into two categories: striated and smooth. You don't eat much meat from smooth muscles (such as the gut), but you do eat the striated kind. These are mostly attached to bones or other pieces of striated muscle. The heart is also a special striated

Chef Sez

A muscle **fiber** is the basic building block or cell of a muscle. A muscle **fibril** is a filament or thread-like part of a muscle fiber. **Connective tissue** holds muscle fibers together and holds meat to bone. Collagen, elastin, and reticulin are the three types of connective tissue.

muscle that you can eat. When they are attached to a bone, they are called skeletal muscle. So, let's talk about skeletal muscles of red meat.

Muscles are composed of long cylinder-shaped cells called *fibers*. Inside the fibers are long strands of muscle *fibrils*. Though not politically correct anymore, if you were to pick up five or six cigarettes and wrap the fingers and thumb of one hand around them, and then hold them up and look at them as if you were using your hand as a telescope, you would see what a fiber and fibril unit is like. The cigarettes are the fibrils, and your hands wrapped around them constitute the muscle-fiber unit.

But any muscle is not just made up of one muscle fiber. Layers of muscle fibers are in turn are made of stacks of muscle fibrils. The layers of fibers are held together by *connective tissue*. This connective tissue is collagen, elastin, and reticulin. Muscles had a big blood supply before they became meat, so most elastin is found in the muscle's blood vessels. Collagen appears as sheets between muscle fiber bundles, kind of like sheets of paper packed between fragile items to keep them from breaking during shipping. Different muscle groups, and therefore different cuts of meat, contain different amounts of collagen.

Crosscut of a bundle of muscle fibers

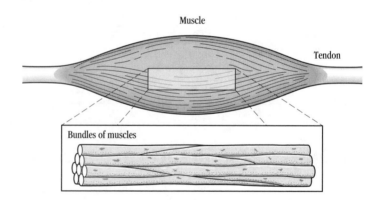

Muscle tissue

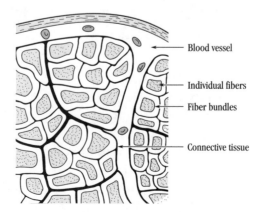

A type of reinforced collagen is found on the outside of muscle bundles. It wraps around the bundles and holds things together firmly. It's called silverskin because it is a shiny, silvery-white membrane. It looks like reinforced packing tape, and is just as strong. Silverskin is tougher than collagen, and it won't cook out with normal heat. We will talk more about how to handle silverskin in different cuts of meat in Chapter 13.

Ligaments are a continuation of the silverskin sheet. Ligaments come together as long cables at the ends of muscle groups. If you take a wet towel and wring it to squeeze out the water, it simulates a bundle of muscles covered by silverskin. The twisted ends of the towel would be analogous to the point where the ligaments begin. The ligaments attach the ends of the muscle group to your bones. It's not just what's on the outside of muscles that is important for meat. The inside stuff is critical, too.

Meat from the Inside Out

One reason why humans and other animals like meat is because it is a good source of protein. In fact, meat has relatively high protein content, from 18 percent to 24 percent. But it's not just total protein that is good; it is also the type of protein. You know that protein is made of individual molecules called amino acids. Meat is complete protein. This means that it contains all the essential amino acids, including the ones your body can't make.

Proteins are responsible for muscle contraction and color. You will learn about the importance of contractile proteins in the next chapter on aging meat.

Food for Thought

Amino acids are the building blocks of proteins. Of the 20 known amino acids, nine are essential. That is, those amino acids must be supplied from your diet. Nonessential amino acids are the ones that are produced naturally by your body. The specific combination of amino acids gives each protein its unique characteristics and properties.

Is Redder Better?

Like typical shoppers, you probably look for the most ruby-red meat you can find in the butcher's case. You might think that red meat gets its color from hemoglobin, the protein that makes your blood appear red. But almost 95 percent of the hemoglobin is drained out of muscle when it becomes meat. Meat color comes from the protein myoglobin, which is a cousin of hemoglobin. Myoglobin is the oxygen-transport pigment of muscle. It ferries oxygen from the blood into the muscle in the live animal.

When myoglobin is in an oxygen-rich environment like open air, it first glows a bright red. It has become oxymyoglobin. Oxymyoglobin, though, loses its rosy glow over time as the protein changes to a substance called methmyoglobin. It turns a dull reddish or purple gray. You usually associate this color with older, less desirable meat, though the meat quality is actually just fine. It is only the myoglobin that is different.

If you scrape off the surface of this purple-gray meat, the myoglobin in the layers below the surface take up oxygen and glow bright red once again. This is often done by meat cutters and butchers to put a "healthy glow" back on meat. This marketing magic is called bloom. Special plastic wraps permit oxygen to filter onto the meat's surface gradually, helping create an oxymyoglobin appearance. But in meat as in life, you just can't stop the clock, and even this meat will start to gray sooner or later.

Magic Marbles

Meat also contains lipids. We say lipids in this context because lipids include fats as well as things like cholesterol. Cholesterol isn't a fat but is in the same general classification. Cholesterol is only found in food from animal origins. The lipid content varies in different meats from 1 percent to as much as 15 percent.

> **Chef Sez**
>
> **Marbling** refers to thin bits of fat located within or between muscle fibers. This fat is desirable because it adds flavor and juiciness to the meat.

Fat content varies by the type of animal as well as the location of the meat on the animal. Beef, lamb, pork, and veal all have different percentages of lipids in various cuts of meat. Young animals develop layers of fat as they mature. When the fat is weaved in between the muscle fibers and connective tissue, it is called *marbling*. Marbled fat is the last type of fat to be deposited in animals as they are fattened for food.

> **Food for Thought**
>
> Beef is often graded for quality based on its degree of marbling, age, color, and texture. The USDA has established eight quality-grade categories, but quality grading is voluntary. USDA Prime is the top of the line; it is produced in limited quantities for sale through the finest restaurants and markets. USDA Choice is the grade most commonly available in restaurants and grocery stores. USDA Select is less-well marbled and lacks the flavor and tenderness of the higher grades. So, if you want to go leaner, then go for USDA Select. The trade-off is that it will be less tender and less juicy than USDA Choice. But the choice, as they say, is up to you.

Because fat is smooth and slippery when it melts, marbling adds juiciness and flavor to meat. When the fat melts, it also tenderizes the meat. That is why you tend to pay more money for prime beef, which has the highest marble content.

Animals also store fat between muscle and skin and on the surface of large muscle groups. Some areas store more fat than others, which shouldn't surprise you if you battle this phenomenon at the gym every day. The back is a prime area for fat storage, as is the rump or butt area. Bet you know all about that problem!

Fighting BAC

Raw meat carries surface bacteria, and ground meat such as hamburger can harbor dangerous bacteria throughout. The only sure way to destroy these critters is to cook the meat to the proper internal temperature. For ground meat, the recommended internal temperature is 160°F or higher. For whole muscle pieces of meat such as a steak or roast, the recommended temperature is 145°F. You can't tell by appearance or time when these temperatures are actually reached. So, to be safe and consistent when cooking meat, get a thermometer and keep it calibrated.

Obviously, these bacteria can easily get on your hands, cutting board, work surface, knives, and so on when you work with raw meat. To avoid contaminating other foods, always wash and sanitize anything that comes in contact with raw meat—this includes your hands—before using it for anything else. Never put cooked meat back onto the same plate that held the raw meat, and keep raw meat refrigerated until ready to cook.

Food for Thought
Fighting BAC is a consumer awareness program sponsored by the FDA in conjunction with food industry and public health officials. Begun in 1997, the goal is to increase public awareness and education about food-borne illnesses and bacterial contamination.

Done by Degrees

While it's true that experienced cooks can tell how well done a steak or thin piece of meat is by touch, this method isn't reliable for everyone. So, how can you tell when a nice tender cut of meat is done?

Not surprisingly, it's all about water, temperature, and time. Set temperature ranges are the most consistent estimates of rare, medium-rare, medium, and well-done. These temperatures correspond to the amount of moisture left in the meat.

Let's look at the extremes first. A well-done steak is cooked to 165 to 170°F. At this temperature, most of the muscle fibers have coagulated and collapsed, squeezing out the water. If you press down on it with your index finger, it will be very firm to the touch. Cut it, and you'll see that it is uniformly brown inside.

At the other end of the scale, rare meat will come in at about 125 to 130°F. It will be very pink in the center with just a hint of brown right under the surface. Rare meat still has lots of water left and it is softer to the touch, but not as soft as raw meat. Medium-rare meat will be a little more cooked toward the center, but still nice and pink. The internal temperature will be about 130 to 140°F. When you get above 140°F and closer to 150°F, you are in the medium zone. Just a little pink left, there's less moisture and the muscle is a bit firmer.

So, how do you get to these temperature zones? We can't tell you to "always cook a steak for X number of minutes" because the amount of time needed will vary depending on the cut of meat, its thickness, the temperature of the meat when cooking begins, and the source of your heat. Broiling a rib-eye is different than grilling a filet mignon, for example. Although a pro would never admit to doing this, it isn't a capital offense to sneak a peak. Just take a small knife and make a cut in the thickest part of the meat to look at its color. Don't be intimidated; go for it. Practice makes perfect, and practice is the best way to learn to cook meat properly.

Applying Heat to Red Meat

Broiling a steak is a prerequisite for understanding the changes that occur when cooking red meat. Broiling is a dry-heat cooking method best suited to tender cuts of meat. In Chapter 13, you will learn where to find the tenderest cuts on an animal, which is really a matter of location, location, location. For now, let's just observe what happens when heat is applied to red meat.

You will need to purchase a steak. The best one to get is a rib-eye. It won't have a bone to confound the experiment. Get a steak that is at least 1-inch thick. Keep the label or make a note of the weight of the meat. You also need a meat thermometer and a kitchen scale. (If you don't have a scale, that's okay; you'll just have to take our word about part of your results.) Preheat your broiler and place a rack about 6 inches from the broiler coils. Spray a broiler pan with a touch of nonstick vegetable spray. You can sprinkle the steak liberally with salt and pepper, but do so immediately before you pop it in the oven. Use your index finger to feel the steak; press it down a bit. Now go wash your hands. Look at the steak; make a mental note of the color. Note the surface moisture. Now plop it on the broiler pan and place the pan on the oven rack.

You are going to cook the steak for about 10 minutes total. Watch the steak cook by keeping the oven door slightly open. Notice what's happening. You want to cook the steak on the first side for six minutes. Then use some tongs and flip the steak over. Cook for another three minutes. When the 10 minutes are up, take the pan out of the oven. Take your meat thermometer and stick the point in one side of the steak. Don't jam it down the top; you want it sticking out the side. To do this safely, steady the steak with the tongs and gently push in the thermometer. Take the reading when the temperature stabilizes. You are looking for an internal temperature of 140°F. This is close to medium in cooking lingo.

 Chef Sez
Resting meat after cooking before slicing it prevents succulent juices from escaping. Cooked muscle fibers relax while resting and let water seep back into the interior of the meat protein.

If you have that temperature or a bit more, just remove the steak from the pan and set it on a plate to rest. If the internal temperature is lower than 140°F, pop the steak back in for another three minutes. Then check it again. When the steak is done, allow it to rest for five minutes. Resist the temptation to cut into the meat right away; it's important that the meat rests undisturbed. Weigh it if you have a scale. Take your index finger and feel your meat again, just like before you cooked it. Then slice the meat into two parts. Take a peek at the center part and note the color. Now enjoy your meal.

The Results

Now let's break down the results from this heat-the-meat experiment. First, analyze what things looked like before you started cooking. Then analyze what happened to the steak as it cooked.

Your meat was a nice red color right out of the package, right? You can see flecks of fat; that's the marbling. There's not much surface moisture. As you began to cook the steak, a couple of things happened pretty quickly. First, moisture started to appear on the surface of the meat. You even saw a bit of what looked like blood seeping from the top surface.

Now, think about what you were doing. You took some food molecules—protein, fat, and water—and applied intense heat from the broiler. That radiant heat struck the surface of the meat, and was conducted to the inside in 10 minutes. It's pretty powerful stuff. Any food molecule that gets in the way of that heat has plenty to deal with.

Recall that when you used the microwave, the energy pretty much just caused water to heat up, and the water cooked the food molecules. This is very different, however. Radiant heat from conventional cooking is one of the dry-heat methods. Temperatures are going to be in excess of 500°F. All food molecules, not just water, are going to feel the heat. They are all going to undergo changes. And those changes are what you are going to see and smell as the meat cooks.

You heard a sizzle. And you saw a bit of steam rise from the broiler pan. The color of the meat changed from ruby red to light brown. Then it got browner, maybe even a caramel-like color. The fat started to glisten and shine and maybe brown on the edges; it melted a bit, too. When you flipped the steak over, it was a light-brown color on that side, too. The heat of the hot broiler pan is doing its thing even on the underside of your steak. Those food molecules were completely surrounded.

And while the meat rested, you saw a bit of moisture seep out onto the plate as it cooled. When you cut into your steak, the interior was a light shade of pink (we hope). The meat was two-toned: brown on the outside, pink on the inside. And, finally, if you weighed the cooked meat, you found that it weighed less than when you started. It probably lost several ounces.

The Rest of the Story

So, what do all these changes mean? The important things that are happening when heat meets red meat are changes in color, water, protein, and collagen. Some of these things you can see and some you can taste. And these changes occur because of heat affecting the basic food molecules. You are getting to the food molecules by breaking down the cellular structure of the muscle fibers.

Water and color are the first things that change as meat is heated. So, as radiant heat from the broiler contacts the proteins on the cut surface of the meat, the proteins begin to unwind. Those long coiled chains of amino acids start to break down. This initial unwinding of protein is called denaturing. Heat denatures, or unwinds, the protein threads within the muscle fibers and fibrils. And as red-meat protein denatures, it browns. The main protein that is browning is myoglobin. It was red when it was fresh, and brown as it cooks.

As the proteins denature, water that was trapped between the protein coils and between the strands of muscle fibers begins to flow freely. That is what you see coming out of the surface of the meat in the first few moments of cooking. Hey, the meat is 70 percent water; when you break down the protein structures, it's gotta go somewhere, right?

These drops of water even appear red. Water now flows not only from the surface of the meat as protein denatures, but it also percolates outward from the center of the steak. Remember, as the surface is getting hotter and hotter, heat is being conducted to the center of your food. So, as water flows out from inside your meat, it carries the red myoglobin protein to the surface with it, and you see red drops appearing.

As the meat continues to heat, more protein and myoglobin are denatured. Now the surface proteins have almost all denatured. What happens next is a process called protein coagulation. The proteins that have unwound now begin to collapse back upon themselves. The strands start to form little clumps of protein. Now, denaturation and coagulation are very closely linked.

It's not as though a protein denatures, hangs around, and then coagulates. Cooking the protein is a continual process of the two events. It's like a politician working a crowd. They meet, greet, shake hands, and move on. Proteins meet heat, they denature, coagulate, and that's that. Of course, if you continue to apply heat, your steak will turn to charcoal. You have cooked all the carbon. But hopefully you won't do that too often.

So, as proteins coagulate, more surface water is cooked away as it is continually freed up from the proteins; now this moisture evaporates. That is why you see some steam, and smell the meat cooking. The water vapor is carrying those volatile meat smells right to your nose's doorstep.

As you cook away more and more moisture from the meat's surface, you increase the browning activity even more. You get the Maillard products. Remember that as protein is coagulating, it is losing some of its building blocks, the amino acids. They just don't sit around. They hook up with that fat, which is melting and cooking, too. The commune of amino acids and free fats creates some of those nice browning products that taste and smell so good.

If you cooked your meat to medium, you successfully stopped before all of the myoglobin was totally denatured and coagulated. At medium, the steak still has a light pink interior. So, by halting the heat energy's march toward the center of the steak, you salvaged some of the reddish myoglobin and some of the water.

When you touched the raw steak, it was soft, almost spongy. The meat-fiber cells were intact and full of water. As the meat cooked, the texture firmed up. The meat fibers lost water in the process of coagulation. Their structure changes, and so does the meat's texture. Cooked protein changes from a pliable, forgiving tissue to a firmer one as heat is applied. This is why cooks with years of grill experience can tell how well done a steak is just by touch.

Shoe Leather to Go

If you had continued to cook your meat to well done, you would have blasted all the myoglobin protein and water right off the map. The myoglobin would have become brown as you denatured and coagulated it, just like it does on the meat's surface. So, myoglobin is one indicator of cooking doneness. The texture would have also reached maximum firmness, maybe even become hard and leathery. You would have squeezed and collapsed the meat fiber proteins to the max.

Had you cooked your meat to well done, almost all of the water that is making the meat palatable would have been squeezed out of your meat, too. Your steak would be drier, and in the end you would taste the difference. So, you see, it really is all about water.

And how did you know that all this water was leaving? Well, first, you can see remnants of cooking on the broiler pan in the form of free water and melted fat. The melted fat came from both outside and inside the meat. And second, if you weighed your meat, you found there was less than when you started.

And what's so important about not cutting into the meat immediately after cooking it? Why let it rest? This is to retain some of the water that is still hanging around. Though some water will seep out, if you had cut into the hot meat without cooling it even slightly, even more moisture would escape. You need to give the meat time to relax, which means letting those cooked proteins settle back down and soak up their moisture. If you do this, water now flows back into the center of the meat, kind of like filling in the spaces, rather than heading onto your plate. This makes for a juicer and moister steak in your mouth, where it counts.

Finally, you might ask, what about the connective tissue? What happens to collagen when heat hits? You are going to meet this meat again in the next chapter. So, stay tuned, and stay hungry.

The Least You Need to Know

- Meat is the edible form of food from muscle.
- Meat is mostly water, protein, and fat.
- Heat applied to meat denatures protein, melts fat, and evaporates water.
- Meat color, texture, and temperature are end points to determine doneness.
- Wash your hands after handling raw meat and before touching any cooked meat.

Chapter 13

Red Meat

In This Chapter

- ◆ From calf to cattle
- ◆ The benefits of aging
- ◆ How heat effects meat

Not all meat is created equal. That is because not all muscles are created equal. Genes set a basic blueprint. All subsequent biological changes that lead to muscle development, and hence meat produced, are controllable. Cattle farmers or ranchers can control the process. They can make an individual animal fatter or thinner, and ultimately can control even the genetic blueprint through selective breeding.

One thing that does stay the same is the fact that each muscle has a certain job to do depending on its location. How that muscle works affects the type of meat it provides. And the type of meat determines the type of cooking that you do. Thus, the biology of muscle to meat is matched to the kitchen.

Growing Beef from the Ground Up

Though not as extensive as maybe it once was, 4-H is still a great activity for kids. Perhaps you were once a participant yourself. Kids in 4-H have a chance to raise livestock from the ground up. It might be a pig or a calf or some chicks. If it is a calf it is likely going to be a *steer*.

Chef Sez _____

A **steer** is a castrated male calf that is raised for beef production to about 12 to 14 months of age. Steers have benefits in management for ranchers, one of which is behavior and easy care.

There's an awful lot you can learn from doing a 4-H project. You actually see food in motion. You can relate to the biology because you have to follow that calf, for example, through a life cycle. And sometimes the end can be a bit sad because you know what the purpose of raising the livestock is all about. It makes you understand that agriculture and food production are a cycle. And you take a great deal of appreciation from it and learn to always give something back.

So, if you haven't built a piece of meat from the ground up, here's your chance. Let's look at growth, and focus on what might happen as meat is produced for food. We'll focus on building muscles for meat, although so many other products will eventually come from our calf.

Steers are miniature models of adult cattle, or so it may seem. Your objective is to raise that animal so that its muscle growth maximizes its genetic potential. Your steer needs proper nutrition and plenty of fuel to grow up right.

For about the first six months of life, the mother supplies fuel in the form of milk, so things are a bit easier on you. Calves are ruminants, which means that they can eat plants you don't, such as grass. So, the young animal munches each day on grass while drinking momma's milk. It is learning how to be a beef cow.

Food for Thought _____

The meat of a young calf that is slaughtered between 8 and 16 weeks of age is called veal. When a calf is slaughtered at one month of age, it is called bob veal. Most veal is produced from animals that are by-products of the dairy industry. Dairy cows must give birth before they produce milk. So, calves that aren't needed in dairy herds (usually the males) become veal. Veal is lighter in color than beef, and has a more delicate flavor. It is usually very tender with relatively little fat.

Your young steer seems to be nothing but bony legs and a head held together by some hide. Oh, there are muscles in there somewhere; it's just that the muscles haven't bloomed yet. The animal's bones are softer, too. In fact, when an animal is young, the amount of connective tissue in its bones is at a higher proportion than it ever will have as an adult.

Chefs prize these young bones. They are used to make veal stock, a foundation of French cuisine that you'll learn more about in Chapter 24. Collagen, as you will see when you look into stock making, is the primary protein that you want to extract. Having softer bones and more of them relative to everything else just makes getting at the collagen a bit easier. But these young animals don't supply just bones and collagen; their meat is also highly prized.

When you finally wean the calf from its mother, it is pretty much dependant upon you for its food and well-being. If you had ample pasture, you could let your animal graze on grass. The steer's digestive machinery can turn this cellulose and other plant components into food molecules to help their muscles grow. In fact, you could raise your steer entirely on grass this way. Grass-fed beef, sometimes called *free-range beef*, has become one method for meeting the commercial demand for beef.

Chef Sez

Free-range beef is synonymous with the practice of allowing animals to graze freely. Animals are not confined. Of course, most beef raised conventionally in the United States also free ranges for a good portion of the animal's life. In traditional livestock beef production, hormone implants are used. The animals are fed antibiotics. Neither may be used in free-range, organic beef. Hormones are below tolerance in the muscle before it becomes meat. In fact, you typically produce more hormones in a single day in your own body than you would eat in the meat. So, enjoy both free-range and traditional-style beef. There is really no nutritional or health-related difference between them.

But more often than not, you might choose to supplement your animal's feed with grains such as corn. Dent corn is used to make a whole host of feeds tailored to livestock nutrition. Throw some soybeans in with the corn and you have a created a livestock diet that improves the nutritional gains of your calf. It is pretty simple; just as you kick start your energy level in the morning by eating cereal, you are giving a boost to the growth of your calf's muscle by supplementing grass with grain. The grass supplies fiber and nutrients, and the grain is a quick source of energy for muscle development.

So, in a little more than a year, as you tend your animal, it will become beef— ready for market. It will weigh over 1,200 pounds, more than 10 times its birth weight. The muscle mass will have increased and filled out with all of those food molecules. You've turned your gangly sack of bones into a formidable animal. The muscle is now ready to be harvested as meat. You have respected life, been a good caretaker, and witnessed one important cycle of food agriculture.

Aging Gracefully

Raising animals humanely is not just the law, it's also an imperative if you want optimum meat production. You know what stress is in your life. Animals feel stress, too, maybe even more than we do. Bad weather, poor nutrition, over-crowded rearing conditions, or mishandling affect how well an animal grows as it matures. And even as important as succeeding in rearing animals properly, the humane slaughter of livestock is essential. It is essential for the honor owed to any animal used for food production, but it also is important to ensure the quality of the meat produced.

You've been to the gym for a workout and know that muscle injuries hurt. For livestock, injury to an animal compromises the ability to function, too. Muscles were designed to do work. Muscles allow the animal to move and to graze. Muscles receive a large amount of blood flow to bring in nutrients and remove wastes. They function as biological tissue, right up until the time that the animal is killed. If any stress occurs to the animal to disrupt this process, it can show up in poor meat quality.

> **Food for Thought**
>
> Meat harvested from beef that has been stressed is not good quality. The condition is known as dark, firm dry (DFD) cutting meat. The muscle fibers have not undergone a healthy progression through rigor but have been subject to abnormal bacterial contamination. This is directly related to stress and the prevention of normal changes in muscle pH. It's unlikely that you will see such meat in your local market, as quality control prevents it from getting into retail channels.

Good quality meat depends upon how the animal is handled during the last few hours before it is slaughtered, and then how the meat is handled after slaughter. Muscles are living tissue that function to contract and relax. In the process, they use energy and produce wastes. Muscles' favorite fuel is carbohydrate or animal starch. As the starch is used up during contraction, by-products including acids are produced. Blood flow flushes the acids away and the cycle repeats itself. This is all very natural to the physiology of the muscle.

Now, imagine the muscle once all of that blood flow and oxygen is removed when the animal dies. The muscle fibers use up its last supply of animal starch. In the process, the acids build up in muscle-fiber cells. But now there is no blood or oxygen to replenish the system. The pH remains low, and the muscle starts to change. The acids break down the muscle-fiber cells. Once that happens, the cell membranes and all that cellular machinery start to unravel. The cellular compartments that are there to keep all the systems working properly can no longer do their coordinated jobs. Things get pretty hectic, and the muscle goes into a state of contraction (this is called *rigor mortis*). The muscles literally stiffen, just like you suddenly getting a cramp in your leg. But, in this case, it's because the tissue is dying.

While all this sounds like something you don't want to happen, it really is a natural and necessary part of meat aging. Rigor mortis in cattle will disappear within 48 to 72 hours under refrigeration. All meats should be allowed to age or rest long enough for rigor to dissipate. This is called resolution of rigor. Hanging is part of the aging process. Hanging stretches the carcass, doing the same thing that stretching your muscles does if you have a cramp. Meats that have not been aged long enough or that have been frozen during this period are known as "green meat." Green meat will be very tough and flavorless when cooked.

Today, most meat is wet-aged, meaning that the carcass is broken down into parts, vacuum wrapped, and shipped to the market. The industry calls this boxed beef. A great part of the aging process takes place while the meat is being transported from the slaughterhouse to the butcher or market. Keeping the meat in vacuum-sealed plastic prevents loss of moisture, and it lowers costs. The trade-off may be less flavor, however. Longer periods of aging are sometimes used, especially with beef and lamb, in order to increase their tenderness and flavor. Pork is not aged further because of its high fat content. Just remember that aging only works if you start with a healthy animal that is humanely slaughtered.

Why is this so crucial? When you are upset, your metabolism increases. You burn more calories, you use up your carbohydrate fuel reserves, and you tire easily. It is no different in animals. Imagine that the animal was under a great deal of stress at the time of slaughter. Their muscles use up all of the starch reserves. Once these are depleted, the changes in pH and acid production can no longer occur when the animal is killed; there is nothing left to make the acids. The lack of acid means fewer natural changes are going to occur. And with disrupted changes, you get the start of a poor aging process in the meat.

Now You're Cooking

Dry-aging of red meat is the process of storing meat in an environment with controlled temperature, humidity, and air flow for up to six weeks. This allows natural enzymes and microorganisms to break down connective tissues and to develop stronger flavors. Dry-aged beef is very expensive to produce and is only available through specialty butchers or restaurants.

Aging your stretched-out beef carcass under refrigeration also encourages something else to happen. The drop in pH of the carcass encourages the growth of good bacteria as opposed to pathogenic bacteria. These good bacteria will populate the surface of the carcass. The bacteria produce acids and other compounds that are essential to tenderize and break down the muscle. Keeping the meat cold helps regulate bacterial growth. And, of course, when you cook the meat with high temperature, you are killing the bacteria before you eat them. Safe food handling is essential to reduce any chances of food-borne illness along the way.

Matching Heat to Meat

You invest your money when you purchase protein in the form of meat. You want to make sure that you use this resource wisely. You want to cook it appropriately and not compromise the quality of your expensive investment. So, what can hedge your bets toward success?

Actually, the most important thing you can do is to choose the appropriate retail cut of meat for the right cooking technique. If you do not choose wisely, all the cooking skill in the world will not help. Retail cuts of meat are produced according to standards of basic muscle geography.

Now, this is not your typical road map. This geography lesson is based on an anatomical map for each domestic livestock species. If you know what part of the carcass a piece of meat comes from, you can understand what the muscle was originally designed to do. And knowing what it was designed to do gives you important knowledge about how to cook it. So, remember: It's location, location, location. The following table is a simplified road map that you can use to help match the best cooking method to the most popular types of meats.

Matching Cooking Method with Popular Cuts from Domestic Red-Meat Animals

Species	Dry Heat	Combination	Moist Heat
Beef	Ground beef	Chuck roast	Brisket
	Rib roast	Sort Ribs	Oxtail
	Porterhouse	Round Steak	
	T-bones	Flank Steak	
	Filet		
	Flank Steak		
	Sirloin		
Pork	Ham	Spare Ribs	
	Bacon	Chops	
	Picnic Shoulder	Back Ribs	
	Chops	Chops	
	Tenderloin	Boston Butt	
	Boston Butt		
	Loin		

Species	Dry Heat	Combination	Moist Heat
Lamb	Ground Lamb	Shoulder stew meat	
	Rack	Breast	
	Loin & chops		
	Leg		
Veal	Ground veal	Shanks	
	Chops		
	Loin		
	Leg	Leg stew meat	
	Round steak		

Visualize any four-legged domestic specie standing up. The further away from the ground a muscle group is, the more tender the meat from that muscle will be. The more tender the muscle, the more appropriate it is to use dry, high-temperature cooking methods. Less tender cuts—those located closer to the ground—contain more connective tissues and will benefit from moist-heat and combination cooking methods.

Food for Thought _____

Primal cuts are large, specifically defined divisions of muscle, bone, and connective tissue produced by the initial butchering of an animal carcass. Retail cuts are the smaller, even, individual-portion cuts that your butcher sells in the market. At one time in America, grocery stores received primal cuts and local butchers cut the meat to order for you. Today, most beef is sold as "boxed beef," which means that it was broken down into retail meat cuts at the processing plant, and then shipped to your market ready for display.

Clearly, leg, rump, and shoulder muscles are designed to work the most. Walking, running, and grazing require movement. When you go to the gym to work out, one goal may be to build up your arm and leg muscles. The more you work your arms and legs, the bigger and tougher those muscle groups become. Cattle and sheep do the same thing as they walk miles each day grazing. Even standing around defeating the forces of gravity is enough to work those leg muscles. And work means more protein and less fat. And less fat means less tender eating for you.

So, if leg muscles get tougher from the ground up, as you move on toward the top and center of an animal the muscles get more tender. The top of the back and the rib cage are the two key areas for tender meat. Those muscles have to work less, which means the muscle fibers can relax more. And since fat tends to build up there in domestic livestock, this marbling adds flavor, and juiciness, and contributes to tenderness. These muscles can withstand high heat for short periods and still retain moisture and flavor. They are well adapted to dry-heat cooking methods.

Like most rules, exceptions do exist. Some cuts of meat can be prepared two ways. This depends on the animal species and age. And most often, these cuts can be cooked by either dry heat or by combination methods. And even that makes sense when you think about it. Combination cooking begins with dry heat and ends with a slow moist-heat process—braises or stews. So, you get the best of both worlds when choosing some cuts of meat, because they are a bit more versatile.

Too Hot to Handle _____

Ground meat must be cooked to well-done temperatures every time. It is simply no longer safe to eat a rare or medium-rare burger. Bacteria that naturally populate the surface of meat as it ages will be killed when a steak, chop, or roast is cooked. When meat is ground these surface bacteria get mixed all throughout the meat, however. The only safe way to serve ground meat products such as burgers or meatloaf is to cook them until the internal temperature is at 165°F for 15 seconds.

Collagen Injections

Some cuts simply must be cooked with moist heat, unless you are prepared to spend hours chewing shoe leather. Take a beef chuck roast for example. Chuck comes from the shoulder, which is a constantly used group of muscles. It contains a great deal of connective tissue, which also means it will be very flavorful. Chuck is the perfect cut for braising or stewing.

The reason goes back to basic muscle biology. Certain cuts of meat have a very high percentage of collagen or connective tissue. Remember that connective tissue is the glue that holds muscles together or holds muscles to bone. And one very important thing about collagen is, it never begins to really break down until temperatures approach 200°F. Then it melts and softens. But 200°F is a hot tamale, so to speak, for meat temperatures; well-done steak is only 160°F, after all.

Think about it this way. Collagen will start to soften when the temperature gets over 145°F, but it is still pretty stout stuff. If you were to eat a chuck roast cooked to 160°F like a well-done steak, the collagen would still be very tough.

So, why don't you just cook it longer, or extend the dry-heat method to a higher temperature, you might be asking? Well, though it seems logical, think what would be happening to the movement of water and the condition of the muscle as you try to soften the collagen more with dry heat. By the time you get to an internal meat temperature of 200°F using only dry heat, the outside of your steak might be approaching charcoal. And the meat would be extremely dry. Oh, you might very well have some soft collagen, but you won't be able to eat any of the meat that surrounds it.

Just remember that collagen dissolves best in moist heat, so tougher cuts of meat—those with plenty of connective tissue—will be best when prepared with moist or combination-cooking methods.

The Sunday Dinner Combo

A beef chuck roast like grandma used to make for Sunday dinner provides a trip down memory lane for some people. And since grandma didn't work for NASA, making one isn't rocket science. Buy a 3-pound chuck roast. Then coarsely chop an onion, a couple of medium carrots, and a stalk of celery. Use a roasting pan or Dutch oven big enough to hold everything without crowding. You'll need a lid, too. Pre-heat your oven to 500°F. Season the roast well with salt and pepper. You can really do any dry spice rub you want, but grandma probably just used fresh cracked pepper and salt.

Lightly rub some oil into the meat; not much, just enough to give it a bit of shine. Then put the meat into the pan and pop it into the oven. Leave the lid off for now. Cook for eight minutes, and then turn the roast over. Cook for seven more minutes. This step sears the meat to add color and flavor. It is the dry-heat part of a combination-cooking method. Now take the pan out of the oven, and move the roast to a plate to rest. Turn the oven temperature down to 325°F. Put the roasting pan on a stove top burner set to medium high. Put your chopped vegetables in the pan and cook them, stirring occasionally so they don't burn, until they take on a nice shine and begin to brown. You might need to add a touch of oil if your pan is too dry, but don't add much; you merely want to sweat the veggies, not fry them.

Now take some water or stock and add to the vegetables in the pan, scraping up all the bits and pieces that might be sticking to the bottom. How much water? A good rule of thumb is to use about 1¹/₂ to 2 cups of liquid for every pound of meat. If you have a big lump of meat or a really large pan, you'll need the higher amount. For your 3-pound roast, 5 cups is a good bet. You only want enough liquid to reach about a quarter to a third the height of the meat, never covering it. As the liquid begins to simmer, place the meat on top of the vegetables. Sprinkle some salt into the liquid and, if you want, toss in a couple of cloves of garlic and a bay leaf. Put the lid on and pop it back in the oven. This is the moist-heat step of the combination-cooking method. You are now braising.

In 45 minutes, you can baste the meat with some unsalted butter. Just rub it across the exposed surface. Fifteen minutes later, turn the meat over. As you do, poke it with a fork. Note that the meat is likely still tough, and might even cling to the fork. Return the covered pan to the oven and keep braising. Check your meat in 30 minutes. If it is still tough and resists your fork, baste it again with more butter and pan juices. Continue to braise until a fork slides in and out effortlessly. Now it is done. Good braises can take two to three hours of slow cooking. When the meat is done, use the procedure described in Chapter 25 to convert your pan drippings into gravy.

Lab Project

To braise a 3-pound chuck roast, preheat the oven to 500°F and find a Dutch oven or roasting pan with a lid. Season the meat with salt and pepper and rub the surface with 2 tablespoons of vegetable oil. Place the meat in the pan and roast, uncovered, for 8 minutes. Turn the meat over and roast for 7 more minutes. Remove the pan from the oven and turn the temperature down to 325°F. Move the roast to a plate and set aside.

Place the roasting pan on a burner over medium-high heat. Add one coarsely chopped onion, two chopped carrots, and one stalk of chopped celery. Cook the vegetables in the pan drippings until they sweat and begin to turn translucent. Add one bay leaf, a pinch of salt, two peeled garlic cloves, and 5 cups of beef stock or water. Bring the liquid to a simmer, and then return the meat to the pan. Cover and place in the oven. After 45 minutes, brush the exposed surface of the meat with unsalted butter and continue cooking. Fifteen minutes later, turn the meat over, checking it for doneness. Continue basting and checking the meat every 20 to 30 minutes until it is tender when pierced with a fork. Remove the pan from the oven and uncover. Allow the meat to rest for 15 to 20 minutes before slicing.

You braise chuck roasts, or other shoulder and leg cuts of meat that have lots of connective tissue, in order to give the collagen time to melt fully. When that happens, the meat will nearly fall of the bone. This soft, gelatinous collagen is one of the real treats of perfectly braised meat. You have added color and flavor by first *searing* the meat and the vegetables. Slow-going then allows the collagen to melt, and the moist cooking environment keeps the meat around the collagen from drying out and toughening up. It is old-fashioned cooking at its best, and well worth your time. One thing you should look for before you start cooking the meat, though, is the presence of silverskin. If you buy a piece of beef with silverskin visible on the outside surface, you should cut it away. Remember, it looks like sturdy packing tape and it will never cook. You can remove silverskin most easily by using a sharp knife to peel it away. Just slide the knife under one end, cut it loose, and lift it up. Then take your knife blade and cut between the meat and the silverskin as you hold the flap of silverskin with your other hand, pulling it in the opposite direction as you cut.

Chef Sez

Searing means to cook meat by high heat for a short period of time to add color and flavor.

Tender Is as Tender Does

If an inexpensive, tough chuck roast can be made tender and flavorful by braising, imagine what braising will do to a cut of meat that is already tender. It's bound to be good, right? Wrong. The factors that make the tougher, close-to-the-ground cuts good for braising aren't present in tender, high-on-the-back cuts such as the tenderloin, strip loin, and sirloin. These muscles don't get as much of a workout as those in the legs and shoulders, so they don't have as much connective tissue. Moist heat isn't needed to tenderize these cuts; they are best prepared with dry-heat methods such as grilling, broiling, and dry roasting. The lack of connective tissue also means that these cuts are actually less flavorful. It's the high-temperature, dry-heat techniques that add the caramel-like flavors we find so appealing in a good steak. In fact, using one of these higher priced cuts in a stew or braise would be a waste of good animal flesh.

The Least You Need to Know

- How an animal is raised and treated affects meat quality because it affects muscle development.
- Muscle function and anatomy determine the best cooking method to use for each cut of meat.
- Cuts with higher amounts of collagen should be cooked by moist heat of combination methods.
- Naturally tender cuts should be cooked with dry-heat methods, such as grilling, broiling, or dry roasting.

Chapter 14

Chicken and Other Tame Birds

In This Chapter

◆ Handle with care

◆ White meat or dark?

◆ Cooking the whole thing

No one has answered the age-old question, which came first, the chicken or the egg? No matter, because chicken has certainly become the first choice for dinner tables and lunch boxes in the United States. You eat chicken in increasing quantities for a variety of reasons. First, it tastes good. And it tastes good in so many different forms, which is another way of saying that chicken is versatile. Second, you like it because it is relatively lean. Third, chicken is relatively inexpensive. What's not to like?

Of course, the world of poultry isn't always about chicken. There are other birds out there on the culinary roost. Turkey, duck, goose, and game hen are all pretty common in today's markets. For the most part, any cooking procedure or information for chicken will apply to these other birds as well. So, let's take a flight into the wonderful world of poultry.

Handle with Care

Life is risky business. So is eating. Bacteria love the food you love almost as much as you do. And usually they succeed in getting there first. Meat is a particular delicacy for bacteria because it is a high-protein food. You like protein because it supplies all the essential amino acids to make you healthy; so can you blame the bacteria for selecting it, also? Of course, meat is high in moisture. It contains about 70 percent water. This is good for you because when you appropriately cook it, the meat is still moist and juicy. Bacteria like nice, juicy, moist things, too.

But probably the number-one reason that meat is a delicacy for microorganisms is opportunity. Bacteria have a chance to get into the action simply because of the way meat is processed. And when it comes to chicken, it seems that the bad microorganisms have a head start.

Problem microorganisms already reside in the bird's digestive track. This is not abnormal or unusual. You have your fair share of bacteria in-house as well. But poultry has an affinity for a particular type of microorganism: Salmonella. You remember Salmonella from Chapter 5. Salmonella just naturally resides in the digestive tract of poultry. Unfortunately, this microorganism can cause a serious illness in humans. Whenever chicken is processed, there is a chance for the bacteria to latch onto the bird's skin or muscles. In additional, Salmonella may also be present in a chicken's reproductive tract. So, you have double-barreled trouble here. Both eggs and flesh can be infected. Careful handling of the birds as they go from farm to dinner table is essential.

Food for Thought

Poultry have been fed antibiotics for many years to reduce bacterial problems associated with decreased growth or loss of health. Reducing antibiotics in your food requires alternative solutions. A new biotechnology-based solution patented recently feeds chickens antibodies rather than antibiotics. The antibodies prevent the loss of appetite and growth while allowing the birds to fight off infection naturally without antibiotics. This solution should reduce any antibiotic residue in the food chain as well. It will also lead to reduced chances for endemic *salmonella* infection; though, as always, vigilance in food-handling in your kitchen is still essential.

Vigilance in following food safety and sanitation rules is absolutely necessary when cooking any poultry products. Chicken should be purchased as fresh as possible, and then kept under refrigeration at all times. And don't put raw chicken on a top shelf in your refrigerator. Poultry of any kind should always be placed on the lowest possible shelf. It should also be kept in a pan or container so that liquid from the packaging doesn't contaminate other items.

Cold Is Good

Chicken is often bought frozen or partly frozen. But even frozen birds carry bacteria. Freezing might slow the bacteria's growth, but it doesn't kill the microorganisms. Never thaw chicken at room temperature. This would encourage any bacteria to grow more rapidly. Always thaw poultry slowly under refrigeration; it takes about a day to thaw out a small bird. So, holding it overnight in the refrigerator is the best solution. And your Thanksgiving gobbler must be thawed under refrigeration, even though that may take two or three days for a large bird. Just plan ahead.

When you are working with poultry to prepare it for cooking, always keep it on a pan of ice. Never leave it sitting on your counter at room temperature.

You must also avoid cross contamination, so never work with raw poultry products along with other things. For example, slicing and dicing onions and chicken together is taboo. And, of course, the most important thing is to always wash your hands before and after handling poultry products. Never touch other utensils or food without washing up first. And if a utensil was used to cut or pick up any piece of poultry, it needs to be washed and sanitized before it is used again. If you simply assume that all poultry is infected with undesirable microorganisms, and then handle it in an appropriate manner, you should have no problems.

Hot Is Better

Because the bad bacteria are already present in your bird, it isn't enough to prevent spreading that bacteria to other foods or keeping it too cold to grow. You have to do your very best to destroy these critters before they reach your dinner plate. The number-one destroyer of bacteria is, of course, heat. Like most pathogenic bacteria, Salmonella die at about 165°F. It's especially important to heat all poultry to this temperature or higher to kill the bad bacteria. Luckily, people aren't generally too fond of rare poultry. Cooking the bird thoroughly, as explained below, will take care of the Salmonella problem and give you a delicious product.

Anatomy 101

Domestic poultry really is a bird of a different color when compared to our four-legged livestock friends. If you haven't done so before, take a few minutes to compare the structure and anatomy of a chicken with a piece of red meat such as a steak.

Fat Matters

The first thing you will notice is that chicken has a different kind of fat covering. Look closely, and you'll notice that all of the fat on a chicken is located outside the muscles. Marbling doesn't exist in the chicken world. Poultry does not lay down fat during growth and development like your favorite ruminant. You will see ample fat around a porterhouse steak, and plenty of marbling or flecks of fat inside the meat.

In comparison, a chicken breast has a fatty skin covering, but peel that off and you have a pretty lean piece of meat. Of course, the nutritional qualities of any meat depend on how it is prepared. Good old southern-fried chicken is probably one of the best culinary creations to ever reach your mouth. A platter of this stuff is likely to make you give up the mantra of boneless, skinless, low fat, and unfried. Just like life, sometimes it's good to sit back and enjoy.

Chicken and other birds build up fat in the abdomen area. Most of us can probably relate to that phenomenon. Chicken fat is also a different kind of fat; it is softer. Compared with the fat of ruminants like sheep and cattle, a great deal of the chicken's fat is less saturated. The ease with which you can peel that fat away no doubt contributes to the popularity of chicken. Stripping the fat and skin off a chicken breast, or removing globs of fat from the body cavity of a whole bird, are routine tasks in preparing poultry dishes.

White Meat or Dark?

When you get past the fat, you'll see that there are other differences in chicken anatomy. Chicken has both white and dark flesh. Of course, dark is a relative term because the meat isn't as dark as, say, beef. In fact, it isn't even really red; it's more of a pale-rose color. Poultry muscles contain myoglobin, the same color pigment in red meat. It's just that the relative proportion of myoglobin differs from muscle group to muscle group, and poultry generally has much less than four-legged livestock. The biological reason for this can be explained by examining what chicken muscles are designed to do.

Muscle fibers come in two basic types. You can have red ones or white ones. Each type has its own function and role to play. Red fibers are called slow twitch and white ones are called fast twitch. Twitch refers to how quickly the muscle contracts and relaxes and then is ready to contract again. It is synonymous with whether the muscle is designed for long-distance performance or short sprints. If you are a red slow-twitch muscle, then you were designed for the long haul. Red muscles help to get you through an extended journey. If you're a fast twitch, then the idea is to get to point B from point A as quickly as possible.

Now, chickens aren't into, nor really designed for, long-distance racing. Take a look at that breast; it's a pretty light color. That breast was made for quick spurts, not for walking. The legs are a bit darker, so they probably have a few more slow-twitch fibers to help the bird walk around. Free-range chickens, especially, must spend a good part of their day pecking around for food. Red fibers in the legs battle the effect of gravity, too. Chicken legs and thighs simply get more of a workout.

Food for Thought

Free range refers to chicken that is raised with access to an outdoor feeding area. Producers of free-range birds may also avoid using antibiotics. Commercially produced chickens are raised indoors, though the birds can move freely and have a healthy living environment. In blind taste tests, panels have found no difference in the palatability of free-range and commercially grown chicken. There is also no difference in nutritional quality. The only consistent difference between free-range and commercial birds is in their size. Commercial chicken is consistently larger with more meat per pound, which means it costs less.

The fat content of muscles with white or red fibers also differs. Take the chicken leg and breast as an example. Slow-twitch red muscle fibers thrive on fat as a metabolic fuel. The muscle fibers break down fats for the long haul. That's another reason the fibers are a bit darker in the chicken leg. It takes more blood and oxygen to break down that fat, which also means more myoglobin, hence a darker color. As a white muscle, the breast thrives on carbohydrates as fuel, they require less blood flow, and they have less fat and myoglobin. These cells don't have time to break down complex fats for fuel.

To understand the concept of slow- and fast-twitch best, though, in poultry, you have to look beyond domestic birds like chicken. Take a gander at a duck. Now you're talking about a big difference in the color of the meat. Ducks are migratory. In the wild, they can fly long distances, sometimes thousands of miles. Their muscles were designed for the long haul. They are built on slow twitch. This doesn't mean that a duck doesn't have any fast-twitch muscles; it just means that most of their muscles are designed to move the bird around a bit differently. If a duck has to escape a predator

Food for Thought

You usually don't expect to meet a bird weighing up to 250 pounds and towering 7-feet tall unless it's playing for a professional basketball franchise. But ostrich and emu are commercially raised poultry that fit that description. These birds are flightless. The meat is lean and low in fat yet high in protein. It tastes almost like beef, only a bit sweeter.

quickly, such as a fox or a 16-gauge shotgun shell, it can kick in its fast-twitch apparatus and get the job done.

It's Time to Cook

The real reason to know about red and white muscle fibers is in knowing how to cook them properly. And cooking them properly is a must for safe eating enjoyment. The versatility of poultry makes it desirable for just about every cooking method known. It's just that some birds are better than others for a particular method, depending on the bird's age and size. The following table lists common categories of poultry based on age, size, and cooking method.

Common Categories of Poultry

Type of Chicken	Age (wks)	Size (pounds)	Cooking Method
Game hen	6	2	Dry heat
Broiler/fryer	13	3.5	All
Roaster	20	4–5	All
Capon	32	8	Roast
Stewing hen	40	4–6	Moist

Note the marketing names given different types of chickens. The names "fryers," "stewing hen," "roasters," and "broilers" correspond pretty well to the cooking methods that work for each particular age of bird. Pretty neat trick, huh?

Modern-day poultry operations grow chickens very rapidly. In as little as a month and a half, a chicken can be ready to eat. Most chicken is only three to five months old when it arrives in your market. Older birds tend to end up in the soup and commercial-product trade.

Chef Sez

A **capon** is a castrated male chicken fed to produce a larger bird with a higher proportion of white breast meat. A **game** hen (a.k.a. Rock Cornish game hen) is the young offspring of Cornish chickens, or a genetic cross between a Cornish chicken and a White Rock chicken. A whole bird is a small single-serving-sized portion.

Is It Done Yet?

Whatever size bird you choose, the key to cooking chicken safely is to make sure that the meat is cooked well done. Three techniques can be used to check for doneness:

♦ Internal temperature

♦ Color of juices

♦ Looseness of joints

When you roast a bird, even in a very hot oven, it takes time for the heat to penetrate through the interior of the chicken by conduction. It's a matter of size again. Meats with lots of bones, like an entire bird, heat more slowly. The bottom line is that it is more difficult to cook a whole bird and get that heat into the joint where the leg meets the body.

Well-done poultry should have an internal temperature of at least 165°F. Let's say you are roasting an entire bird. You should insert your trusty thermometer at the thickest point of the thigh and leg, making sure to avoid the bones. You want the real internal temperature at the coolest, thickest part of the bird. Wait a minute, you say. Granny never used a meat thermometer in her life. That's probably true, but you are eating a lot more chicken than in granny's day so there is more of a chance of exposure and risk. The incidence of Salmonella caused foodborne-illness appears to be more common today than even 20 years. And temperature is the only sure way to know that your bird has gotten hot enough to destroy these bacteria. Granny did have some tricks for determining doneness that you can use, also.

Wiggling the joint where the leg meets the thigh is another way to check for doneness. If it is a bit loose, like a weak handshake, that is a good sign. If not, you may want to cook the bird a little longer.

Finally, after taking the temperature of the bird, and just to supplement your thermometer reading, check for the flow of juices. Take a small pairing knife and gently make a cut on the joint at the point where the leg meets the body. You do not need to take off the leg, just open up the joint and take a peek. If you see any blood-like drippings or light-pink tissue, you need to cook the chicken more. The bottom line is that the juices will be clear, not blood-like, when the bird is done.

Ready to Roast

Producing a roasted chicken with a beautiful golden exterior and moist, tender interior is a delight. To do so, get yourself a 3-pound roasting hen and preheat your oven to 500°F. Slice one small onion and one small lemon in halves or quarters. Melt 2 tablespoons of butter and stir in 1 tablespoons of orange blossom honey and 2 teaspoons of extra-virgin olive oil. Set aside a handful of fresh parsley, two sprigs of thyme and two cloves of garlic. Have some fresh cracked pepper and salt handy.

Remove any giblets from the bird's body cavity, and rinse the inside of the bird well with fresh cold water. Pat dry inside and out with paper towels. (Then throw the towels away!) Season the inside and outside of the bird liberally with salt and pepper. Stuff the lemon, onion, garlic and herbs into the body cavity. Truss or tie the legs in toward the breast. Rub the honey and fat mixture over the breast and legs of the bird. Place the bird on a rack in a roasting pan and pop it into the hot oven.

Cook for 10 minutes. Open the oven door, turn the temperature down to 375°F, and then close the door again. Continue roasting the chicken until the internal temperature reaches 165°F. If the bird seems to be browning too much, fold a piece of aluminum foil over the top and continue to cook. Baste the bird with your honey and fat mixture about 30 minutes after first putting it in the oven. When the bird is nicely golden brown and done, remove it from the roasting pan. Set it aside to rest for 10 to 15 minutes before carving. Untie the bird and remove the aromatics from the body cavity. Take a quick peek, too, to see if the juices are running clear, another sign of a completely cooked chicken. Now make yourself some gravy according to the techniques explained in Chapter 24.

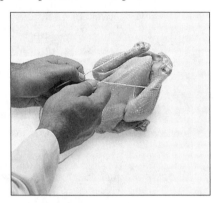

To truss a chicken, cut a piece of butcher's twine about three times the bird's length. With the breast up and the neck toward you, pass the twine under the bird just in front of the tail.

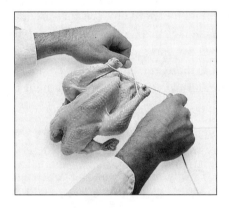

Bring the twine up around the legs and cross the ends, creating an X between the legs. Pass the ends of the twine below the legs.

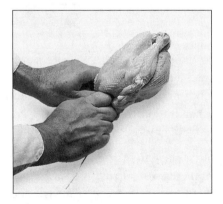

Pull the twine tightly across the leg and thigh joints and just above the wings.

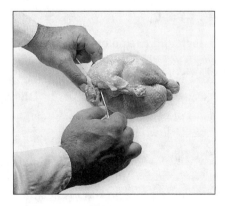

Pull the string tight and tie it securely just above the neck.

Lab Project

For a roasted chicken, preheat the oven to 500°F. Remove the giblets from the chicken's body cavity and rinse the bird thoroughly. Pat dry with paper towels and season liberally with salt and pepper. Cut one lemon and one small onion into halves or quarters; combine with a small handful of fresh parsley, two springs of fresh thyme, and two cloves of garlic. Fill the body cavity with these aromatics. Truss the bird. In a small bowl, stir together 2 tablespoons melted butter, 1 tablespoon honey, and two teaspoons extra-virgin olive oil. Brush or rub this mixture over the breast and legs of the chicken. Place the bird on a rack in a roasting pan and place it in the hot oven. Cook for 10 minutes. Reduce the oven temperature to 375°F and continue roasting until the bird reaches an internal temperature of 165°F. Allow the bird to rest for 10 to 15 minutes before carving.

What Happened Here?

You used some basic food chemistry to roast this chicken. By mixing carbohydrate from the honey with fat and proteins in your butter and oil, you increased browning. Dry heat, starting with very high temperatures, created a multitude of Maillard reaction products. These browning products provide the flavors and aromas characteristic of a good roasted bird. Stuffing your chicken with aromatics—herbs, onion, and lemon—perfume the meat with volatile compounds. These aromatics also add moisture, preventing the meat from becoming too dry. It's also a safer stuffing, less susceptible to causing food-borne illness than breadcrumbs with sausage or oysters. Now, go and enjoy a crispy beautiful treat.

The Least You Need to Know

- All poultry have surface bacteria and must be handled with utmost care.
- Never thaw whole birds at room temperature; always thaw in the refrigerator.
- Fat is external to the meat in poultry and can be removed to lower fat content and calories.
- Dark and white meat differ because of the type of muscle and presence of fat.
- Poultry are always cooked to an internal temperature of 165°F.

Chapter 15

Game vs. Tame

In This Chapter

- ◆ Game day players
- ◆ Your game sense
- ◆ Liquids meet meat
- ◆ The cutting edge

You probably limit your hunting and gathering prowess to forays in the wilds of your local grocery store. The opportunity for finding ranch-raised game meats such as venison and rabbit there has increased considerably in the last few years. Game meat has become a fixture on restaurant menus, also. If you are a real hunter, however, then you go into the woods to harvest your meat. This may be as close as anyone can get to enjoying and participating in true seasonal eating. That's because most state and local governments control well-defined hunting seasons to limit when and how much game can be harvested.

So, whether you sample your game truly wild or enjoy it from a ranch, game has unique attributes that are important to understand. And it really is no different than understanding quality factors for domestic livestock. It comes down to a consideration of muscle biology and how that affects the way meat is prepped and cooked.

Our Furred and Feathered Friends

Game refers to nondomesticated animals and birds that are hunted for sport or food. The term covers a bunch of different birds and animals. Large furred game includes deer, elk, and antelope, all of which may be called *venison*. Small furred game includes rabbits and squirrels. Feathered game includes upland birds such as pheasant, quail, or grouse, and aquatic birds such as duck or geese. In the United States, game sold commercially must be farm or ranch raised and must be government inspected. In addition, New Zealand, Germany, South Africa, and China have large game-ranching operations, and products from these countries can be imported to the United States.

It's important to distinguish between farm- or ranch-raised game and truly wild critters that you harvest on your own. Game farms typically raise their animals in smaller pastures more typical of domestic livestock methods. Game ranches usually cover wider areas and raise the livestock free-range style. The flavor of ranch-raised game is more similar to wild game, though neither domestic practice will give the earthy flavor found in truly wild game. Commercially raised products, which are available in groceries and restaurants, are tenderer, slightly fattier, and have a milder flavor and aroma than their wild cousins.

> **Chef Sez**
>
> **Venison** refers to the flesh from any member of the deer family, including antelope, elk, moose, reindeer, red-tailed and white-tailed deer, mule deer, and axis deer.

Why Game Is Gamey

Though game meat, particularly venison, doesn't have a high percentage of fat, the fat it does have packs a punch. These fats contribute a great deal to the overall flavor and aroma of game.

> **Food for Thought**
>
> Flavor is actually a combination of senses. It starts with the usual suspects like sweet, sour, bitter, salty, and umami (the richness of meaty flavors). But flavor also includes things like aroma or smell, texture, and mouth-feel. Try holding your nose and tasting a cold soft drink. You can feel the cold and the carbonation, but all you taste is wet. You don't know if it's water, lemon, or cola flavored. Only the nose knows. A piece of perfectly cooked, lean venison is going to feel different in your mouth than a USDA Prime beef rib-eye steak. And without its specific aroma compounds, you wouldn't know what you were enjoying.

Most meat—game in particular—owes its unique flavor properties in large part to the fats it contains. There are general meat flavors, and there are species-specific flavors. This means that all meat has certain flavor characteristics that simply make it meat, instead of carrots, for example. Beyond these basics are special compounds that distinguish venison from lamb from beef. So, what are some of these unique flavors?

To some, the flavor of game meat is like an old pair of sweaty gym socks. You might find the aroma attractive. Others might disagree with you. The primary fatty acid that contributes to this flavor and aroma is called *methlyocanoic acid*. That's a big mouthful, but the fatty acid is just a small one in the fat world. It's only eight carbons long compared with its big brothers that have 12 to 18 carbon units. And it's volatile, which means that you can get a good whiff of the stuff before, during, and after chewing the meat.

You also might also get some goat-like flavors in certain wild game. One substance, *ethlyoctanoic acid*, is the culprit here. Again, this may be either objectionable or attractive to your palate. If you like gamey goat cheeses, then you are in aroma nirvana with ethlyoctanoic acid.

Venison also has some of the properties of fatty acids and general flavor patterns that are common to domestic ruminant meats. *Alkylphenols* are a whole family of substances that provide a flavor base for meat and milk products from domestic red-meat animals. These compounds make the sensation of the meat what it is to your nose and mouth.

Of course, these substances do not exist in a vacuum. Cooking changes them. And the application of heat to game, or to any meat for that matter, creates the particular smells that you sense. If you cook lamb, you already know that it has a really distinct smell. You are cooking the volatile fatty acids as well as protein and fat. Venison and other game meats react to heat to produce their characteristic odors, too. Your own senses and perceptions determine whether this food chemistry is pleasurable and mouth-watering or objectionable to you.

Marinade Science

You might find the gamey smell or taste of wild game objectionable. Or you might find that it needs a little kick to impart some different flavors or textures. If an animal is under stress when it dies, its muscles will be tighter. Acidic *marinades* are used to help break down and tenderize these tissues. Marinades can also be used merely to add flavors. A marinade affects both the flavor and the texture of meat. Whatever your pleasure, marinades can be a great addition to your game cookery skills.

Marinades are simple mixtures of ingredients that may be cooked or uncooked. Often, when using wine-based mixtures, it is necessary to cook off the alcohol to improve the flavor of the final marinade. Virtually all marinades include certain types of ingredients:

Chef Sez

A **marinade** is a highly seasoned liquid that contains acid. Food is marinated (soaked) in marinades in order to add flavors and improve its texture.

- Acids
- Aromatics
- Seasonings
- Oil

Acidic ingredients include such items as lemon juice, yogurt, vinegar, wine, and tomato products. Acids are used to help soften connective fibers, thus tenderizing tough cuts of meat. Acids can also cook meats, such as what citrus juice does to fish in a ceviche. Be careful not to leave food submerged in high-acid marinades for too long. An over-marinated piece of meat will become gray and flabby.

Aromatics include onions, garlic, shallots, or citrus zest, always finely chopped, of course. Seasonings include the herbs and spices that add the flavors you crave, as well as whole or ground peppercorns. By the way, salt, normally a universal seasoning, is not recommended for meat or fish marinades, as it can draw too much moisture from the tissues. The flavors in a marinade are up to you. Juniper is a classic flavor partner for game meats, but just choose a flavor profile that you like or that complements what you're cooking.

Most marinades also include some oil. Just a touch of oil can help the marinade's flavors cling to the food. In this regard, vinaigrettes (which you will learn about in Chapter 27) make good marinades. Rich marinades made with milk, cream, or yogurt are sometimes used to tame the strong flavors of wild game meats.

Marinades affect the unique flavors of game's volatile fatty acids. These fats are susceptible to the process of oxidation. This means that continual exposure to air can make them change chemically, producing off-flavors. The covering layer of liquid marinade protects the meat from the air during storage. But maybe more important, herbs, spices, and acids in the marinades interact with these chemical fats to change the way they taste to you. The seasoning in the marinade can counter any strong off-flavors naturally. This often tempers these acids and makes them more palatable to you.

As meat is affected by the marinade, so, too, is the marinade affected by the meat. It's a two-way street. Any meat has bacteria growing on its surface. Some of these critters can get into your marinade. For that reason, never reuse a marinade without first taking some precautions. If the marinade has been at room temperature for four hours or more, toss it. If the bacteria have a four-hour head start, it's not worth the risk. If the marinade has been properly refrigerated, you should still boil it for five minutes before reusing or even tasting it. Since many marinades get very strong from the boiling, it might be even better if you just make a fresh batch.

Too Hot to Handle

Acids react with metals as well as with foods. For example, you know what battery acid does to your car battery. While you will never make a marinade as strong as battery acid (we hope), acids in marinades can eat away at certain metals. This is a particular problem with aluminum, because aluminum can be toxic when ingested. Besides, aluminum can change your food to a nasty gray color. To be safe, always use glass or stainless steel bowls and utensils when making marinades. Heavy-duty resealable plastic bags are good for marinating foods—when you're finished, just throw the bag away.

Making a Marinade

A basic red-wine marinade is a good thing to use for stronger-flavored game meats such as wild venison. To make a basic marinade, coarsely chop one small carrot, an onion, and four garlic cloves. Add $1/4$ cup of vegetable oil, 1 teaspoon dried thyme, a couple of bay leaves, and 2 teaspoons of juniper berries. Dried juniper berries can be found in the spice department of some markets and specialty stores. If you can't find them, add a splash of good gin to your marinade. Finish off your marinade with 1 tablespoon of whole back peppercorns, $1/2$ teaspoon of dried sage, one bottle of a full-bodied red wine (cabernet sauvignon or merlot works well), and $1/2$ cup of red-wine vinegar. If you want to decrease the alcohol content of the wine, simmer it in a saucepan for 10 minutes first. This also deepens the color and concentrates flavors.

Too Hot to Handle

Never eat a raw marinade after it comes in contact with any meat product. Any harmful bacteria that were on the meat will have contaminated the marinade. If you want to use leftover marinade in a sauce, be sure to boil it for five minutes first to destroy the harmful bacteria.

Now mix everything together in a nonaluminum container. You can marinate your meat for as little as an hour or as long as two days. If the meat is strong, do a longer period; if not, less is better. Remove the meat from the marinade when the time is up, pat it dry with clean paper towels, and proceed with the cooking.

Lab Project

For a red-wine marinade, simmer one bottle of full-bodied red wine in a saucepan for 10 minutes. Remove from the heat and add one carrot, chopped, a small onion, chopped, and four cloves of garlic, minced. Now add $\frac{1}{4}$ cup of corn or vegetable oil, $\frac{1}{2}$ cup of red-wine vinegar, 1 teaspoon dried thyme, 2 bay leaves, 2 teaspoons dried juniper berries, 1 tablespoon of whole black peppercorns, and $\frac{1}{2}$ teaspoon of dried sage. Allow the marinade to cool completely before adding the meat. Store in a glass, stainless steel, or plastic container.

At the Cellular Level

It isn't hard to understand the science of marinating meat when you think of meat as a biological tissue. Meat, like plants, is composed of cells. You know that heat will affect the cells by denaturing and coagulating proteins, and causing water to move out of the cell.

In a lesser way, acid marinades can do similar things. Though the cells do not cook fully, acids do affect the proteins that they come into contact with on the meat's surface. Just as acids helped break down the muscle fiber and tenderize meat during ageing, acids applied via marinades continue to break down some meat-cell proteins. One of these is myoglobin, the meat-color pigment. If you look at a piece of meat before you place it in the marinade, then after it comes out of the acid, you will notice a distinct color change. The meat is not as bright red, a sure indication that the acid has denatured some of the protein myoglobin. You've darkened the color and affected the protein structure.

Acids also help to soften connective tissue. This softening of connective tissue, as well as the softening of the muscle-fiber proteins, acts to tenderize the meat. This can be a benefit to game meat. If game was harvested from the wild, it likely was from an animal that had to do a lot of foraging for food, or escaping from predators. This means that its muscles were working a lot harder than those of domestic livestock. Working muscles also burn fat. So, the combination of less fat and firmer muscles gives you ample reason to consider a marinade soak to soften what is a naturally tougher piece of meat.

Going Against the Grain

It must be tough being a muscle. Muscles were designed to produce tension. You may have a negative connotation associated with the word tension: tension headaches, tension in everyday life, tense situations. Tension equates to the inability to relax. It is a measure of stress. And nobody wants a stressed-out piece of meat. But some tension is good because it adds texture to food. But overdoing it is just not palatable when it comes to a steak.

Any muscle can be stressed out if improperly cut or prepared. It's just a fact that game meat is particularly susceptible. You can take a choice steak from a baby beef and sometimes it is more forgiving of your preparation and cooking errors. This is not the case with a steak from a deer. You just basically have to look at each piece of meat to understand the whys and wherefores of this difference.

Food for Thought

One attractive reason for adding more game to your diet is its nutritional benefits. A 3-ounce portion of game meat—from a variety of species—is less than 150 calories. It supplies nearly 20 grams of protein and less than 5 grams of fat. This means that the percent of calories from fat is extremely low. In addition, the amount of saturated fat is only about 10 percent as much as other red meats. Game can be a delicious, healthful, alternative meat. If you cover your venison with a butter-enriched cream sauce, however, you'll have to deal with the fat police on your own.

All muscle has a grain. This doesn't mean that it has wheat or oats or barley inside of it, it means it has a pattern of arrangement of the muscle fibers. Look at the next roast or steak that you bring home from the grocery store—you can actually see the grain. Turn it around and examine it from different angles. You will find a cut side and a smooth side. The cut side is where the butcher sliced it off from something else. Compare the differences in the cut edge and the smooth surface.

You will see that the cut end has a speckled texture. You are looking right down the barrel of the muscle fibers. As you learned in Chapter 12, these fibers are arranged into long narrow cords. Just like a wet towel all twisted up from end to end. All skeletal muscle has a grain.

The grain is the arrangement of the muscle fiber to do its work: contraction. So, when you think about it, when a muscle contracts, which means it gets some tension, it's really trying to decrease its length along the grain. Now, your piece of meat isn't going to start contracting on you naturally. You've aged it properly as you have learned, and it has gone through its relaxation phase of rigor.

But when you cook it, the grain is still there. And the heat of cooking can make the meat shorten up along its grain. It's just doing what a muscle was designed to do, which is to pull itself together along its grain. It is reacting to the heat rather than contracting naturally, but the effect is the same: a tough, chewy piece of protein.

So, when you slice meat, always cut across or against the grain. Cutting with the grain makes long strips that can really coil and ball up when heat is applied. Cutting across the grain shortens the length of the fibers. The result is that there is less of a chance that your meat is going to shorten and get tough on you when cooked. And when your meat is relaxed, so are you and your dinner guests.

Game's Grain

This process of cutting across the grain is really important for game meat, especially things like venison steak. It's important for a couple of reasons. The first is that game animals have a much higher ratio of meat to fat. This is another way to say that game is leaner.

So, you are going to have more muscle fibers concentrated in any given area with less fat in venison than you would for the beef. And knowing what you just learned about tension and grain, the chances of getting meat to toughen up through shortening seems intuitively more probable for a piece of game than for beef.

Fat Matters

But leanness has another important aspect besides muscle-fiber concentration in the meat. There is less marbling within a piece of venison, and less fat covering around the meat, as compared to beef. You also know that fat melts when heated. Fat melts inside the muscle, too, when you apply heat. And the fat located between muscle fibers along the grain acts as a shortening agent during cooking. It liquefies, adding lubrication and slipperiness to the meat fibers.

So, when a piece of red meat from game is cooked and it has less fat, it has less lubrication. Your piece of prime or choice beef loaded with marbled and surface fat literally seems to melt in your mouth. This melting fat adds the intangible quality of mouth-feel and juiciness to your enjoyment of the steak. You can get this same effect with venison or game, but you need to work at it a bit more.

You measure the sum of all these changes in your mouth when you chew a piece of meat. If your venison has been cooked too well done, and is very dry, the force you need to chew with is very high. The meat has a high shear tension. If the venison is cooked perfectly, and is firm yet soft, needing only a little bit of chewing to break it down, then the shear is less.

So, what the combination of muscle fibers and leanness means for game meat such as venison is that the cooking must be much different. Game is susceptible to being overcooked and dry. It does not have the fat lubricating properties to the extent of beef, or the fat insulating properties to prevent water loss. And even though the water content of game tends to be higher than meat from comparable domestic livestock, the chances of cooking this water away are much greater.

Turning on the Heat

Probably the most important thing in game cookery for larger animals like deer or elk is picking the proper cooking technique, and then applying it properly. This is particularly true for game harvested wild. Think about it. The animal is likely foraging for food and working a lot harder at it than farm-raised game. So, that means the muscles are working more every day. And hard-working muscles mean more protein and less fat. Because of this, you really need to apply the rules for matching location and cooking technique.

Game meats should only be cooked one of two ways. For very tender cuts from the loin, rib, or back, dry, high-heat cooking methods are really the way to go. For tougher cuts, such as cuts from the shoulder or leg, which do most of the work of movement, it is just like cooking a Sunday chuck roast. You need to go very slow and easy. Combining moist-cooking methods like braising and stewing with marinades, *larding*, or *barding* will improve your chances of cooking your tougher cuts of game properly, while retaining flavor and palatable textures.

When you lard or bard game meat, you are adding fat that the growing animal wasn't able to store for itself. And adding fat is also a way to short-circuit toughness and dryness when you apply heat to the meat. The fat will melt, bringing with it flavor, juiciness, and improved mouth-feel. Of course, you don't want to overdo this or you'll lose that advantage that game brings to the table—its leanness.

The popularity of game is due in part to its low fat content and high meat-to-fat ratio. But because game is naturally lean, it can overcook quickly and end up dry, mealy, and tough. Two classic techniques can be used to prevent this problem: barding and larding. Barding is wrapping meat with solid fat. You can use bacon strips or thin slices of fatback. Game birds such

> **Chef Sez**
>
> **Larding** is inserting long strips of fat into lean meat to increase its moistness and tenderness during cooking. A larding needle or sharp thin knife will assist with this process. **Barding** is tying a thin piece of fat or bacon across lean meat or poultry, especially game. The fat adds moisture and tenderness during cooking.

as quail are especially appropriate for barding; just wrap a couple of bacon strips across the bird's breast before roasting. Larding is inserting strips of fat into thicker pieces of meat using a larding needle. You can also poke a small incision into the meat with a knife and stuff the cavity with strips of fat. Barding and larding add flavor and mouth-feel, and protect the meat from drying out.

Barding a pheasant with fatback.

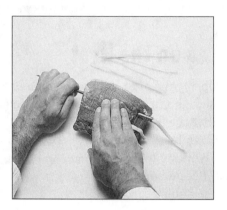

Larding a lean roast with strips of fat.

The Least You Need to Know

- Game includes a variety of nondomesticated species of animals, from large four-legged beasts to small birds.
- Meat from game is very lean and requires either quickly applied dry heat or moist-heat cooking methods.
- Marinades help tenderize, protect from moisture loss, and soften gamey flavors of the meat.
- Never eat uncooked marinades after using to soak raw meat. Either boil or preferably discard them.
- When making acid marinades, never use aluminum pans or utensils.
- Covering or inserting fat into meat helps retain moisture, and it adds flavor.

Part 4

The Aquatic Cook

Fish tales have jumped to new levels of respectability in the nutrition world of late. Seafood lovers may not need any other reasons to appreciate aquatic sources of protein, but now even they can enjoy the fact that fish food is good for you. It's not just protein, though; now fat from fish is in vogue. Yes, it is true. Not all fat is bad for you. You can enjoy fish two or three times a week. And consuming fish just might keep you from swimming with the fishes as a result of afflictions such as heart or blood-pressure problems.

And don't think that you will get bored with eating the same old types of fish. Fish are diverse. They come in all shapes and sizes and colors. There are lean ones with less fat, and fatty succulent ones that are just perfect for certain cooking techniques.

Chapter **16**

Swimming with the Fishes

In This Chapter

- ◆ Going the distance
- ◆ Not always fishy
- ◆ Ice is nice

You probably are eating more fish these days. This is good for your health. You may not think about it when you eat fish, but what you are mostly eating is muscle. Oh, you may be a person who loves to chow down on a crispy fin from a whole fish like it was a potato chip, but most of the time you are going for the muscle.

Muscles from fish differ quite a bit from those land animals or birds. They have some things in common, too. But it gets right down to what the fish was designed to do, which ultimately affects how you cook it and what it tastes like. Edible meat even from fish depends upon muscle biology.

First, let's take a look at where fish live and how that affects the types of muscles they have. In the next chapter, you then will appreciate why you need to handle and cook fish in very different ways than other kinds

Chef Sez

Roundfish have a backbone on their top or dorsal area and an eye on each side of the head. Trout are a typical example. Flatfish have a backbone in the center of the fish, with muscles above and below it. Both eyes are on the top of the body. Dover sole and halibut are examples.

of meat. And before you leave the water, the last chapter on fish covers some skeletons in the fish closet that are very unique to uncover.

Cruisers, Darters, Dinner

If you didn't know anything else about fish, you probably could come up with at least one big difference of why they are not beef cows. And that one difference is that fish live in water. Though it appears rather simple and obvious, this one little fact is really quite profound when it comes to the fish's muscle biology—and your food.

Bone structure of a round fish

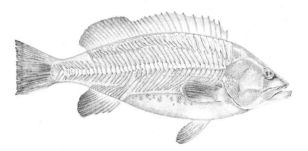

Bone structure of a flatfish

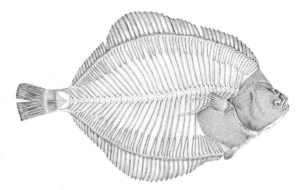

Water Babies

Fish live in water and are adapted to swimming. You, on the other hand, might swim, but you are adapted to land. Your muscles and pretty hefty skeletal system keep you from falling down because of the force of gravity. And, together, they move you along quite nicely. Fish, on the other hand, don't need to worry much about falling down since water is pretty buoyant. And that heavy skeleton you lug around, forget it; fish don't need that extra baggage because they're not walking anyway.

As fish don't have the energy cost of lugging around a big skeleton to fight forces of gravity, they can put a little more effort into their muscular anatomy. In fact, when you get right down to it, a roundfish like a trout is pretty much a pair of long muscles draped around a spinal column of soft bones, with a head at one end and a tail at the other. This muscle sandwich is designed to move the fish through water.

But fish are not devoid of mechanical challenges. Moving through water is no cakewalk; in fact, water presents more resistance to movement for a fish than air does for you or a beef cow.

Chef Sez

A **fish fillet** is a boneless piece of flesh cut from the entire side of a fish. Each roundfish has two fillets; each flatfish has four. A **fletch** or quarter is a piece of fish muscle from flat fish. There are four fletches from every flat fish.

Color Coordinated

Fish have solved the challenge of swimming in two basic ways. And those solutions determine the type of muscle they have. Some fish are cruisers. Other fish are darters. Cruisers are built to move long distances and cover big chucks of territory. Darters want to go from point A to point B quickly. They are more concerned with the now than with the future.

If this scenario sounds a bit familiar to you, it should. The analogous situation occurs for muscles in poultry. Recall the migratory duck compared with the barnyard chicken? Ducks migrate and have mostly red fibers, chickens a preponderance of white ones. Light and dark meat exists in the fish world, too. This function and form go hand in hand for fish, too. Cruisers are mostly migratory fish. Cruisers depend upon those red slow-twitch *myotomes* for the long haul. Au contraire for darters; they are mostly pure white. Darters represent just what your mind's image says a fish should look like. And because their flesh is basically white, you know they have mostly fast-twitch myotomes.

Chef Sez

Myotomes are the bundles of muscle-fiber cells of fish.

There are other things that go along with the cruiser and darter scheme of things. Dark-fleshed cruisers also have more fat in their muscle. The fat is used as fuel. Darkness is also caused by more myoglobin. This iron-containing molecule is the same one that gives that nice rosy bloom to red meat. Just not in as high a concentration as you find in red meat, it nonetheless contributes to the darker flesh of cruiser fish. Salmon and tuna are the kings of the migratory species. For salmon, these fish spend part of their life in freshwater, and part in saltwater. They can travel thousands of miles.

In contrast, darters with white muscle fibers have less need for myoglobin. They typically are your bottom dwellers and freshwater-pond species such as bass, bluegill, and catfish. They prefer staying pretty close to home.

In life as in science, "all" and "never" are dangerous words. Cruisers are not, therefore, devoid of fast-twitch white muscle, and darters are not always white as the driven snow with fast-twitch muscle fibers only. There are mixtures of both in each class of fish.

For example, the greatest concentrations of slow-twitch red fibers often are found near the tail or along the fins, even in fish that are mostly white fleshed, which makes sense when you ponder it a bit. The tail of fish always seems to be waving back and forth. If you have an aquarium, take a look at your fish. Swishing that tail back and forth keeps the fish stationary and stable. So, too, the fins; they have a duty to move from side to side to stabilize that body in position. So, these areas tend to be darker in color because that is where you will find more of the slow-twitch, red fibers. Though, as you know, red is a whole lot different in fish. You might call them dark muscles. And interspersed in even these dark areas will be some fast-twitch white fibers.

So, the next time you are dining on Ahi tuna or salmon, pretty good examples of cruisers, think slow twitch. And the next time you are having catfish and hushpuppies, think fast twitch. Muscle biology never tasted so good.

Food for Thought

Fresh fish and other seafood are not only nutritious high-quality protein sources, but are also neutraceuticals. Neutraceutical foods provide health benefits beyond simple nutrition. Cold-water types of fish such as tuna, mackerel, and salmon are rich sources of the omega-3 fatty acids. These substances have been linked to lower blood cholesterol, fewer heart attacks and strokes, and overall lower levels of hypertension. These benefits accrue to you from only one 3- to 5-ounce serving of fish each week. Eating more fat is not much to ask for heart health, is it?

Why Fish Taste, Well, Like Fish

You eat and like fish for the taste. And when fish really tastes fishy, the whole world turns up their noses. In that case, all those flavor substances that give fish its appeal have gone bad. It's all about fish-food chemistry and proper handling.

Of Melons and New Mown Grass

You might agree that fish have the most distinctive flavors of just about any form of edible meat. This covers their aroma, taste, and texture. There are two reasons for this. One is that fish have their own unique fingerprints of chemicals. The second concerns the relative freshness of the fish.

You smell the fresh fish aromas because of the presence of certain fatty acids. In fish, these are small six- to nine-carbon volatile fats. They are found in muscle as a part of the normal cell activity. If you want to really be a namedropper at a dinner party, just mention that the fish is amazing for its fresh notes of aldehydes, ketones, and alcohols.

Curiously, you might even get a hint of melon or grass-like aromas in a very fresh piece of fish. This is because these compounds are very similar to substances found in fresh fruits and vegetables that are undergoing ripening. This just goes to show you some of the overlap in the palate that Mother Nature uses to build life.

Food for Thought

Ensuring quality of fresh seafood is a combined effort of the federal government and the seafood industry. Since 1997, the Food and Drug Administration has adopted safe handling techniques for domestic and imported seafood under the application of hazard analysis critical control points (HACCP). The HACCP controls are preventive measures that seek to avoid food-handling problems associated with seafood safety as it is processed and before it is delivered to markets. Inspectors at seafood plants monitor the hygiene of processing and sample seafood to determine chemical contaminants, microbial pathogens, pesticides, food additives, and fish and shellfish toxins. Once the seafood is at a retail outlet, the responsibility shifts to the retailer, and to you, to ensure safe handling and preparation.

When Fish Go Bad

So, what about the fishy fish tale? Well, fish that is going bad smells a lot like ammonia, or it should. That's because as fish or seafood ages, a substance called triethylamine oxide breaks down. Ultimately, as this substance breaks apart, it forms formaldehyde. You'll recognize formaldehyde from Biology 101. It's that horrendous-smelling liquid used to preserve specimens. It has a nasty, penetrating odor. Bad fish does, too.

There are a few other things that you smell in bad seafood. These give the fish that "fish-oil" aroma. And not surprisingly, they come from the aging of unsaturated fats and oils in the fish meat. So, you want to be a name dropper again? Just call them decatrienals for short.

> ### Food for Thought
> Did you ever wonder why fish have so much unsaturated oil and no visible satu-
> rated fat really hanging on the fillet? Oh, you will see fat on some internal organs, but
> even that is oily. Fish oil prevents freezing. Think about it. If you were swimming around
> in near-freezing temperatures, what would you rather have, oil that stays fluid, or lard that
> turns you into a frozen piece of fat? The fish oil serves the same purpose that antifreeze
> does in your car in winter. It keeps the pipes open and the machine running. So, the oil
> in fish is good for them, and science is showing that this fat is good for your health, too.

Fresh to Frozen: Cold, Hard Facts

Fish live in a cold-water environment. On the surface, you would think that this fact would make them easier to freeze and good keepers in your freezer. But it is just the opposite.

On the High Seas

Commercial fishermen battle the freshness issue all the time. From the time fish are hooked and landed into the boat, there are things being done to suspend those fish muscles in as fresh a state as possible.

After catching the fish, commercial fishermen gut and bleed them out. Since waste products would accumulate in these areas, removing them prevents by-products from accumulating in the fish carcass. This small step is the first one to reduce those off-flavors you know all about.

Fish are also chilled on ice as quickly as possible. Lower temperature is also your best bet for keeping high quality fish in your home. Fishing boats are equipped with lots of ice, and some even have low-temperature freezers on board.

So, why would you want to give so much attention to the fish as soon as they are caught? Well, fish are living creatures that start to deteriorate as soon as they die. This battle is not only against bacteria, which you know want to be the first in line at your food party, but the war is against the natural deterioration that occurs in fish tissues.

Because fish live in the cold, their entire enzyme system is designed to function just fine at lower temperatures. Fish are cold blooded, not warm blooded. So, slowing down the metabolism of a fish is very different from chilling a beefsteak. While deterioration is going to happen in each piece of meat, fish are more susceptible to it. Their cells keep churning out products even at low temperatures. In fact, even after freezing, fish muscle cells are making products that have decidedly off-flavors and aromas.

The best fishermen do a good job of slowing down the deterioration of fish flesh. And the things that they do, you can even do, if you catch fish on your next fishing expedition.

In Your Home

You come face to face with fish at your local market. You can begin the selection process for high-quality fish right there.

When fish are delivered to a reputable market, the chilling process practiced by the fisherman should be continued. When buying whole fish you can judge a good fish market by how the fish are displayed. Fish should be packed in ice in the swimming position. This allows any liquids or melted ice to flow away from the body cavity and not accumulate in the meat.

Food for Thought

Fish muscle is more delicate than that of red meat and does not freeze as well. Part of this problem is actual physical damage of the connective tissue that holds the muscle fibers together. Fish fillets that have deteriorated in the freezer undergo what is called gaping. The flesh literally separates and large open pockets will be noticeable on the side of a fillet. Improper handling of fish before freezing them, by exposing the fish to high temperatures, might be one factor that causes the problem.

Your fish should also not smell fishy or have that ammonia odor. The skin should not be slimy. The color should be bright, not faded or brown. You can equate slime and smell with bacterial contamination. And when you look into a fish's eyes, they should be clear and not cloudy or sunken. A fish with good eyes will give you love at first sight; it says "take me home." So, take the fish home, preferably packed in ice. And one important thing when you buy fish: do it last. Don't pick up the fish and put it in your shopping cart first, if you have other things to buy. Make the fish food your last stop, and don't forget that ice.

The ABCs of selecting fresh whole fish are the following:

◆ An ocean smell, not a strong fishy odor

◆ Bright clear eyes

◆ Scales that are shiny and cling tightly to the fish

◆ Pink or red gills, if present

◆ Fillets should be moist, no brown, dry edges

◆ Fillets should be firm, not spongy

Stowing It Away

If you are successful at getting a really good fresh fish, eat it as soon as possible. Of course, keep it stored in the refrigerator on the bottom shelf, covered in ice, in the swimming position, too—at least until the oven is warmed up. Keep ice around it, because, more often than not, you have your frig set at about 38 to 40°F. Most fish and seafood do better around 34°F.

But you know that sometimes it just isn't possible to eat all the fish fresh. Freezing fish is almost always a necessity. So, you need to follow some helpful tips.

Size matters when freezing a fish. If your fish is small like a trout, it can be frozen whole. If the fish is large, it's usually best to cut it into about 1-inch-thick *steaks* or pieces. You can do this by cutting cross sections through the bone, from the front to the back toward the tail. A good sharp knife is necessary.

Chef Sez

Steaks are cut from round-fish by slicing cross sections of a 1- to 2-inch thickness across the body from head to tail. Steaks include a piece of the backbone.

Your fish or pieces of fish should be clean and free of blood. Then you have a couple of packaging options. The first is good old plastic wrap. This should cling as tightly as possible to the fish, with no air pockets. Air is the enemy here; it causes the meat to deteriorate. Then wrap the fish next in freezer paper or aluminum foil. This double wrap of plastic and paper or foil is your best bet to seal out air.

If you use freezer bags, press as much air out of the bag as possible before sealing it. Don't overstuff the bag with fish. It will only cause air pockets to form. You should wrap the freezer bag in foil or freezer paper, too, as an added precaution.

Fish can also be frozen in water blocks. You can even use old milk cartons, or get fancy and use commercial plastic containers. Layer the fish into the plastic and cover with water. Then seal the top. The ice will protect the flesh from the air.

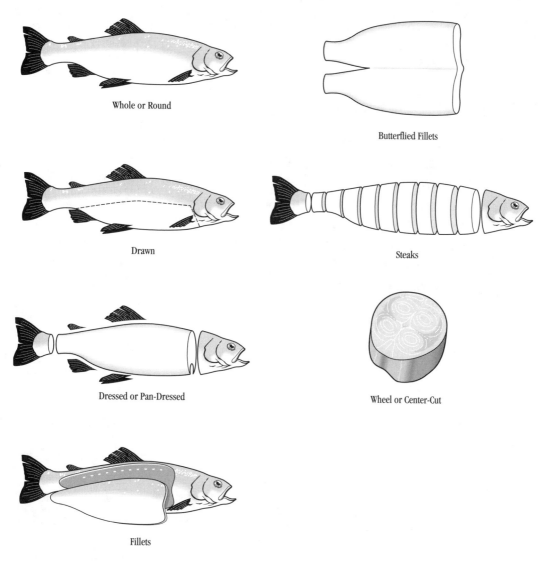

Whole or Round

Butterflied Fillets

Drawn

Steaks

Dressed or Pan-Dressed

Wheel or Center-Cut

Fillets

A roundfish can be cut into steaks or fillets.

Vacuum-packaging of fish fillets is also recommended. The availability of the vacuum machines is much more common, and they are usually a snap to use.

So, if you can't eat your catch, then by all means freeze it. Fatty fish like salmon will keep for three months, and white, lean fish like trout or catfish for five months. When you thaw the fish, remember that it must be done in your refrigerator and not at room temperature. This will give the best thaw results and be the safest from a food-borne-illness standpoint. But eating fish fresh is the best solution and use of this valuable protein source. So, whenever possible, go fresh, not frozen.

Now that you've hooked a fish, it's time to explore cooking. The next chapter covers how to make that valuable fish flesh edible. Cooking fish properly is very different than cooking red meat, as you will see.

The Least You Need to Know

♦ Fish should always be kept as cold as possible and preferably packed on ice to keep the meat fresh.

♦ Use your senses when picking out whole fish, including sight, smell, and touch.

♦ Fresh fish fillets should be moist, not dry or brown on the edges. The meat should be firm, not spongy.

♦ The smell of "fish" is the first sign of decreasing freshness; good, fresh fish should smell like the sea, or have a hint of freshly mown grass or of melons.

♦ Fish frozen properly can last three to five months, depending upon the type.

Chapter 17

Look Ma, No Legs

In This Chapter

- Just heat and eat
- Batters and protective coatings
- Cooked without heat

Although real fish don't pump iron, they are literally muscle power packs. They have a higher proportion of meat to bone, nearly two thirds of their body weight, compared with domestic livestock. Fish raised in a pond by aquaculture convert more feed to edible muscle. This means that, let's say, domestic livestock might need 1 pound of feed to grow and maintain 5 pounds of flesh; fish can do it with less than half the amount of feed. Said another way, they can go further on the same tank of fuel. But even though fish are muscle bound, their edible meat isn't that tough. Tenderness is one of the things we love most about fish.

Heating Quick and Easy

Your mantra for cooking fish is pretty simple: fish cook fast. It's really a matter of how their edible muscle is put together that makes it so.

Your fish friends haven't put a lot of time and effort into arranging their muscles around heavy bones and connective tissue. So, the idea that you have to take a lot of time to drive heat energy through skeletons and around connective tissue to loosen things up just doesn't hold water for cooking fish. Fish muscle is pretty exposed when you think about it.

When you fillet a fish, you are separating one side of the muscle from the backbone. If you then remove the skin, you have the exposed muscle. There is no heavy fat covering, such as you might find on a piece of beef. There is no tough connective tissue sheath or silverskin to deal with here. You don't see any tendons or ligaments. It's just a clean piece of edible muscle.

If you look at a roundfish fillet, you will see a shiny side and a more opaque side. The shiny side is the one the skin was attached to. Looking at the opaque or internal side, you might locate some bones. You can feel them by running your index finger lightly back and forth across the fillet. They might feel like little barbs or pins, which is a good term, because they are called pin bones. They are pretty soft, and you can pick pin bones right out with a pair of tweezers.

Starting at the head end of a fillet, use your fingertips to locate the pin bones, and use pliers or tweezers to pull them out one by one.

So, what you are left with is a very delicate arrangement of myotomes in your fish fillet. If you use the point of a paring knife, you can actually separate the myotomes a bit. They are arranged in sheets running from top to bottom. They appear as thin lines that give the fillet its textural look. The only connective tissue to deal with separates these bundles of myotomes. The connective tissue is called *myocommata*. It's pretty insubstantial and very soft. You really can't see it like you can silverskin. But it is there doing its job.

Chef Sez _____
Myocommata is the connective tissue layers found between fish muscle groups.

Applying heat to meat like fish is a pretty direct shot. There is very little standing in the way of the energy that's coagulating proteins and moving water around. The only thing you now have to consider is what is the shape and form of the fish you are cooking. That will make a bit of a difference on how you approach things.

Parts, Pieces, and Protective Coatings

One size doesn't fit all when cooking a whole roundfish. You can be dealing with something fairly small like smelt, which are fingerling-type or bite-size fish, or maybe something a bit larger like a *pan-dressed* brook trout. Or you might be dealing with a king salmon that weighs 12 to 15 pounds. So, the shape of the package that you're cooking is a consideration for heat transfer.

> **Chef Sez**
> **Pan-dressed** fish are drawn fish that have the fins, head, and tail removed. Some smaller fish such as trout may still have the head and trail attached.

You Caught One How Big?

Small fish can be *drawn* or opened up enough to expose most of the muscle. That means that the conduction of heat is going to be rapid from outside to inside the fish. Not so with big fish. Large fish present you with the problem of overcooking the outside and undercooking the inside. This is best solved by slashing through the skin with several cross cuts up and down the body. It opens up the meat so that heat can be transferred more efficiently.

> **Chef Sez**
> **Drawn** refers to a fish that has been gutted but still has its head and gills attached. To **scale** is to remove the scales from fish using a fish scaler or knife. You do this before skinning the fish.

Of course, with the skin on, you want to remove the *scales* and thoroughly clean the outside of the fish. Scales are almost indestructible forms of protein similar to your fingernails. You do not want to tackle eating this form of protein.

Whole fish can be cooked with dry or moist heat methods that are applicable to the size of the fish. So, size matters for practical purposes. You aren't going put a 15-pound king salmon in a deep fryer. You can bake it, though. You can grill it. You can even use moist-heat cooking and poach it whole or in parts.

> **Food for Thought**
> Fish lend themselves to all manners of cooking methods. It depends on size of the fish, type of fish, and your creativity. Steaming is an excellent way to cook fillets or steaks, preserving the simple taste of the food. Doing steaming in a piece of baking parchment paper, or even in aluminum foil, is called cooking *en papillote*. Fish are usually layered atop vegetables, with seasonings, oil, and a splash of white wine. Then the package is sealed and baked in an oven. The moisture from the food and wine delicately steams the proteins. The package is served, and the diner gets to cut into the paper to release all those wonderful steaming aromas.

Remember the mantra, fish cook quickly. The end point for large fish is 140°F. This is the temperature that will keep your fish moist while still cooking it to doneness internally. Because fish collagen has long-since melted, at about 110°F, the target of 140°F enables you to exceed the danger zone for any food-borne pathogens. (Remember that the bacteria that cause food-borne illnesses can thrive if the temperature is between 40 and 140°F, hence the term danger zone.) And in fish, this means things like worms and other parasites, not just bacteria. Whole fish are targets for parasitic infections.

Naked Fish Exposed

So, what about parts and pieces of fish? The same target temperature holds true. The difference is that it takes very little time for heat to penetrate a naked fillet. Dry heat and moist heat work well. So, you might pan fry or sauté; or you might poach in a little seasoned liquid.

As the proteins in a fish fillet cook and coagulate, you will see a noticeable change in appearance. Flesh that was soft to the touch becomes firm. The myotomes become more pronounced. Edible fish muscle changes from a translucent shiny appearance to opaque as it cooks. You often cannot take an accurate temperature of small fillets. So, your best bet for gauging doneness is by touch and sight. You can feel how firm the muscle has become, and you can gently peel apart the myototomes to take a look. If there is no appreciable shiny surface, then the fish is cooked.

You do not want to overcook your naked fish fillet. This happens when the surface looks pale and dry. You will see cooked protein coagulated as beads on the surface. This is protein and water that has literally knotted together from the heat. The muscle is falling apart. If you want to overcook a fillet to see what it really looks like, then give it a whirl. The contrast between a properly heated fish fillet and one that is overcooked is striking. It is the best way to observe and learn about the effects of applying too much energy.

Dressing Up Naked Fish

Because your fillets are easily damaged when naked, you can give them some clothes. A batter or crust is used on fish to protect the delicate muscle when using a dry-heat cooking method. Of course, it also adds flavor and texture.

A *batter* is a liquid–like pourable mixture. In baking, you will make dough. Well, think of a batter as a more liquid form of the basic dough. Its basic components are starch, liquid, and fat. Usually flour is the starch, milk or water the liquid, and egg or oil or both provide the fat. You can get crazy with batters, too. Just substitute beer for the liquid and create the infamous beer-battered fish.

Batters applied to fish do not last indefinitely. This means that you are not going to batter your fillet in the morning and cook it later that day. So, you need to coordinate the heat with the batter and the meat. Batters also stick better when they are cold. Remember, liquids flow more when warm, so by chilling your batter before dipping the fillet in it, you can create a better surface coating. So, right before you fry, dip the fillet in the cold batter, shake off the excess batter, and immediately fry, baby, fry!

> **Chef Sez** _____
> A **batter** is a semi-liquid, pourable mixture usually made from flour, milk, and eggs. It can be used to coat and protect foods for deep-frying.

The heat to use is dry heat in the form of hot fat. Think about it: Batters are pourable semi-liquids. They do not go well with moist-heat methods that use water. You need hot oil to immediately gelatinize the flour base in the batter coating. Any proteins in the batter are also immediately coagulated. And the oil should surround the food. If you fry in a pan, use enough oil so that the fillet literally floats in the hot fat. You want even, immediate, and complete contact of the fat and the batter-coated fish. What you get is a beautifully browned crust with your moist, nicely cooked fish inside. Battered fillets should be drained of fat as soon as they come out of the fryer. This will help keep them crisp.

Battered fish does not keep well, at least from a palatability standpoint. The outer coating gets soggy. This makes some sense when you think about it. You are dealing with starch. Starch loves moisture. So, if the starches cool in the batter, they can tend to pick up moisture from the air as well as from the cold fish. It's best to eat your batter-dipped fish soon after cooking it. If you must wait a bit, at least do not wrap it up. This will prevent escaping steam from causing it to become soggy.

Tailoring Crusty Coats

Breading are a different form of coating for fish fillets. Breadings are dry, not moist like batters, and they give a more delicate crunch. Because your fish is a delicate piece of meat, you never want to overdo the coating. Do you really want to bite into a 3-inch piece of hard coating to get to the nice 1-inch soft fillet?

> **Chef Sez** _____
> **Breading** is a three-step process of coating food with fine or coarse crumbs after dipping the food into flour and a liquid egg-water mixture. Breading adds flavor and coats and protects delicate foods when they're being fried or baked.

The classic method for breading fish is called the "standard breading procedure." It is easy as a snap to do. You need some flour, an egg beaten with 1 tablespoon of water and a pinch of salt, and the breading. The breading can be anything, from standard bread crumbs to corn flakes to chopped nuts. Just make sure the coating is finely ground, especially for fish.

To build a basic breading, just roll the fish fillet in flour, dusting off the excess. The flour's starch helps the egg proteins and fats adhere, which is your next step. Dip the flour-coated fish into the egg. Again, let the excess drip off. Then gently roll the fillet in your crumbs. You can do the breading ahead if you like. In fact, chilling the fillet is recommended. You can also freeze them, and you need not thaw them before cooking. This can be a real time-saver.

When you are ready to cook the fish, get the fat hot and drop in the breaded fillet. As was the case for the batter method, have plenty of oil so the fillet is surrounded by heat. When the crust is nicely browned, the fillet should come out of the fat. Drain off excess fat on paper towels or a metal rack. Sometimes for thicker pieces of fish, or fish that is frozen, the outer crust will brown faster than heat is conducted to the center. If this happens, the solution is simple. Just have a preheated 375°F oven handy. Remove the fillet from the hot fat and finish baking it in the oven. *Oven finishing* allows the interior to cook without overcooking the outside.

> **Chef Sez**
>
> **Oven finishing** is completing the cooking of foods internally that have cooked sufficiently on the outside. It is done in a hot or moderately hot oven for a short period of time. **Ceviche** is raw fish marinated in lemon or lime juice. The acids partially denature and cook the protein.

Of course, if you want to bake the breaded fish to avoid all that deep-fryer fat just place them on a cookie sheet sprayed with vegetable spray to prevent sticking. Bake them in a hot oven until they are nicely browned and done in the center.

Effective Acids

Denaturing and coagulating meat protein by applying heat energy is one form of cooking. Because fish is naked protein with a high moisture content and very little connective tissue, acid treatments can also cook the proteins.

Acids work on proteins to cause them to denature. You have seen examples of this in the chapter on red meat. When red meat is aging, the acids produced as the meat decomposes and the acids of the bacteria cause cell membrane proteins to unwind. Digestion of the tissue is happening to some degree. Acids in red meat marinades do a similar thing. The surface is cooked to a certain degree. You even use acids such as lemon juice or vinegar to denature egg-yolk proteins when making mayonnaise and hollandaise sauces. Acids were also an option for you in cheese-making.

> **Too Hot to Handle** _____
> Acid treatment of fish does not efficiently kill parasites called nematodes, which raw fish can harbor. Though the risk may be low, it nonetheless exists. You can get severe gastrointestinal problems called *anisakiasis* from these nematodes. To enjoy lightly marinated fish or raw fish in sushi, you should first freeze the fish for at least 24 hours. If you are dealing with a large fish, freeze it for five days. Freezing to -4°F will destroy nematodes completely. If you eat raw seafood in restaurants, ask if the fish has been properly frozen. For the same reason, do not feed raw fish to your dog or cat.

Because fish are very delicate, adding acids, such as citric acids from lemons or limes, to fish muscle will cause the proteins to denature. You can actually see the changes in opacity or color. Raw, diced fish will be soft and spongy but, when soaked in citrus juices for as little as 15 minutes, become white and firmer.

Acids work on proteins in the meat and connective tissue of the fish to soften them. Remember that collagen, like muscle, is protein. Fish start out with much less connective tissue and protection to begin with, so when you dice up raw fish and add acids, you are exposing a lot of surface area to low pH. You can easily denature the proteins, and you see this effect as the fish changes from translucent to white and opaque. It is kind of like watching egg albumin change from clear to white when you fry it.

Remember, you are not adding heat when you denature proteins with acids. But don't take it easy just because there is no heat there; you can still overdo it. If you soak tender chunks of fish too long, you can coagulate proteins too much and the texture becomes rubbery. So, this form of fish cookery takes attention, too. And remember, if you are not using heat, you are not cooking harmful microorganisms. So, freezing it before using it in acid marinades is highly recommended.

The Least You Need to Know

- Fish cooks quickly; appearance and touch are often used to gauge doneness in fillets, though whole fish should be cooked to an internal temperature of at least 140°F.
- Batters and coatings protect fillets when high-temperature, dry-heat cooking methods are used.
- Batter-coated fish is cooked immediately, while breaded items can be frozen.
- Fish frozen for at least 24 hours, preferably for five days for whole fish, are safe for light acid marinade-type cooking.

Shell Game

In This Chapter

- ◆ The flip side
- ◆ Love me or leave me
- ◆ Playing it safe

You either love them or you hate them. You consider them safe or unsafe. You think they might improve your love life. You associate some of them with prestige and expensive dining. There isn't a middle ground when it comes to shellfish. But in this chapter, you will learn that we have a lot of ocean to cover.

Skeletons Outside, Muscles Inside

Just when you think you have this whole muscle, bone, and connective tissue thing sorted out, along comes a ringer.

So, let's get this straight: First there were muscles held together by connective tissue, draped around and over big bones, held together by more connective tissue, everything covered by skin, giving you one big lumbering beef cow on land. Now, take away the land, the heavy bones, and most of the connective tissue, drape a muscle power pack around a lighter version of a backbone, add water, and you have a fish. Now, let's drape a skeleton around a muscle, and what can we call it? A mussel is one possible answer. Let it live in or out of water and we can call it a lobster or a crayfish or an oyster or a scallop.

This just goes to show you that food is truly diverse in form, function, and context. And what you call food or seafood is defined by a whole lot of circumstances.

> **Chef Sez** _____
>
> **Shellfish** are a diverse group of freshwater or saltwater aquatic animals that have a shell in some form. In crustaceans and mollusks the shell is on the outside as armor. Cephalopods have a thin internal shell called a pen or cuttlebone imbedded in the muscle.

Shellfish cover three basic classes: crustaceans, such as lobsters, shrimp, and crayfish; mollusks, which includes snails, oysters, and clams; and an oddball group called cephalopods, which includes squid and octopus.

But no matter what the basic anatomy might be, shellfish as food is nothing but protein, fat, water, and maybe some carbohydrates. And that is consistent with beef, fish, or any food you might compare.

All in the Family

You may not realize it, but crab is in the top 10 of most preferred seafood. And the native crabs that grow on the two coasts in the United States are unique treasures. The two with a mystique all their own are the Dungeness and the blue crabs.

Dungeness crabs have been harvested for over 250 years on the west coast, from central California through to the Gulf of Alaska. The name Dungeness refers to a tiny fishing village on the Strait of Juan de Fuca in Washington. The crabs are truly wild, and are harvested between December and August. They are caught in steel traps called pots.

Only males make it to your table, and the industry is pretty keen on staying sustainable for you and your grandchildren. You might be lucky to enjoy whole fresh crabs in season. If not, you can also find these crabs as whole cooked, frozen whole cooked, frozen clusters of cooked parts, frozen legs, or a very popular form of vacuum-sealed crabmeat. Fresh vacuum-packed crabmeat is best eaten in about a week, while frozen meat that is vacuum sealed will keep for four to six months in your freezer.

Now, switch your attention to Louisiana, the Chesapeake Bay, and North and South Carolina. Here you're in blue crab country. Blue crab is romantically called the "savory beautiful swimmer." They have one pair of legs just for swimming, and three more pairs just for walking. They can really boot, scoot, and boogie with those muscles. Just as Dungeness are harvested, blue crabs are caught in pots. Crabs are harvested commercially all year long, but mostly from October to December.

Even a recreational industry exists for catching blue crabs. In South Carolina you can have two pots; more than that and you become a commercial fisherman. If you go crabbing, never put your crabs in water to store them after catching one or two. They will suffocate in stale water. And stale crabs are not safe to eat, nor very palatable. It's best to simply keep them on ice and cook them as soon as possible.

Cooking blue crab is a snap. The preferred way is steaming, using a double boiler. Water is brought to a boil in a lower pot, and the upper covered pot holds your fresh crab. Cook them about 20 to 30 minutes until they turn bright orange (see all those flavenoids) and the meat is pearl white and nicely firm. Once done, have some cold, highly seasoned water ready. Just drop the crabs in the cold water to stop cooking (recall water has high specific heat) and to let them soak up all those spices. What you mix up from the spice rack is your business; maybe Creole spice mix tonight?

You also can cook crab the way you do lobster by just boiling them submerged, or steaming in a covered pot with a touch of water. You should put the spices directly into the water in those methods. If you are really brave, you can clean the fresh crab and cook only the meat. But be careful; they can really pinch. Whatever method you choose, happy eating.

Shellfish Cross-Dressers

Some shellfish available at your local market isn't really shellfish. If you enjoy imitation crab meat, lobster, or scallops, then you are eating surimi. Surimi is fish paste made from either Pacific whiting or pollock. Over one million metric tons of pollock is harvested in Alaskan waters each year. While over-harvesting is an issue, some of the fish is used to produce fish oil, and some eventually is dried and turned into a fish meal. And some goes into the fish paste that eventually is fashioned into imitation shellfish food. Leaner fish are used to make surimi because the paste stabilizes better.

Surimi is produced by finely mincing fish muscle, and then passing it through a series of washing and filtering steps. Just like making grandma's meatloaf, this produces a paste that sticks together. Meatloaf sticks together as you force the meat proteins and things like egg and cracker binders into a bound product. This is why meatloaf might be called a force meat. It isn't going to form on its own but takes some work from you.

After the fish paste is formed, it goes to food companies that make the surimi products. The paste is first cooked until it forms a gel, which is not unlike cooking a

Food for Thought _____

A knock on shellfish has always been that they are high in cholesterol. They really aren't. Compared with a large egg, they have only one third to two thirds as much. And your dietary cholesterol has very little relationship to your blood cholesterol level. Saturated-fat intake increases cholesterol, and shellfish have mostly unsaturated fat, including the good omega-3 fatty acids.

lean hamburger patty until it sticks together as the proteins coagulate. The cooked surimi is then flavored and shaped into various forms as textured artificial shellfish.

So, you can appreciate that shellfish are very diverse. You have the real shellfish and the surreal surimi. As food species, they differ in a number of nutrient profiles. But some members have been maligned as being dangerous or unhealthy to consume in any large quantities. There are unsubstantiated "facts" about their nutrition and misinformation that needs to be considered suspect. So, what are some myths and what are some facts and figures about shellfish?

Seafood with Amore, Armor, and Allergies

Shellfish really do love you (see the table that follows). They give you everything you need in a relationship with your food; low calories, lots of protein, and little fat. Add in the fact that they never will argue or talk back to you, and it truly sounds like a match made in heaven.

Food Molecules and Calories of Selected Shellfish

Type	Kcals	Fat	Protein (g)	Carbohydrate (g)	Cholesterol (mg)
Crab	100	1	20	0	90
Clams	100	1	22	0	55
Lobster	80	.5	17	1	60
Oysters	100	3.5	10	0	115
Scallops	120	1	22	2	55
Shrimp	80	1	18	0	165

Per 3-Ounce Uncooked Portion

So, let's say you want to have a relationship, what constitutes a good-looking shellfish? Well, if you are looking for fresh live ones, there are certain things to check for right off. Let's say you're shopping for lobster or fresh crab. They should be active and moving. Belly up is not a good sign. When you pick up a lobster, it should curl its tail underneath the body. Remember, you are dealing with a live muscle here. It should have reflexes just like your knee does.

For oysters and mussels, look for a closed shell. There should be no chips or broken shells, either. All seafood should have a sea breeze or a newly mown lawn smell. An ammonia smell is a bad sign. And if you are ever in doubt, all reputable seafood purveyors must have the shipper's tag, which details the catch and gives information about seafood inspection. Ask to see those tags.

When you get live shellfish home, do not immerse it in water. In fact, the best thing to do is to pack the shellfish on ice and cover with some wet paper towels. Of course, your shellfish need to be kept in a cold refrigerator on the lower level to prevent any cross contamination with other foods.

> **Chef Sez**
>
> A **toxin** is a substance that, when consumed in sufficient quantities, is poisonous to your health. **Vibrio vulnificus** is a pathogenic bacteria that can colonize shellfish and cause severe gastroenteritis in humans who consume raw products.

Raw: A Steaming Debate

Your greatest risk in getting a food-borne illness from shellfish fall into three general categories: bacterial pathogens, parasites, or natural *toxins*. For two of these risks, cooking the shellfish properly eliminates the problem. In all three cases, buying shellfish from reputable seafood purveyors greatly reduces the risk.

Why cooking? Well, you know that bacteria do not like high heat. So, in all cases of bacterial risk, including such things as Salmonella, Listeria, *Vibrio*, or even parasitic worms, cooking shellfish until an internal temperature of 145°F is reached for 15 seconds does the trick. The following table lists the FDA-recommended cooking times to safely consume shellfish.

FDA-Recommended Cooking Times for Safe Shellfish Consumption

	Moist Heat	**Dry Heat**
Shrimp (1#)	Steam 3 to 5 minutes	Fry @ 375°F for 7 to 10 min.
Shucked*	Simmer 3 minutes	Fry @ 375°F for 10 min.
		Bake @ 450°F for 10 min.
Scallops	Simmer 3 minutes	Sear 3 minutes
Lobster	Boil 5 to 7 minutes (until the color turns to red)	

Shellfish are shucked. Cook all unshucked shellfish until the shell completely opens. Never cook shellfish that have broken or open shells that do not close when tapped lightly.

And cooking is easier to do for the various classes of shellfish than you might think. For crustaceans cooked in the shell, such as shrimp and lobster, the surface turns bright red and the meat becomes a bright, pearly white color. For scallops, the flesh changes from a translucent glistening shade to one that is milky white, and the meat gets very firm.

And what about the bivalves like mussels and oysters? First, you only keep ones that have shells that are closed and unbroken. If the shell is open, give it a little tap. Live bivalves close up. Dead ones should be discarded. You need to only steam the oysters, clams, or mussels until the shells open up. This can be done fairly rapidly in a covered pan on the stove top. Of course, you may want to add some aromatics, or even some white wine to fully enjoy this steamed delicacy.

But what about toxins? Cooking does not destroy toxins. They are bombproof proteins that still pack a punch. So, hot clam chowder or oyster stew that is tainted is not a good situation. Toxins arise from algae blooms in the water where shellfish live. The shellfish are exposed as a natural part of the food web. Fortunately for you, inspection and regulation are primary ways to greatly lower the risk. The seafood industry, local government, and federal agencies monitor algae blooms and intercept contaminated food. Toxins are only a problem if the toxic levels reach a threshold that can do harm. Your awareness is the most important thing to keep you safe from this risk. And the old adage of buyer beware is your best bet; buy from reputable dealers only.

So, shellfish, as with all natural foods, have inherent risks associated with eating them. But they also have major advantages. Using proper techniques, and being educated about the pros and cons, are your best bet to enjoy, not avoid, shellfish as part of a healthy diet.

The Least You Need to Know

- Shellfish are a high-protein, low-fat food that is very diverse in form and use.
- Though certain shellfish can be consumed raw, cooking minimizes any risk of consuming them.
- Persons with known food allergies to shellfish must avoid them at all times.
- Shellfish should be purchased from reputable purveyors, be fresh, and always stored under refrigeration.

Part 5

Beautiful Baking

Don't let the concept of sugar-plum fairies and cream puffs fool you; it's a disciplined world in the bakery. The science of measures and weights reigns supreme here, and understanding why will make you a better baker. So, jump right in because a little knowledge of baking science reaps sweet rewards.

You will learn the ups and downs of bread-baking and the importance of cooking with gas. You'll take a walk through candy land. And you'll learn to appreciate the fact that an egg isn't just a way to make another chicken; it's the basis for foods such as custards.

Firm Abs but Flat Buns

In This Chapter

- ◆ Bakery ingredients
- ◆ Gluten's role
- ◆ Batter vs. dough
- ◆ Weights and measures

Nostalgia is probably the reason we love baking. You might actually remember a time when fresh bread was baking, or cinnamon rolls came popping out of the oven, or you found that plate of peanut-butter fudge as a surprise on the kitchen table after school. But more likely, it wasn't real-life baking experiences that you recall. It is just the hope of these memories, maybe from others relating them to you, or reading about them, or late-night reruns of June Cleaver and Hazel.

But don't kid yourself. The bakery is a real science jungle. You might get away with a pinch of this or a splash of that, making soup. But you are not going to be so successful improvising in the bakery. Bakery science is spit and polish and attention to detail. Oh, there's plenty of creativity to go around, too. And you must admit that the presence of cinnamon and sugar and chocolate sure does make this aspect of kitchen science appealing.

Bakeshop Ingredients

Flip through the baking recipes in any cookbook. You'll see a few ingredients that appear over and over: flour, sugar, butter, and eggs. The selection of lab supplies starts to look pretty limited. But think of all the different products that can be made from a limited list of ingredients. What this means is that the four food molecules really come to life in the bakery. Proteins, carbohydrates, fats, and water really are your primary ingredients, your foundation. And with a strong foundation and some basic techniques, you can do lots of stuff. It's form and function and chemistry and science, but most of all it's tasty and fun.

Flour Children

Flour is probably the first thing to think about when you think about baking. Why? Well, it's not just that cute image of a doughboy. Flour contains all of the food molecules in one tidy package. And not just any flour will do. Although there are a bunch of flours, the one you must focus on is made from wheat.

Food for Thought

The word "flour" can take on lots of modifiers. Most refer to additives and procedures approved by FDA. *Enriched* means the flour is supplemented with vitamins and iron. *Presifted* means sifted when milled. *Bleached* whitens flour and speeds up the natural aging process. *Unbleached* is flour that ages in air naturally. *Patent* flour is the highest grade of flour commercially. *Organic* flours are made from grains not treated with herbicides or insecticides, or flour that has no fumigant treatment or other additives during processing. *Bromated* means the flour was treated with potassium bromate to strengthen its proteins, although this technique is rarely used these days.

Wheat is made into flour by grinding the berries and separating out the bran, endosperm, and germ. This should sound familiar from Chapter 10, of course. All wheat has this basic anatomy. Different flours come from combining the parts and pieces back together again. And when you have different types of wheat, you end up with a bunch of different combinations.

Wheat can be a hard red winter, hard red spring, soft red winter, hard white, soft white, or durum. What counts is the difference in the protein content. When wheat has lots of protein, we say that it is hard. More protein means more *gluten*-forming potential. The softer the wheat, the less protein it contains, decreasing its ability to form gluten. And, as you will soon learn, it is gluten that makes bread bread. And it is having the right amount of gluten that makes those cakes, cookies, and biscuits look right and feel right in your mouth.

Now you need to think about all the different types of wheat flour that your grocery might have. You can get a general idea of the types of flour and their applications by looking at the following table. The basic one everywhere is all-purpose flour, AP for short. It is made from hard wheat or blends of hard and soft wheat varieties. Protein varies from about 8 to 11 percent. It's called all-purpose because it can be used for all sorts of things. It may not be perfect for everything, but it works just fine for a broad range of applications.

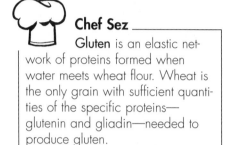

Chef Sez _____

Gluten is an elastic network of proteins formed when water meets wheat flour. Wheat is the only grain with sufficient quantities of the specific proteins— glutenin and gliadin—needed to produce gluten.

Flour Types and Applications

Type	Percent Protein	Best Used For
All-Purpose	8–11	General baking
Bread	12–14	Yeast breads
Cake	7–9	Tender cakes
Pastry	8–9	Pie crust, biscuits
Whole wheat	13–14	Bread
High Gluten	40–45	Blended bread baking

Think of all-purpose as the midpoint on a scale; protein content either goes up or down from there. Flour might be a lot like you. You can work out at the gym and build up that muscle protein and look and feel one way: strong and intimidating. Or let the protein be a little less strong on that body and look and feel entirely different: maybe more soft and supple. So, one day you might feel like a nice, thick, strong loaf of bread, and the other times, like a fine French pastry. You and flour do have a lot in common.

Flour is more than just powdered protein, however. It packs a bunch of carbohydrates, too. And starch is as important in the baking process as protein. The higher the starch content, the lower the protein content, and vice versa.

> **Now You're Cooking**
>
> Do you know how to tell the difference in flours by feel? Take a handful each of bread, all-purpose, and cake flour. Squeeze each one separately. You will see that bread flour falls freely away. Cake flour clumps up and cakes. All-purpose flour is somewhere in between. The higher starch in cake flour causes it to clump up. Strong or high-protein flours tend not to attract moisture from your hand, so the flour falls away more freely. This is one reason why rolling out dough with bread flour makes the dough less sticky.

Flour is an important ingredient, and you need to treat it well to keep its properties functioning properly. Flour starches love water, so keep flours in a cool, dry place with an airtight lid if possible, but not in the refrigerator. Refrigerators are too moist, and all that moisture can ruin your flour. Flour will keep about six months at moderate room temperatures. As for whole-wheat flour, well, it contains more fats and fiber than other flours. And those fats can turn rancid more quickly, which means that they spoil. Storing whole-wheat flours in the freezer is a good idea. Just let it warm up to room temperature before using it.

Sweet Cheeks

Where would a bakery be without sugar? Sugar, in all its various forms, is a foundation ingredient of the bakeshop. It provides flavor, color, moisture, and texture for baked goods.

Table sugar, as you know, is glucose and fructose. It's called sucrose, and it comes from refining sugar beets or sugar cane. Molasses is syrup that comes from the repeated cooking and refining of the cane juice. That nice brown color is from the browning products created when molasses is refined through heating, centrifuging, and reheating. Blackstrap molasses is the darkest, strongest type of molasses.

Brown sugar is a blend of molasses and granulated sucrose. The myth that brown sugar is more natural or unrefined is just that: a myth. Brown sugar is just sugar crystals with a coating of molasses on the surface. When you have more molasses clinging on it, you call it dark brown sugar; less molasses gives you light brown sugar. Turbinado sugar is one of the first refined fractions from washing the crude cane juice with steam. It is similar to brown sugar, but less refined. Somehow it gets marketed as a pure sugar, but it's just good old sucrose with a tan. Your body's metabolism treats them all the same way—sucrose is sucrose is sucrose.

Food for Thought

Most kitchen cupboards contain several liquid sweeteners in addition to molasses. *Honey* contains the same monosaccharides as table sugar: glucose and fructose. The ratios of free sugar molecules combined with special manufacturing (thank you, Mrs. Bee) give honey its distinct flavors and colors. *Maple syrup* is mostly sucrose, plus water and amino acids. Cooking maple sap produces browning reactions and the colors and flavors of real maple syrup. *Corn syrup* is the most consumed sweetener in the United States, thanks to our love affair with soft drinks. It's basic glucose or double units of glucose, called maltose. *Corn sweeteners* are jazzed-up versions, with more fructose added to heighten that sweet sensation. Corn syrups are used commercially to help baked goods stay moist.

The biggest difference between brown sugar and table sugar is good old water. Brown sugar has about a third more moisture, so it loves water; it is hygroscopic. That is why it lumps up and is so nice and soft. Until, of course, you leave the brown sugar container open. Then all the moisture evaporates and you are left with rock-hard sugar. Always store your brown sugar in an airtight or well-sealed package.

Take a long look at granulated sugar and you'll see that it is crystalline. That crystalline structure is important in some baking processes because it enables you to incorporate air. It also has a sandpaper quality that can actually help break down smooth things such as eggs and make them creamy. The crystals can cut through egg fats and proteins.

And, of course, sugar is a food. You like it, and things such as yeast and bacteria like it. So, when you use helpful yeasts and bacteria to make things, sugar feeds these living creatures.

Because sucrose is a simple disaccharide, it dissolves easily. You can use it to make simple syrups or candies, or cook it all the way to very dark caramel for sauce or flavoring. You'll learn more about sugar in Chapter 21.

Soft and Sweet

Of course, there are times you don't want your sugar to be coarse; you want something finer. Powdered sugar is nothing more than finely ground table sugar, with a little cornstarch added to absorb moisture and prevent caking. You can't make powdered (a.k.a. confectioner's sugar) at home because you don't have the sophisticated grinders and sifters that the chore requires, however.

Because powdered sugar is so much finer than granulated sugar, it takes much more of it to get the same sweetening power. Don't try to substitute powdered sugar for granulated sugar in a recipe; you'd only have about half as much sweetness and none of the texture. Powdered sugar is great for making smooth creamy icings, sweetening beverages, and decorating cookies, cakes, and such.

Fat Chance

Fat performs a number of essential chores in the bakeshop, and with good scientific reasons. Whether saturated, unsaturated, hydrogenated, solid, or liquid, the type of fat helps determine how it should be used. The following table shows an array of common fats you will use in the bake shop.

Fats and Their Use in Baking

| Fat | Percent Fat Type | | | Room Temp | |
	Sat	Mono	Poly	Form	Function
Shortening	25	46	29	Solid	Leavener, nonstick
Butter	65	31	4	Solid	Flavor/texture
Margarine	20	45	35	Solid	Butter substitute
Lard	42	42	18	Solid	Flavor/texture/leavener
Corn oil	13	25	62	Liquid	Texture/moisture

Shortening is good for preventing things from sticking because it has very little taste or aroma. Unlike butter or margarine, solid shortenings contain virtually no water, and water can cause sticking.

Other fats might be used because they have specific flavors, such as butter, lard, or olive oil. Fats react with protein and sugar so they are useful for creating structures and textures. They don't like water so they are useful in creating barriers. And fats melt at different temperatures, so they release water and steam into baked goods during cooking. All of these physical or chemical properties occur at different levels for different fats. And you mix and match them to the job when you choose which to use. Some will be good for some jobs like bread-making, while others are better for pastries and cakes. Versatility is a big function in the fat family.

Technique Matters

Part of the fun of baking is mixing stuff together. Some things need to be combined gently and slowly; other things need to be worked vigorously to incorporate lots of air. Sometimes you might be making a mistake to undermix ingredients; other times it can be easy to overmix them. It all depends on what you are trying to achieve. Like science, mixing methods have their own lingo:

- *Beating* is stirring rapidly to incorporate air or develop gluten; this usually requires an electric mixer or a strong arm with a spoon.
- *Blending* is gently mixing ingredients to distribute them uniformly. Just about any tool can be used, depending on the ingredients you have to work with.
- *Creaming* is aerating fat and sugar by beating.
- *Cutting* is incorporating fat into dry ingredients until lumps of a certain size remain. This can be done with pastry cutters, fingers, or two forks.
- *Folding* is very gently mixing to preserve aeration. An example is incorporating whipped cream or whipped egg whites into a batter, usually with a rubber spatula.
- *Kneading* is working dough in a vigorous folding-and-turning pattern in order to form gluten. You can use your hands, or an electric mixer with a dough hook.
- *Sifting* is passing dry ingredients through a wire mesh to remove lumps, combine ingredients, or reduce particle size.
- *Stirring* is the gentle mixing of ingredients until well blended. It is usually done by hand.
- *Whipping* is rapid beating to maximize aeration. A whisk or electric mixer with whip attachments is necessary for this.

Being a successful baker means knowing what recipe instructions and terminology really mean, and then following these instructions carefully. It would be a shame to ruin your carefully selected fats, flours, and sugars by improper mixing, now wouldn't it?

Gluten Maximus

Let's get into the thick and thin of things. First, let's talk gluten, and then take a peek at a batter. To understand one is to really understand them both.

Gluten is the child of two proteins—glutenin and gliadin—that are found in the endosperm of wheat. Gluten is created by mixing moisture into wheat flour. Gluten is essential for trapping air or carbon dioxide gas inside your cake or bread or buns; and without air, your cake or bread or buns would be flat and dense and unattractive.

Gluten is special because of the chemical charges that these proteins have in relation to water. Yes, baking has a lot to do with water, also. Remember that water is polar; it has a charge. It also forms and reforms bonds, sort of ticking away, like a digital watch counts off seconds. The forming and reforming of bonds at the molecular level are called hydrogen bonds. This bonding produces a three-dimensional stacking of water, which makes it stable and unique. You might say that water bonds with itself; it is water loving, or as chemists say, hydrophilic.

As it so happens, gluten also has hydrogen bonds. The bonds in the protein are attracted to one another just like water attracts itself. But gluten is a complex protein. It also has hydrophobic bonds, which is a chemist's way of saying it has water-hating bonds. You've met other water-hating molecules along the way, namely fats. Finally, you should be aware of one other bond—a sulfur-to-hydrogen bond. In chemist's lingo, it's called a sulf-hydryl. It's an important bond in gluten, as you will see shortly.

Dough Land

The funny thing is that you would never know these three different bonds exist in wheat proteins until you try to mix in some water. Water is the polar molecule moving into the gluten neighborhood. Now, you just don't add any amount of water. What you need to do is combine three parts of flour to every one part of water. Or, said another way, add 3 cups of flour to 1 cup of water.

Now things begin to happen. First, the wheat proteins unwind because some of them love water. They begin to shake hands with water, saying, in effect, "Welcome to our place, man." This is fine until you realize that living on the same block as the water-loving proteins are the water haters. These hydrophobic dudes dislike water, so they form their own little enclave. You can already tell what's going to happen, right?

If everything were hydrophilic, then as soon as you add water, the flour would dissolve. Just like sugar in water. But because of the hydrophobic protein, all that really happens is that a clump of *dough* forms. Basically, with just a little water in the mix, you have a nonsoluble mixture of flour and water.

So, now you're asking (well, maybe you're asking), what about those hydrogen and sulf-hydryl bonds in the proteins? They turn out to side with the hydrophobic crowd. They actually help the water haters fend off those water-loving parts of the protein. And, in doing so, they make the gluten stronger. In fact, those sulf-hydryl and hydrogen-bonding dudes actually line up the hydrophobic proteins into cords or threads as you mix the dough. You might say they organize the water haters' resistance group.

When you make dough, the water disappears in hydrophilic land and is surrounded by sheets and cords of hydrophobic protein. As you work the dough back and forth, a process called kneading, you are working out the alignment of the hydrogen and sulf-hydryl attachments to make the dough even stronger. The hydrophobes are in charge.

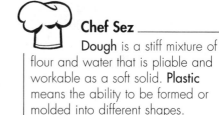

Chef Sez

Dough is a stiff mixture of flour and water that is pliable and workable as a soft solid. **Plastic** means the ability to be formed or molded into different shapes. **Elastic** means the ability to snap back when tension is applied.

Of course, now the hydrophobes are in for a little exercise. They love it when you stretch and pull them. The dough becomes *elastic* and rebounds as you stretch and fold it. And it is *plastic* because it enables you to move it into different shapes. Both elasticity and plasticity are related to the strength of the gluten. And since gluten development depends on how much protein was in the wheat to begin with, stronger dough requires high-protein flour. That's why higher-protein flours are better for making bread dough.

But don't overwork those hydrophobes. Just like you can over-stretch and strain your muscles, gluten can strain. And once you break those sulf-hydryl and hydrogen bonds, you've weakened the gluten. It tears and loses its elasticity, and once that's gone, it's gone for good.

Batter Up

Let's recap: We mix water with flour and create dough. The magic formula for that is three parts flour to one part water. That produces an insoluble, plastic, and elastic gluten ball.

What would happen if you simply added more water? Say, equal parts? Well, what you'd get is not a plastic and elastic ball of dough but a mixture called a batter.

Batters are the pourable, semi-liquid mixture of flour and water. Now, what you've done is move more water into the gluten neighborhood. The hydrophobes, sulf-hydryls, and hydrogen-protein crowds don't have the upper hand anymore. They can't just segregate and wall off the water-loving crowd. In fact, the water-loving proteins are free to go flowing around, running here and there. Water lovers now envelope the gluten and become the leaders of the pack. The result is that gluten can't form those strong elastic and plastic bonds. And with less gluten, the batter is really soft. And it's all about water.

Now, you probably realize that when you make tasty breads or flavorful batters, you add more than flour and water. But that is just adding icing to the cake. The basic food science is in the foundation of water and flour. Anything you add to the mix has to play second fiddle to these star performers.

So, in the end, the whole gamut of differences in batters—cake, crêpe, or pancake—differs by the amount of water you add. And it's the same idea with breads. You take the basic foundation of flour and water and create anything from chewy French bread to tender biscuits, from cookies to pasta. Flours, fats, sugars, and liquids can vary; mixing times and techniques can vary. But the flour-water foundation still determines what you build. And it all gets back to the chemistry of good ol' water.

Heat Helps

It would be a shame to mix up a dough or a batter and leave it at that. With the exception of chocolate chip cookie dough, few things are really better raw. So, add some heat and cook it. In the next chapter you will build on this foundation of unleavened dough and batter and move into the wonderful realm of baking with gases. You will go from unleavened to leavened. For now, though, it's back to basics with a look at precision measuring.

A Final Word: Weights and Measures

When you're making soups and sauces, it can be easy and fun to add a pinch of this or a dab of that. There's no need to measure, because your taste buds tell you how much to add, right? You and your dinner companions can even add salt or other seasonings at the table to fix any problems.

That's fine for some things, but don't even think about winging it in the bakery lab. Here, accurate measurements are essential for success. So much of what happens in baking involves precise chemical reactions. It's important to follow such recipes carefully (bakers even call them formulas to sound more scientific). For example, if you leave out the salt, or double up on the baking powder by mistake, you can't stop baking a cake in the middle to repair the damage. You may not realize your mistake until the cake is on your plate, when it's too late to make adjustments. Simply reading and following bakery recipes carefully will go a long way toward making your kitchen a successful bakeshop.

You also need to understand some measurement fundamentals. First, weight refers to the heaviness or mass of something. When you step on a scale, you find out just how much mass or heaviness your body has. If your scale is precise enough, you can weigh anything. The units might be pounds, ounces, grams, or kilograms. Weight is the most accurate way to measure something. It is a constant. They don't weigh semis on the Interstates for nothing.

Second, volume refers to the space occupied by a substance. Volume has height, length, and width. A cup, gallon, quart, or bushel measures volume. Teaspoons and tablespoons also measure volume and are good to use because, let's face it, you don't want or need to weigh everything that small. Now, the important point here is that weight and volume are not the same. A cup measures 8 fluid ounces by volume, but the contents of that cup may not weigh 8 ounces on a scale.

The old saying that "a pint's a pound the world around" only holds true for water, and a few other things like butter, eggs, and milk. A cup of flour does not weigh 8 ounces; it only weighs about $4^{1}/_{2}$ ounces, depending on how loosely you filled the cup. Likewise, a cup of chopped apples will weigh different amounts depending upon the size of the pieces. So, real bakers and scientists beware! Do not flip-flop between measurement systems. The point is, when a recipe specifies an ingredient by weight, weigh it. If it says volume, get out the measuring cups.

> **Now You're Cooking**
> One of the most scientific yet practical tools you can add to your kitchen is a simple scale. For less than 20 bucks, a spring-operated balance scale can make all your measurements more accurate. Fancier platform scales cost less than $100. Old-fashioned balance-beam scales can often be found at garage sales and flea markets. These offer the added advantage of looking really cool on your counter.

Oh, you can also count some ingredients. Sometimes you might be told to use a lemon. Fine, use a lemon. Or your recipe might say to beat six large eggs. That's fine, too. Most of the time, you won't need to worry about count, unless you become some fancy TV celebrity chef who wants to count his or her money.

We'd like to make one final point about measurements; take the time to learn metric conversions sometime. A table of metric equivalents is included in Appendix B. It isn't rocket science, and you'll feel so much smarter if you ever vacation in France.

The Least You Need to Know

- Flour, sugar, fat, and water are important baking ingredients.
- Different flours contain different amounts of protein, thus differing in their ability to form gluten.

◆ Various mixing techniques are used to achieve different results.

◆ Batters differ from dough by having more water in proportion to flour.

◆ Fats and sugars are added to batters and dough to produce different textures, flavors, and cooking properties.

◆ Be true to your measures of weights and volumes, and they will be true to you.

20

The Quick and the Dead

In This Chapter

- ◆ Now you're cooking with gas
- ◆ Speed up with quick breads
- ◆ Slow down with yeast breads
- ◆ Going stale

In the previous chapter, we explained how wheat flour and water become a batter or a dough. Unless your dough is for chocolate chip cookies, however, you probably won't find it too appealing until heat is applied. Heat is the magic that transforms a lifeless-looking ball of dough or a bowl of sticky batter into bread or cake or muffins. Heat makes it edible. But before popping your creation into a hot oven, you need to breathe life into it.

Bread has been raised from the dead for a long time now. Even the ancient Egyptians added fermented grains (beer, that is) to make their breads lighter and tastier. Long before anyone understood the science behind the process, lifeless, heavy breads were transformed into airy and texturally pleasant products by the addition of gas. Now we know that the type and amount of gas that goes into a batter or dough depends on what's being made. Your job as a scientifically oriented baker is to match the method to your foundation ingredients.

But before you look at what leaveners bring to your bread, some general information about the process of baking will help you understand why you should worry about gas in the first place.

Baking 101

You have mixed your basic food molecules according to a standard recipe. You have some protein, some starch, some fat, and some water. The final task is to apply some energy in the form of heat. You are going to cook it, or, said more appropriately, *bake* it. Baking is a process of cooking food in an oven surrounded by dry heat. Heat energy from the hot air will be conducted into the interior of the product to transform these food molecules. Scientifically, the process is the same whether the item is a loaf of *yeast* bread, a chocolate chip cookie, or an angel food cake. When heat hits, food molecules change in very routine ways.

> ### Chef Sez
> **Baking** is a dry-heat cooking method that cooks food by surrounding it with hot, dry air in an enclosed chamber such as an oven. The same process may be referred to as roasting, depending on the food item being cooked. For example, meat and chicken are roasted; cakes, bread, and fish are baked. **Yeast** are microscopic fungi that eat sugars and produce carbon dioxide and alcohol through a process known as fermentation.

Gases to Go

Baked goods get a great deal of their texture and shape from the gases that are present in the dough or batter. When gases get hot, they expand. As they expand, the batter or dough rises, developing the airy textures we find so appealing. Most baked goods contain three types of gas: air, steam, and carbon dioxide.

When you mix the ingredients for your bread or cake, you introduce air. You might even see some air bubbles forming when you mix and combine things. And as you knead and slap that bread dough around on the table, you are also folding air into it.

Water also contributes gas to your baked goods. This gas is steam. Steam develops when the bakery product is heated. It is not unlike heating water to make a cup of tea. When the water boils, you can see the steam escaping. The heat of baking likewise transforms liquid water into a gas inside your dough or batter.

The third type of gas you sometimes use in baked goods is carbon dioxide (CO_2). Carbon dioxide is created as a by-product of chemical and biological leavening agents. Recipes that use baking soda, baking powder, or yeast do so in order to add carbon dioxide gas to the mix.

Balloon Ride

For now, let's just assume that all three of these gases are in your dough or batter. They are ready to do what gas always wants to do—escape. This tendency is easy to illustrate. Just blow up a balloon but don't tie off the end. When you let go of it— swoosh—the gas blows away. Gases like to exert pressure. You can see that pressure form as you blow up the balloon. The skin of the balloon keeps the gas in a nice little package. Tie off that balloon, and you can entertain your cat or dog for hours. Forget to tie off the balloon, and all that gas says sayonara.

The gases in your dough want to do the same thing—escape. Don't blame them; escaping is just their job. But you are smarter. You have created gluten (that elastic network of wheat proteins we talked about in Chapter 19) to trap them in the dough or batter, just like you trapped air in the balloon. If you're making yeast bread, you can actually see how gases are trapped. The dough rises even before you bake it. A batter might even get a bunch of bubbles on the surface if you leave it sitting around awhile.

Applying Heat

Once gases are formed and trapped, you are ready to rock and roll. Or, said another way, you are ready to bring a little heat action to bear on that batter or dough. And when you apply dry heat, say from a 350°F oven, you already know what will happen to the starches and the proteins.

Heating that bread means heating the water inside it. When water reaches about 140°F and gets next to some starch, well, things start happening. And what happens is gelatinization. The starches cook. And when starches cook, they transform themselves into a soft gel. Just like cornstarch in water going from a liquid to a gel, the same thing is happening in your bread. And this starch-gel barrier is a line of defense against the escape of those gases.

Proteins coagulate when cooked, or, in this case, baked. As the heat is conducted from the surface of your baked good to the inside, proteins denature or unwind. The surface proteins cook first, just like the ones in a steak placed on a hot pan. As soon as they reach 100°F, in fact, those proteins begin to denature. And when they get above 160°F, they coagulate.

When we talk about coagulating proteins in things containing wheat flour, we are really talking about coagulating gluten. Eggs provide some proteins, too, of course. But the real foundation of your baked good is gluten. It gives your bread structure. And structure helps trap those gases. Just like tying off a balloon, the coagulation of protein and gelatinized starch closes the gate. These gases begin to exert pressure on the coagulated protein and starch structure. They push against it and make the product rise.

If you aren't a low-fat freak, your recipe may have included some fat or oil. So, fats are doing what fats do when the temperature gets hot: They melt. And when fats melt, say butter, for example, the water that was inside of them turns to steam. This steam is another gas that contributes to the rise of your bread, cake, or muffins.

When fats melt, they don't disappear; they just find another home. Remember those hydrophobic proteins in gluten? Well, melting fats look them up and move into their neighborhood. And when they slide in there, they lubricate and soften the gluten proteins. They keep them from stretching too much. They shorten them. This shortening effect helps things relax.

By now, several things are happening inside your baked goods: Gases are being created and trapped, starches are gelatinizing, proteins are coagulating, and fats are melting. Heat is being conducted toward the center of the food, and the interior is beginning to steam. Water is turning to steam and evaporating.

Getting Crusty

As the temperature of your dough or batter goes up, all those tasty sugars begin to caramelize. You'll learn more about the cooking of sugars in Chapter 21, but for now it's important to understand that this is where that beautiful brown crust on the top of your bread comes from.

Because the surface of the dough or batter received a prolonged direct blast of oven heat, it has become dry and, you guessed it, crusty.

So, when you pull your dough or batter out of the oven, you have done a lot of good things. But, of course, it is still very hot. In fact, it is still baking even as it cools. Internal heat produces what is called *carryover cooking*, which puts the finish on your baked goods. That's why you probably should take your

Chef Sez

Carryover baking is the effect of residual heat from hot items removed from the oven. Foods continue to cook and finish, even if slightly underbaked. **Leaveners** or leavening agents refer to anything that causes a baked good to rise. This includes steam, air, and products that create carbon dioxide gas such as baking soda and yeast.

cookies or biscuits or bread out of oven when they are still just a wee bit underdone. Carryover cooking will finish the job. Now that you have been through the baking process, let's go back and look at the gas situation more closely.

Breads in a Flash

Chemical *leaveners* find a happy home in the kitchen when making quick breads. This makes sense because quick breads are quick to make and quick to bake. So, they require gas that is also quick to develop. You can't fuel a quick bread with anything that is going to take a long time to generate gas. If you do, the bread is baked long before the gas can do its job.

You have two basic choices to gas up a quick bread: baking soda and baking powder. Some recipes even call for both. Do not, however, substitute one for the other in a recipe. The chemistry necessary to make them work requires specific ingredients and ratios. Think of it like salt and pepper; both flavor your food, but in different ways. Likewise, baking powder and baking soda both produce carbon dioxide gas to leaven baked goods, but they do so in different ways.

Bicarb on Tap

Baking soda is sodium bicarbonate. You can heat baking soda and liberate the CO_2 gas. But this isn't the best way to make it work in your quick breads. What you'll get is a salty, soapy aftertaste. It's far better to combine the baking soda with an acid to produce CO_2. Sodium bicarbonate is basic, which means it has a pH above 7.0. Acids have a pH below 7.0. Put them together and they neutralize one another, producing CO_2 as a by-product.

Acidic foods are those that give you free hydrogen ions (H+). Things like buttermilk or yogurt are acidic and often do the trick in quick-bread recipes. When the free hydrogen from these foods comes in contact with the baking soda in that moist, quick-bread batter, CO_2 is produced. The food acid and sodium bicarbonate base neutralize one another, and you get your gas with less aftertaste.

Two things you need to keep in mind. First, because this is a chemical reaction, it can go

Too Hot to Handle

Self-rising flour is all-purpose flour that already contains salt and leaveners. It should not be substituted for regular all-purpose flour (or vice versa) without making careful adjustments. One cup of self-rising flour contains the equivalent of $1\frac{1}{2}$ teaspoons of baking powder and $\frac{1}{2}$ teaspoon of salt. It's a convenience product best reserved for recipes that are specifically designed for it.

very quickly. This means that you can't be dawdling around after mixing all of your ingredients together. Once you set the chain of chemical reactions in motion, gas is being produced. To trap that gas, you need to get your quick bread into the oven quickly so that the starches can gelatinize and the proteins can coagulate and the carbon dioxide can be trapped before it escapes.

Second, you need to measure these chemicals accurately. If you don't add enough baking soda, the bread won't rise properly. If you add too much baking soda, there won't be enough acid to neutralize it, resulting in leftover sodium bicarbonate, which you'll taste as a bitter, soapy afterthought. So, follow your recipe directions carefully.

A Baking Powder Keg

You can also get your leavening in another form, called baking powder. Baking powder contains both sodium bicarbonate and an acid (usually something like cream of tartar) in an easy-to-measure powder.

Baking powder is a bit more complex than simple baking soda because you have fast- or slow-acting versions. The fast stuff starts reacting when it comes in contact with the moist ingredients in your batter. This is called single-acting baking powder because it only produces one reaction—with moisture.

Double-acting baking powder contains a third chemical, which produces a delayed reaction when heat hits. Can you see the advantage to using double-acting baking powder? You get the first quick pulse of CO_2 as the chemicals react with moisture.

Then, you pop the bread in the oven and start the heating process, which triggers the second chemical reaction. Those chemicals can be either sodium aluminum sulfate or anhydrous monocalcium phosphate. Either of those two acids is only turned on by heat. So, they liberate their H+ and start the second reaction to produce CO_2 as the bread bakes. By this time, your quick-bread structure is nicely established and you are able to trap those gases inside the banana bread where it belongs.

Mixin' and Fixin'

Quick breads are quick and easy to put together. All quick breads can be made using one of three basic mixing methods: the biscuit, muffin, or creaming method.

Each method is important for creating the final texture and characteristics of the specific product. Of course, all quick breads should be tender. You aren't out to achieve a maximum gluten structure—save that for chewy yeast bread. You get tenderness by choosing the correct proportion of food molecules and then applying the proper mixing method.

It's a Cold, Hard Fat

The biscuit method gives you one very flaky type of quick bread. For this, you combine all the dry stuff with cold, solid fat. Cutting the fat into the dry ingredients enables you to control particle size. In this case, you want chunks of fat in your dough. Remember the baking process? When the fat melts, it creates steam, and this steam will help the biscuits rise.

The fat also finds a home in the gluten, shortening it and making it tender. So, each little piece of fat creates a small, tender spot that we see as a flake. Flakes are what make biscuits biscuits, and pie dough, pie dough. In both products, flakiness is the result of the way you combine fat with the dry ingredients. Once the fat is in place, knead the biscuit dough as little as possible. You don't want to smash down all those fat particles you worked to create, or make the gluten proteins too strong by overworking them.

Lab Project

For biscuits, combine 3 cups all-purpose flour, 1 1/2 teaspoons salt, 2 tablespoons granulated sugar, and 2 tablespoons double-acting baking powder in a bowl. Cut in 1 cup (two sticks) cold butter, working it in until the mixture looks mealy. Stir in 3 cups milk, mixing only until the mixture holds together. Knead the dough gently five or six times on a floured board. Roll the dough out to 1/2-inch thick; cut with a floured biscuit cutter and place the circles of dough close together on a lightly greased cookie sheet. Bake at

Liquid Fat

The muffin method produces a very different type of quick bread. For this you use a liquid fat such as oil or melted butter. The liquid fat flows in and around the gluten proteins, shortening them and making your bread very tender. To keep your bread tender, don't overmix the batter. Overworking the batter toughens up the gluten and incorporates too much air. In fact, tunnels can be created, which are pockets of air that leave holes in the finished product. This is not a pretty sight. What you want to achieve here is a slight lumpiness when you finish mixing. These lumps of ingredients bake into a coarser crumb that creates the texture you expect from muffins.

Beginning bakers often overmix muffin or cake batter in an effort to make sure it's just right. This overmixing shows up in the finished product as a rough surface or as internal tunnels or large pockets of air. The technical name for this is tunneling, because it looks as though something has been burrowing tunnels inside your baked goods. Overmixed quick breads will be tough and spongy as well. The best advice is to stop mixing before it's too late.

Lab Project

For basic blueberry muffins, sift together 2 cups all-purpose flour, $1/2$ cup of granulated sugar, 2 teaspoons double-acting baking powder, and $1/4$ teaspoon salt in a large bowl. In another bowl, stir together 2 eggs, 1 cup milk, 1 teaspoon vanilla, and $1/4$ cup melted butter. Stir the liquid mixture into the dry ingredients. Do not overmix. Gently fold in $3/4$ cup fresh blueberries and 1 tablespoon finely grated lemon rind. Portion in to greased or paper-lined muffin cups, and bake at 350°F until lightly browned and set, about 14 minutes.

Soft Fat

The creaming method produces products similar to those from the muffin method, but with a higher fat content and finer texture. Creaming is the technique of beating sugar and fat, usually softened butter, together to incorporate air. The crystalline structure of granulated sugar works like sandpaper, literally grating the fat into a creamy texture and leaving tiny pockets where air can be trapped.

When fat, combined with sugar, meets gluten, you are giving gluten a double whammy of shortening. With the creaming technique, it's also important to add the liquid and dry ingredients alternatively to the fat. That means you add some dry stuff to the creamed fat, and mix. Then add some liquid stuff and mix. Then go back to the dry, and then to the liquid. Do this until everything is used up. This will help you to mix things evenly without overmixing the batter or causing the creamed fat and sugar to break.

Lab Project

For cake-like sour-cream muffins, cream 1 cup (two sticks) of softened butter with 1 cup of granulated sugar. Add 2 eggs, one at a time. In a separate bowl, sift together $1^1/2$ cups all-purpose flour, 1 teaspoon baking powder, 1 teaspoon baking soda, and 1 teaspoon salt. Measure out $1^1/4$ cups of sour cream and stir in 1 teaspoon vanilla. Add the dry ingredients to the creamed butter, alternately with the sour cream. Portion the batter into greased or paper-lined muffin cups and bake at 350°F until light brown and set, about 20 minutes.

Slowing It Down

You can also produce gas by using the natural biological process of microorganisms. We are talking about yeast, of course, which is used for yeast bread, beer, and wine. What valuable little critters!

Yeast are fungi; they are from the same family as mushrooms. Yeast eat carbohydrates; sugar and starch are their preferred food. They then produce carbon dioxide and alcohol. There are two primary kinds of yeasts, based on how much CO_2 or alcohol they make. Brewer's yeast produces more alcohol with less CO_2 under conditions of limited oxygen. Baker's yeast is the opposite, favoring the production of CO_2 in a well-aerated environment. Of course, the story is more complex than that because there are many strains of yeast, especially in the brewing business. Each one of them gives unique flavor and composition to the end product. For now, we'll just focus on bread-making yeast, however.

Food for Thought

You can create fermentation using only water and flour and patience. This is known as sourdough starter. Left uncovered to ferment at room temperature, the mixture "sours" because yeast and bacteria that naturally reside in the air around us cultivate it. The starter should be fed with more flour over the course of several days, which give these microorganisms the starch they crave. After about four days, the bubbling brew has grown very acidic. The acids give the distinct sour flavor to the bread when the starter or "mother" is used to leaven bread dough. Commercial sourdough starters usually combine a strain of *Lactobacillus sanfrancisco* with the yeast strain *Saccharomyces exigus*. This leaves less to chance and controls the fermentation more than just relying on open-air cultures.

Form over Substance

Baking yeast can come in two forms: fresh compressed or active dry. Compressed yeast is fresh, good old-fashioned yeast in a white crumbly cake. It should smell like yeast and not have any ammonia smells or off color. This yeast is most active between 70 and 90°F. It will keep refrigerated for about three weeks.

Active dry yeast is the same as fresh yeast, but with water removed. The little yeast cells are sleeping, just waiting for you to add some warm moisture. And when you add moisture, it really needs to be warm. But don't scald them with boiling water, or you'll have DOA yeast. Their optimal temperature for gas production is 105 to 115°F.

Instant dry yeast is another dehydrated form. Its advantage is that it can go directly into your dry mix ingredients; it is activated with very warm water at about 125 to 130°F. In fact, you must mix the yeast with the other ingredients. Plopping instant yeast directly into hot water can destroy their effectiveness. And it's important to remember that all yeast will die at about 138°F; and dead yeast produce no gas. So, be careful not to add liquids that are too hot. The yeast in your dough should die naturally as the bread bakes.

Mixing It Right

Making yeast breads is dependent upon following mixing procedures correctly. It takes time for carbon dioxide to develop. Let's face it, you're growing a population of living, breathing fungi inside that bread dough. You have to give them time to do their thing. Yeast have a definite growth and temperature curve. So, the mixing and resting and shaping stages of bread-making all have a purpose. The stages in making yeast breads are as follows:

- Mixing the ingredients
- Kneading the dough
- Fermenting the dough
- Punching down the dough
- Portioning and shaping the dough
- Proofing the dough
- Baking the bread

Chef Sez

The **straight dough** method means to simply combine all the ingredients together and mix. The **sponge** method is a two-stage process in which a batter is first made with part of the flour, liquid, and yeast. This batter ferments, and then the remaining ingredients are added to complete the bread-making process.

Most yeast breads will be mixed using one of two methods: *straight dough* or *sponge*. The straight-dough method is just a fancy way of saying to put all the ingredients in a mixer bowl and turn it on. The sponge method requires two stages and is often used with rye, whole wheat, or multigrain breads. The first stage allows the yeast to ferment a portion of the dough before all of the ingredients are incorporated. You can mix it all up by hand with either method, of course. Just be sure that everything is well combined before you begin kneading.

After mixing your dough, the fermentation reaction needs time to develop. After all, you just fed your yeast and put them in a big mass of flour and water to grow. As they populate the dough, they are giving off CO_2, which gets trapped within the gluten network during this initial fermentation stage. So, cover the dough and let it rest in a cozy, warm place.

You can actually see the results of fermentation when you check back after an hour or so. The dough should double in size from all the gas given off by your yeast. Now you want to redistribute the result of your work; you want to spread that gas through the dough, which means you have to punch down your beautiful work. Punching down the dough also relaxes the gluten. Can you imagine keeping your arm flexed for hours at a time? The muscles get tired. Well, gluten proteins get tired and need a break, too.

Next, you divide the dough into portions and shape each portion as you see fit. Measurement and speed are important. Weigh the dough if necessary, so that you get the correct amount in the pans or so all your dinner rolls end up the same size. You want to work quickly so that the dough doesn't become dry. Moisture is always evaporating. So, the faster you can work, the less time the dough has to dry out.

You gently round the outside of the dough to form a nice stretched-out layer of gluten on the surface. Why is this important? This will help keep the gases inside your bread, just like a balloon traps air. And it will also keep the dough uniform and not rough. It justlooks more professional, too.

Now You're Cooking

Hard, crusty bread recipes usually tell you to dock the rolls or loaves before baking. Docking means to slash or cut the top of the bread with a razor or sharp paring knife. This improves the appearance and relieves gas pressure. Hot gas will find a way to escape; if you don't cut an escape valve in the surface, the gas may burst out the sides, leaving you with an uneven, unattractive product. Beside, docking lets you decorate your bread with all sorts of neat designs.

The Proof Is in the Pudding

After shaping your yeast bread, you proof it. Proofing means you are letting the yeast have one final round at making more CO_2. Ideally, you want to do this uncovered in a moist, warm environment. After about an hour, press the dough with your finger; the indentation should not spring back too quickly. The bread should also have doubled in size.

If you don't proof your bread long enough, the yeast won't have time to do its thing, and your final bread will be flat, dense, and tough. If you proof your bread too much, the yeast will have produced too much gas and too many acid by-products. The gluten will also be stretched too much. Your bread will end up with a sour taste, pale color, and poor volume.

Finally, you get to bake your bread. And we will have come full circle, back to the beginning of this chapter. You might wonder what happened to the yeast. Well, when you pop the bread in the oven and the yeast experience that first couple of minutes of dry heat, they really start to churn out CO_2. This causes an immediate rise, called oven spring. But as the temperature of the bread approaches 139°F, the yeast are killed. Though the yeast die, they are not forgotten. The products they produced contributed to the success of your baking. And the special yeasty flavor of the bread comes from the yeast cells and all the good things they left behind.

Lab Project

For soft yeast dinner rolls, combine 10 tablespoons warm water and $1/2$ ounce (two packages) of active dry yeast in a small bowl and set aside. Combine 3 cups (approximately) of bread flour, $1\frac{1}{2}$ teaspoons salt, 2 tablespoons sugar, 2 tablespoons nonfat dry milk powder, 2 tablespoons vegetable shortening, 2 tablespoons butter, and 1 egg in the bowl of an electric mixer. Add the water-and-yeast mixture and stir to combine. Knead the dough with the dough-hook attachment until smooth, about 8 minutes. Place the dough in a lightly greased bowl, cover, and let rise until doubled. Punch down the dough and divide it into 16 to 20 pieces. Round each portion into a smooth ball and place on a baking sheet lined with parchment paper. Proof uncovered until doubled. Carefully brush the rolls with egg wash (1 whole egg mixed with 1 tablespoon water), and then bake at 400°F until medium brown, about 12 minutes.

Why Bad Things Happen to Good Bread

Unfortunately, both you and your bread are aging. Bread ages a bit faster, however. In fact, aging begins as soon as you take bread out of the oven. To understand staling is to revisit the concept of gelatinization and remember the changes that occur when starches cool.

Baking bread gelatinizes starch. Starch becomes more soluble as it traps water and forms a soft gel. This is no different, really, than the process that happens when you thicken a sauce. The gelatinized starch contributes to the texture of bread. When starches cool, the amylose and amylopectin reorganize. And in doing so, some water gets squeezed out. This is all part of the natural cooling process. The squeezing out of water and formation of new starch granules is the process of starch *retrogradation*.

Retrogradation takes a few days to complete. So, the starches, which begin as soft gels and give bread that pleasing texture, begin to firm up. They get harder. When bread firms up, you call it staling. You can't blame it all on the starches drying out, though. Protein is also losing some water, and this, too, contributes to the undesirable firming of the bread as it ages and stales.

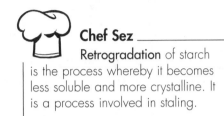

Chef Sez _____
Retrogradation of starch is the process whereby it becomes less soluble and more crystalline. It is a process involved in staling.

Once the water is squeezed out of its happy home with the starches and proteins deep inside that loaf of bread, it starts to seek a new home. It migrates to the surface of the bread. There it comes into contact with the dried-out starches in that firm, crunchy crust. The water softens the outside crust, making it leathery. This is a sure sign that staling has done its dirty deed.

You can rescue staling bread with a one-shot solution. You can cover it and reheat to 140°F. This is not a made-up temperature; it's the temperature at which gelatinization occurs. As you heat the covered bread, water that had migrated to the surface is driven back into the interior starches, rather than escaping as steam. Unfortunately, this same heating process causes the bread to lose some water, and you further dry out the crust. So, reheating is a one-time-only rescue.

What about keeping your bread in the fridge? Won't that help? Nope. Retrogradation of starch occurs during cooling and begins as soon as the bread leaves the oven. So, it shouldn't be surprising to learn that bread kept in the refrigerator will stale even faster. Simply never store bread at 40°F.

What about freezing bread? Freezing is fine, if you do it quickly. You want your bread to spend as little time as possible in the dead zone between 40 and 32°F. And make certain that the bread is well wrapped. This will help reduce moisture loss and prevent freezer burn. Breads with more fat freeze better because fat helps retain more of the water. Lean breads such as French bread are poor choices for freezing. They are best eaten as fresh as possible.

The Least You Need to Know

- ◆ Baking bread is a process of trapping gas within a network of cooked starches and proteins.

- ◆ Measure chemical leavener accurately to optimize the rise in breads and minimize chemical off-flavors.

- ◆ Yeasts perish above 138°F, so never put them in hot liquids.

- ◆ Baked goods continue to cook out of the oven.

- ◆ Breads stale quickly in the refrigerator; keep them well wrapped at room temperature, or freeze for longer storage.

Chapter 21

Sticky Fingers:
Sweets for the Sweet

In This Chapter

◆ Sugar's sweet attraction

◆ A couple ways to make caramel

◆ Creating candy and forming fudge

◆ Welcome to a chocoholic's dream

Your taste for sweet things developed in the womb. Newborn babies, as well as offspring from most mammals, come into the world with a preference for sweet. Milk is sweet and satisfies this craving early in life. As you grow older, the cravings for sweet grow with you. According to USDA Research Service figures collected from 1994–1996, an average person consumes about 3 ounces of caloric sweeteners each day. Of that total, about $1\frac{1}{2}$ ounces is pure sugar. That means you eat about 35 pounds of sugar each year.

Simple sugar (sucrose) is made into many things. From hard candy to soft caramel, the process of transformation is truly amazing. It shows that grandma has been practicing complex food chemistry with her old pots and pans. You don't need fancy degrees to work with sugar, either.

Sugar Solutions

Sugar is one of those water-loving food molecules. It's hygroscopic, which means it attracts water. And because it's water loving, you can easily mix it with some water and make what is called *simple syrup*. We can demonstrate lots of science with just some granulated sugar and cold water. If you can understand this process as well as granny did, you can become a super candy- and caramel-maker.

Measure out 1 pound of sugar and 2 pounds of water. (Remember you can also use volume when measuring water, by recalling "a pint's a pound the world around.")

Stir the water and sugar together in a saucepan and heat it just until the sugar dissolves. Then boil it without stirring for exactly one minute. You now have simple syrup. The water contains a certain concentration of dissolved sugar molecules. You don't see the crystals any longer but they are in there. Think of them lined up like little soldiers with molecules of water standing between them.

> **Chef Sez**
> **Simple syrup** is a mixture of sugar and water. Syrups may be light, medium, or heavy depending upon sugar concentration.

Now change the ratio of sugar and water by adding 1 more pound of sugar to the syrup. This means you now have equal parts sugar and water. Stir it and heat it just until the solution clears. Then boil it for a minute without stirring. This new syrup has twice as much sugar as water and twice as much sugar as the first solution. Now, imagine those sugar soldiers all lined up but with fewer water molecules between them. Things are a bit cozier now, and the syrup should look thicker or more viscous. This type of syrup has many uses in the bakeshop, and can also be used as stock or bar syrup. Mint juleps, anyone?

Now, let's make one more sugar solution. This time, take 1 pound of sugar but add only a $1/2$ pound of water. Stir, heat, and dissolve again. Then boil it for one minute undisturbed. This version contains twice as much sugar as water. Many more sugar soldiers are lined up in half as much water as the last syrup, and only one fourth as much water as the first syrup. You might say that those sugars are packed together about as tight as they can get.

These experiments illustrate the principle of concentration and saturation. In your first syrup, let's call it *light syrup*, you had twice as many units of water for each unit of sugar in the solution. That sugar had plenty of room to spread out. As you halved the water in the next syrup, and halved it again the next time, the amount of space between the sugars was also being halved. You created a *medium* and then finally a *heavy syrup*.

In fact, you completely saturated the solution of water with sugar last time. If you added even half a pound more sugar to that heavy syrup, you would not be able to dissolve it. There would not be enough room, which is another way of saying not enough water, to separate those little sugar soldiers. So, they would fall to the bottom of your container. They would precipitate out. Why does this occur?

Crystal Blue Persuasion

You know what precipitation is when it is raining, right? The air can't hold any more moisture, so it falls out as rain. Well, your syrup would become so saturated with sugar that it would literally rain sugar to the bottom of the pan.

Another way to say that the sugar is precipitating out of your syrup is to say that it is recrystallized. Remember, you started with crystals of sugar. Crystals are geometric solids of a pure molecule that fit together structurally. You have salt crystals, ice crystals, snowflake crystals, and, of course, sugar crystals. When you dissolve a crystal that is soluble in water, the water steps in to shake hands with the crystal, so to speak. Water moves the solid crystal apart and it dissolves. Add back enough sugar crystals so that you push the dissolved ones closer together, and suddenly they start to reform. They begin to interact as crystals again. They merrily go falling back, hand in hand, to the bottom of your pan. They precipitate out because you have overcome the liquid's ability to keep them apart. You have reached the saturation point in your water-sugar solution.

But it's not just about how sugar molecules saturate the water and recrystallize. Temperature and movement within that sugar-water solution is also critically important. Granny developed a forearm like a heavyweight boxing champion making you homemade candy. Why? Because she understood the principles of crystal formation, saturation, and crystal size. Even though she missed her shot at going a few rounds with Smokin' Joe Frazier, she was one tough cookie when it came to making candy.

Boil, Bubble, Toil, and Trouble

So, it's not just the amount of sugar you have suspended in your heavy syrup that makes it saturated; how fast it's moving also matters. And movement means heat energy and convection in that boiling sugar syrup.

When you make heavy simple syrup, you stop the boiling after one minute. As long as you don't stir the syrup at this point, you have a relatively clear, viscous solution. But why not stir it or agitate at this point? Well, the little sugar soldiers are lined up and separated by water, but they are teetering on the saturation point. Now, suppose you dip a spoon in there and start stirring things up. What you are doing is moving the soldiers around, increasing the chances they are going to bump into one another and recrystallize. In fact, that spoon is a gathering point for the crystals to latch on to. And when they latch on to the spoon, they concentrate themselves enough to latch on to one another. Whammo, you're growing a crystal garden. Your nice clear syrup is now resolidifying into a gritty, grainy, lumpy mess.

Normally, you aren't going to make heavy syrup and call it quits. If you're interested in making candy or caramel sauce, you need to cook that syrup further to get rid of some of the water. And as you do, it is going from a *saturated solution* to a *supersaturated* one.

> ### Chef Sez
> A **saturated solution** is one that contains the absolute maximum amount of a substance that can be dissolved and still have a stable solution. A **supersaturated solution** is one in which the substance dissolved in a liquid teeters on the edge of insolubility.

Supersaturated solutions result as you evaporate water from the syrup by heating. What you're doing is crowding those little sugar soldiers together as the water departs. As the water evaporates and the sugar gets closer together, it teeters on the edge of recrystallizing. Those crystals are so close together now that they are looking for any opportunity to rain down and form crystals on the sides or bottom of your pot.

The principles of candy and caramel sauce-making are then just different degrees of how supersaturated you let your syrup become before you stop cooking and do something with it. If you go all the way, and heat the syrup until it reaches 338°F, you make rock-hard golden-brown caramel. If you stop concentrating your syrup at specific temperature points along the way, you can fashion that syrup into the multitude of confections called candy.

Caramel Sauce

Making caramel sauce is a process of cooking sugar until it breaks apart from the high temperature into that unctuous, sticky, wonderful thing that some people claim is better than sex. You can do this two ways. (Make caramel, that is.)

You can heat sugar in a pan over direct heat. This is the dry method. A much better and safer way is to dissolve the sugar with some water, or as you just learned, make sugar syrup. This is the wet method. Make sure you start with a big sauce pot. When the sugar is nicely caramelized, you'll need room to add cream and butter to turn it into caramel sauce.

Inverting with Acids

You already know that as you boil away the water, your sugar solution is becoming supersaturated. And as you heat the supersaturated solution, you are running a risk that the least amount of agitation will cause the sugar crystal to precipitate out. One easy way to hedge your bets that this doesn't happen is to add a bit of lemon juice or vinegar when things first start to heat up.

The acid does something very special to the process. First, it splits sucrose into its two monosaccharides: glucose and fructose. This is called *inverting the sugar*. Now your syrup has three different sugar soldiers in solution. You have a bunch of sucrose that isn't converted, plus you have a bunch of free glucose and free fructose molecules running around. What this diversity in sugar populations does is decrease the chance of forming crystals. Why?

> **Chef Sez**
>
> **Invert sugar** refers to sucrose that has been partially broken down (inverted) into glucose and fructose with an acid. This inversion prevents crystallization and makes smoother candies, frostings, and confections.

Well, sugar crystals like to keep their form pure. When the neighborhood only has sucrose around, it's pretty easy finding another sucrose to shake hands with as the water exits stage right. Inverting the sugars puts some fructose and glucose soldiers in the neighborhood, so to speak. They interfere with sucrose getting back together. And because there aren't enough free fructose or free glucose soldiers around to run into one another, there is less chance of them forming crystals. It's all probability and chance. Say you were only one of five people waiting to win the lottery; you might have a good chance of cashing in. But chance says you're one out of a million, so your odds go down. Inverting sugar just increases the odds that one sucrose molecule will not find another sucrose molecule to hook up with.

> **Too Hot to Handle**
>
> Because sugar reaches such high temperatures, it can cause very bad burns. Syrup clinging to the thermometer or splattering from the pan can stick to fragile skin, leaving you blistered or worse. If you do come in contact with hot syrup, immediately run the affected area under cold water. Do not try to wipe it off; this will just spread the syrup and cause an even worse burn.

Another thing that decreases the probability of getting crystal lumps is to paint cold water on the inside of the pan with a clean pastry brush. This will redissolve any crystals that might form there as water boils and evaporates from the pan.

So, now you're cooking your sugar syrup slowly, all the while watching it get thicker and thicker. You added a spoonful of lemon juice and washed down the sides with water. If you have a candy thermometer, you can watch the temperature increase. When it gets near 320°F, you will see a distinct color change in the sugar. It changes from thick clear syrup to a golden color, similar to a cup of weak tea. When that happens, take the pan off the heat and start watching it. The residual heat in the pan will continue to darken the caramel as the temperature climbs toward 338°F.

If you were to leave the caramel cooking on direct heat, it would turn a very dark brown, going well above 338°F. It would scorch and burn and smoke very quickly. At these high temperatures, the sugar has broken down into hundreds of small carbon molecules. And carbon can ignite, just like a carbon charcoal briquette. So, stop cooking when the solution becomes light tan.

Brown Is Beautiful

At this point, your caramel is a soup of interesting compounds caused by the breakdown of simple sugar. Things like furans and pyranone and benzene and other alcohols and esters. You might smell aromas of ripe fruit, yeast, beer, or butter. In fact, your nose would be correct, because many of the compounds formed by cooking are very similar to things you love in nature. For instance, ripening fruit produces many of these same compounds. Or when yeasts and molds break down food molecules, they produce similar things. So, the smells and attractions in caramel are just like food memories you have experienced elsewhere. Caramel, of course, tastes as bittersweet as it smells, and its specific flavor combo is unique.

Lab Project

For a caramel sauce, combine 2¼ cups granulated sugar with 1 cup of water in a large saucepan. Stir to combine, and brush down the sides of the pan to remove any sugar crystals. Bring to a boil over medium heat. Add 2 teaspoons of lemon juice and continue cooking until the sugar caramelizes, turning dark brown. Remove the pan from the heat and gradually add 2 cups of heavy cream. Be careful, as the hot caramel may splatter. Add 2 tablespoons of butter. Return to the heat for about 2 minutes, stirring to melt the butter and blend all the ingredients. Cool completely at room temperature. Stir before using, and keep refrigerated for up to three weeks.

Plain sugar cooked to the light-tea color isn't caramel sauce yet. Now you take the pan off the heat and let it cool for two to three minutes. Heat some heavy cream to a simmer. You want to heat about a pint of cream for every pound of sugar you melted. Carefully pour the heated cream into the caramelized sugar, stirring as you do. Add a dollop of butter, and then cook and stir it all together for one or two minutes. Cool it a bit and share the warm sauce with friends and family. Anyone for ice cream?

Candy Man

Let's go back to the future now. If you start over and begin to heat more simple syrup, but don't heat it all the way to 338°F, you will see all the various stages for candy-making. Each point on the sugar saturation trail corresponds to the correct temperature, and, ultimately, to the correct sugar concentration, to fashion the syrup into things like fudge, hard candy, taffy, caramels, or brittle.

Lucky for us, it's really been worked out. All you need to do is measure the temperature with a candy thermometer or use the tried-and-true ice-water test to tell what stage your sugar has reached, so that you know when to stop the heat. The following table shows the temperature of the syrup and the type of candy that you can create.

The Stages of Sugar for Candy-Making

Syrup Temperature in °F	Candy	Cold Water Test
230–234	Syrups	Thread: Thin, no ball
235–240	Fudge & Fondant	Soft ball: Easily flattens
244–248	Caramel	Firm ball: Will not flatten
250–266	Nougat & Divinity, Rock	Hard ball: Flattens, but plastic
270–290	Taffy & Butterscotch	Soft crack: Separates into threads, not brittle
300–310	Brittle	Hard crack: Separates into threads, brittle
320–338	Caramel	Clear liquid turns amber then dark brown

To do the cold water test, get a cup of ice water and a teaspoon. As you boil the syrup, periodically drop a bit of it into the water and see what forms. Pick up the cooled sugar drop, and roll it around on your fingers to test it. You can demonstrate all the forms if you work quickly and go all the way.

It's important to understand that once a temperature has been passed, the syrup won't revert to that same stage as it cools back down. Temperature is used here to indicate the amount of water remaining in the solution. Once a stage has been passed, the water won't return, just because the temperature falls back to some magic number again. In other words, if you overshoot the mark in trying to make soft-ball syrup (240°F), you can't pull the pan from the heat at, say, the soft-crack stage (270°F) and wait for the cooler temperature to return. The water is gone; you must start over.

Fudging It

Let's say you want to make creamy fudge. You would stop heating the syrup when it reaches 235 to 240°F, which is the soft-ball stage. And how did grandma get that nice smooth, silky fudge instead of that granular stuff that maybe you've ended up with? Well, it all goes back to forming those crystals again; time to recall those little soldiers of supersaturated glucose. Remember, they are now on the edge of teetering into crystals. Of course, what you do next determines whether the crystals grow big or grow small together.

And what you do next is beat the dickens out of the candy after it cools down a bit. Or, more likely, you beat the dickens out of it after it cools down a bit with other flavoring ingredients added into the mix.

You will add in some milk, butter, peanut butter, or maybe some chocolate. And what do these fats and sugars do besides flavor the fudge? Well, they keep the crystals from growing large as you beat the syrup into fudge. Just like lemon juice interfered with crystals forming when you made caramel sauce, these flavor additives do the same things in fudge recipes. The fats and sugars make it more difficult for the crystals to stick together in large clumps. Imagine those little soldiers trying to shake hands with a bunch of greasy, fat-laden palms. Not too easy to hang on, is it? Hey, they might be able to form pairs handshaking, but the fat greatly reduces the possibility of long lines of sugars sticking together to form big crystals.

How fast you beat it is important, too. If you just lollygag around and stir the fudge like you are out of energy, you are giving the crystals time to grow large and grainy. You are moving the soldiers too slowly, so, what happens is that as soon as the first few soldiers latch on to one another and form a crystal, others are just floating by and can hop on their backs. This gives you a big ball of crystals and a nasty lump of fudge.

If you beat the dickens out of it, though, you are whipping those soldiers around so fast that they are lucky to latch on to one buddy, not five. So, the smaller crystals will surely fall out as the fudge cools, but you control the smaller size by going faster as you beat it. Grandma was no dummy, and she sure knew how to beat the pants off of fudge to get small crystals, not large ones.

Chocolate 101

Chocolate evokes emotions. It has a romantic past and represents love today. It kindles passion, lust, desire, satiety, and feelings of well-being. It is craved and carnal. And if that isn't enough to juice you up, the science of chocolate is steeped in controversy, sometimes as hot as the drink you make from it.

Cocoa beans, which are crushed to make chocolate, were once used as money and were considered more valuable than gold. Today, chocolate is big business. Once the privy of gods, kings, rulers, and saints, it is now marketed in voluminous quantities and forms. Though chocolate is a contemporary food without class distinctions, it retains the aura of godliness. Chocolate, and the possession of it, is still revered by lots of folks.

Food for Thought

Imitation chocolate is made using vegetable fats rather than pure cocoa butter. These fats melt at higher temperatures, making the chocolate more durable and less expensive.

From Crush to Candy

Unfortunately, you aren't going to grow cocoa plants in your backyard garden. Most of the world's cocoa beans come from West Africa or Brazil, within 20 degrees north or south of the equator. Beans are harvested, dried on the ground, and allowed to go through a mild fermentation, which helps break down the bean while adding flavor. The beans are then roasted. Roasting browns the cocoa bean and creates over 400 different chemicals. Phenols, our antioxidant friends, actually make chocolate a healthy food.

Chocolate candy doesn't just come oozing out of cocoa beans, however. After fermenting and roasting them, the beans are cracked into small pieces called nibs. The nibs are further ground and heated, creating very thick chocolate liquor or mass. Then this magic elixir is separated into cocoa butter and cocoa powder. The powder is formed into cakes, which may be ground a third time into a very fine powder. Cocoa powder is now used to make beverages.

The development of Dutch-processed or alkalized cocoa was pioneered in the 1800s. In this process, the nibs are exposed to an alkaline solution that raises their normally acidic pH from 5.0 to 8.0. This less-acidic cocoa powder has a milder flavor, darker color, and dissolves more easily in liquids. This process is typically done to contemporary cocoa powders, especially for hot-chocolate mixes. In some mixes, sugar and lecithin, an emulsifier, are added, which further enhance the ability of the cocoa power to dissolve.

Creamy and Dreamy

But what about that stuff called cocoa butter? Well, this fatty extract from the cocoa bean is used for everything from cosmetics to candy. It resists oxidation because of the nature of the saturation of the fats. It is highly saturated, so oxygen has less of a chance of snatching off hydrogen. And the structure of cocoa butter plays the old crystal game just like sugar. Cocoa butter forms a variety of crystals, each with a well-defined melting point. When cocoa butter melts in the mouth, it has a pleasant cooling effect as it takes up heat in the process. You know what happens when you add water to ice. The heat draws from the water into the ice and you taste cold water; same thing with cocoa butter. As it melts in your mouth, heat moves from you to it. The richness, smoothness, and cooling effect of the fat are some of the attractions of chocolate.

The Chocolate Palate

You can have your chocolate either white or dark. The difference between them is how the cocoa butter is blended with other ingredients. A commercial confectioner use various recipes or blends, much the same way a winemaker mixes grape juices to create nuances in taste, aroma, and color.

To make a rich chocolate for use in confectionary work, cocoa butter is added to the chocolate liquor to enrich it. If no sugar is added, it is unsweetened chocolate. This is great for baking purposes, but probably isn't anyone's first choice as a confection. By adding various amounts of sugar, the chocolate flavor progresses from unsweetened, through bittersweet, semisweet, and sweet. In addition, vanilla or other flavorings, milk solids, and emulsifiers such as lecithin may be added enhance the flavor and help keep everything together.

The difference between bittersweet and milk chocolate depends upon the ratio of cocoa solids to sugar and milk solids. Bittersweet chocolate has a higher percentage cocoa solids (40 to 60 percent) and lower sugar content. Sweet milk chocolate has more sugar at the expense of cocoa solids (30 to 40 percent).

> **Now You're Cooking**
> Different brands and different countries produce different styles of chocolate. For example, German bittersweet chocolate is actually somewhat sweeter than French or Italian semi-sweet products. The only way to determine which style you prefer is to taste a wide range of chocolates from various countries. Tough work, but only you can do it.

White chocolate is about an equal mixture of cocoa butter, powdered milk solids, and sugar. It doesn't contain any cocoa solids, so some people don't even consider it to be chocolate. White chocolate is more susceptible to spoilage and off-flavors because it contains no cocoa solids. Those extracts contain things like phenols. Recall from Chapter 7 that phenols are color pigments and antioxidants found in vegetables. Phenols do the same thing for chocolate that they do for you: keep oxygen and oxidation at bay. So, low phenols in white chocolate equates with more chances for rancidity.

The Shining

The beauty of chocolate is its spit and polish shine. The pros use a chocolate called *couverture*. You might say that great chefs who dabble in chocolate leave nothing to chance. To get that shine, the cocoa fat must be tempered. Chocolate contains four primary types of butterfat crystals: alpha, beta, beta prime, and gamma. Tempering is a process of creating beta crystals in the greatest percentage concentration. Your objective is to grow plenty of beta crystals. And if you are successful, they crowd out all the other crystals and give the chocolate a beautiful shine and smooth mouth feel.

> **Chef Sez** _____
> **Couverture** is professional quality chocolate that is extremely smooth and glossy. It contains a minimum of 32 percent cocoa butter.

It's all a matter of knowing the melting point of each crystal. The alpha crystal melts at 70°F, gamma at 63°F, and beta prime crystals at 81°F. Beta, the one you want, melts at 95°F.

The trick, and it can be challenging, is to encourage the beta crystals to outgrow everyone else. It is the story of the little soldiers all over again. As long as you can separate out the crystals you want in a gradient of temperatures, you can be successful. You then can encourage the crystals you choose to hook up more frequently. So, whether you are tempering chocolate crystals or making fudge with small crystals, you are in control by what you do, or don't do.

So, to temper the chocolate, you first melt it to a temperature of about 110°F. This melts all of the crystals in the butter fat. You now have a blank slate. You then cool down the chocolate, while adding in some tempered chocolate as you do. This is called seeding. Seeding is a process of adding back the type of crystal that you want to end up with, a little trick to give you an edge. Since tempered chocolate has more beta crystals, you are stacking the deck toward beta already.

Now, you need be careful to never let the temperature of the chocolate cool to 81°F, the point at which beta prime crystals form. Nor do you want to go above 95°F, where the beta crystals will melt again. So, the happy medium between those temperatures is where you want the melted chocolate to live.

Once the beta crystals are formed and stable, and your chocolate has cooled, they dominate over all the other crystals. But all things do not last forever. If your chocolate loses temper, it takes on a dull, sometimes milky white appearance called bloom. This occurs if the chocolate is mishandled. Like the story of the three bears, it might get too hot or too cold. This lets the other crystals get back in the ballgame. So, storing tempered chocolate at room temperature (around 70°F) is best. Also, keep it well wrapped to prevent the fat from absorbing odors.

Never store chocolate in the refrigerator. Here you will cause bloom, but it can be another kind. Now, what happens to your chocolate is that sugar rather than fat seeps out. In sugar bloom, moisture condenses on the surface of the cold chocolate and dissolves sugar. When the water evaporates, a white dust of sugar crystals is left behind. It won't be pleasant to look at or to eat.

The Least You Need to Know

- Simple syrup is simply sugar dissolved in water.
- Temperature and sugar concentration determine what kinds of confections can be made from simple syrups.
- Small crystals are encouraged to grow in fudge by rapidly stirring cooked sugar with fats and other ingredients.
- Caramel is the result of cooking sugar to the point of caramelization, when hundreds of browning products are formed.
- Various types of chocolate candy are based on different blends of chocolate liquor, cocoa butter, sugar, and milk solids.
- Chocolate should never be stored in the refrigerator. It holds best when well wrapped at room temperature.

22

Custard's Last Stand

In This Chapter

- ◆ What's in an egg?
- ◆ Eggs and heat
- ◆ Custard: to bake or to stir

Eggs are an amazing food. There is no doubt that the entire French repertoire of techniques for cooking would be severely limited if it were not for the egg. Eggs are the foundation of a book full of savory and sweet preparations. One area where eggs are absolutely essential is when you dive into the realm of custards. Making custard is one of the many variations on egg cookery. So, you need to understand a little about the egg before you move on to custards.

The Chicken or the ...?

Eggs are seeds. You've already looked at seeds as grains, legumes, and nuts. Those plant seeds look quite a bit different than the egg. But, like any good seed, eggs are designed to produce the next generation. While chickens are a culinary wonder themselves, cooks intercept their eggs and use them in wonderful ways, also.

> ### Too Hot to Handle
>
> *Salmonella* is potentially found on the surface of eggs and, in less than 1 percent of all eggs produced, on the interior of the egg. So, to prevent food-borne illness caused by this microorganism, safe handling is essential. Eggs must be kept refrigerated. This will keep organisms from multiplying unchecked. Wash your hands after working with eggs, avoid cross contamination between raw eggs and other foods, and cook eggs to at least 140°F for 3½ minutes to greatly reduce or eliminate any health risks.

The Package

The egg contains three of the four primary classes of food molecules. It is 50 percent water, 34 percent lipid, and 16 percent protein. When you look inside a chicken egg, what you see are two major zones: the so-called *yolk* and the *white*.

The yolk is about a third of the weight of an average egg. This is a handy little fact to know. The average large egg weighs about 1.6 ounces. So, the yolk will weigh one third of that amount, or just over ½ ounce. If you encounter recipes that tell you to add so many ounces of eggs, now you can figure out the approximate number of yolks you will need. Most recipes call for large eggs, but if it isn't clear, be careful. Using small, medium, or extra-large eggs obviously can affect your recipe outcome.

> ### Chef Sez
>
> Egg **white** is the clear, translucent part of an egg. It is comprised of three different albumin proteins, vitamins, and minerals. Egg **yolk** is the central, yellow part of an egg. It is a thin membrane filled with proteins, lipids, vitamins, and minerals.

The yolk contains every bit of the egg's lipids and half its total protein. Egg yolk gets its color from xanthophylls pigments, and the color can vary, depending on what the chicken was fed. The yolk was designed to nourish the developing embryo, so it contains many vitamins and minerals.

The white is the albumin of the egg. Egg whites have half the total protein content of the egg. The appearance of egg white as a translucent gel-like mass is due to the types of proteins found there. You can look at a fresh egg and see that the white has sloping ridges; it sits up more around the yolk. The thick protein closest to the yolk is called the chalaziferous white proteins, while right next to them is a thin zone of inner white proteins. Next, there is a thicker ridge of outer white proteins surrounded by thin outer white proteins. This alternating thick and thin anatomy of egg whites tells you the relative freshness when you crack an egg open. Older eggs will be runny and thin, which indicates that the thick proteins have aged and lost firmness. The main proteins of egg albumin are ovalbumin, conalbumin, and globulins.

Now You're Cooking

Meringue is produced by whipping egg whites into a foam, usually with the addition of sugar. As you whisk egg white, the proteins denature to give structure. Denatured protein traps millions of air bubbles and water in a lattice network. Overbeating egg whites will break down the protein lattice, causing meringue to weep trapped water. Room-temperature whites give greater volume. An acid such as cream of tartar (use 1/2 teaspoon per 2 egg whites) will improve stability. Sugar adds flavor and shine, and coats the proteins to improve stability. Fat, even a tiny bit of egg yolk, is the enemy of meringue, as it decreases the foam's surface tension.

The egg yolk and whites are anchored together by chalazae, which are thick protein chords. The chalazae keep the yolk stably positioned within the whites. Thick, prominent chalazae indicate that you have a fresh egg. A thin membrane called the vitelline surrounds the yolk contents and keeps this little package of goods intact and separate from the white.

Of course, covering everything is the egg shell. It is surprisingly porous, which means that air can flow into and out of the egg. The egg is breathing. The air cell, found at the fat end of the egg, is the built-in respirator designed for the chick as it grows. The space actually gets bigger as the egg ages. Old eggs float in water; it's another way to test freshness. By the way, the color of an eggshell only signifies the breed of chicken. The nutritional content and flavor of brown and white eggs doesn't differ in any way. So, no matter which little package you prefer—brown or white—how they cook will be identical.

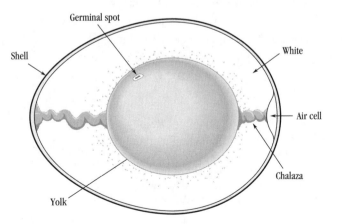

The parts of an egg

Germinal spot

Shell

White

Air cell

Chalaza

Yolk

Food for Thought _____

Eggs are sold by grade and size. Grades are based on interior quality. Both AA and A eggs are good for any use; B eggs are better for baking, scrambling, or in bulk products where appearance won't matter. The size of the egg corresponds to its weight in ounces per dozen. Six sizes make their way to market: Peewee, Small, Medium, Large, Extra Large, and Jumbo. Each change in size corresponds to an increase in 3 ounces per carton. A dozen Large eggs weigh 24 ounces; Medium are 21 ounces; Extra-large are 27 ounces, and so on. Most recipes call for Large eggs. So, if you substitute a different size egg, be sure to do the math to adjust the number accordingly.

It's Solid Gold

Before you tackle custard, it's best to understand how an egg cooks. This simple experiment will illustrate the process. Begin by having your first cup of coffee some morning, and then get out a small frying pan (nonstick is best), eggs, and some butter.

Melt the butter in the pan on high heat until it just starts to foam. If you add a drop of water to the pan and it sizzles, you know the pan is hot enough. Now turn the heat down to low and crack the egg into the pan. You will see an almost-instant change in the outer edges of the egg white. The heat of the pan is cooking the egg-white proteins. The thinnest part of the egg starts to cook first, so you can see the heat work its way from there toward the center. As the proteins denature and coagulate, they change from clear to opaque and become firm. Eventually, the yolk will also become firm and change to a matte yellow. Within two to three minutes, you have a nicely fried egg.

You can repeat the experiment by cleaning out your pan and frying another egg without butter or oil. Of course, this works best if you use nonstick cookware. Again, heat the pan on high, checking the temperature with a drop of water after a minute or two. The water should scoot around, sizzle, and evaporate. Now turn the heat to low and cook another egg. You will see the same changes. But what is important here is that you have added nothing to the pan except the egg.

In both of the eggs—cooked with butter and dry—you should have seen steam rising as the egg cooked. In fact, when both eggs are done, you see a little bit of water left in the pan as well as on the surface of the egg. Obviously, in the egg cooked dry, this had to come from the egg, not the butter.

Water is being cooked out of the egg. As heat is conducted into the center of the egg, proteins all along the way are denaturing and then coagulating. You control how rapidly it occurs by the amount of heat and the duration of cooking. And as the proteins denature and coagulate, they squeeze out water. So, just like cooking meat proteins, you are affecting the movement of water. The longer it cooks, the more water is squeezed out, and the more dense and dry it becomes. You can get to a point that the egg is like rubber, as you have collapsed all the proteins and cooked out most of the water.

If you could measure the temperature from the outside edge of the egg, right on through to the yolk as it was cooking, you would find a gradient. Thin and thick egg-white proteins coagulate between 145 and 150°F. As they cook, light can no longer pass through them. They coagulate and turn white, reflecting light back. The proteins in the yolk begin to set at 160°F. They change from shiny to dull yellow. By this time, the temperature has reached 180°F, and the egg-yolk protein has firmly coagulated. So, to make a sunny-side-up egg, you would need to stop cooking it before all the egg-yolk protein coagulated, which is somewhere between 160 and 180°F.

Custards

Now that you know what heat does to egg proteins, it's time to think about cooking *custard*. And your objective now is not to make scrambled eggs, but to use those eggs to thicken a liquid to a smooth consistency. Though custards can be made using whole eggs, or even the egg whites, typical recipes involve only egg yolks.

Custards can be sweet or savory. Sweet custard might be served as flan, crème brûlée, or vanilla custard sauce. Savory custards are made in the same way, but are flavored with herbs, cheese, vegetables, or meat.

> **Chef Sez**
> **Custard** is a liquid thickened by the denaturing and coagulation of egg proteins.

For simplicity's sake, let's just say that you are going to cook egg-yolk proteins to make a sweet custard. The principles will be the same for savory custards, only the flavoring ingredients will vary. In most (but certainly not all) custards, the liquid being thickened is milk, cream, or half-and-half. Sweet custard also involves sugar. So, egg yolk, milk/cream, and sugar are your basic ingredients. What happens when you mix them and add heat?

That depends. Custard can be made by one of two methods: on the stovetop in a saucepan, or baked in the oven. The method you choose makes a significant difference in how you control the denaturing of the egg proteins.

Getting Stirred Up

Let's first think about what happens when you make *stirred custard*. You know what would happen if you put an egg yolk in your saucepan, turned up the heat, and began to cook. It would quickly look something like scrambled eggs, which is not what you want in creamy custard. Combining that mass of cooked scrambled-egg protein into milk and sugar is not going to be a pretty sight.

Chef Sez

A **stirred custard** is cooked to a creamy, pourable consistency by stirring it in a pan on the stovetop.

So, to get the creamy, pourable texture that you want in stirred custard, you have to combine the ingredients in a certain way. You need to protect the egg proteins from the heat. And the way to do that is by tempering them. This means you are gradually going to introduce the egg yolks to heat. You are going to do so by heating the milk or cream, and then using that to warm the eggs.

Custard Sauce

Temperature control is important from start to finish. So, before you begin, run some cold water into the sink and throw in some ice cubes. You will soon see why it's important to have this ice bath ready. Now bring your milk to a simmer. Milk simmers between 180 and 205°F, so when it just starts to bubble around the edges, it's ready.

While the liquid is heating, whisk together the sugar and the egg yolks. Whisking the sugar into the eggs gives them their first protective coat. Sugar coats the egg proteins, delaying the effect of the heat. It's kind of like putting on sunscreen before going to the beach. You gradually tan and don't burn. You want to gradually cook the egg protein, not harden it up right away.

When the milk is hot, gradually add it to your egg yolk-sugar mixture, stirring constantly. It's easiest to pour part of the hot liquid into the egg yolks and sugar while whisking them together. After incorporating about half the hot liquid into the eggs, pour the tempered egg mixture back into the saucepan with the remaining hot milk. Put the pan back on the stove and cook over medium-high heat, stirring continually with a whisk or heat-resistant rubber spatula.

As you stir, the mixture will begin to thicken right before your eyes. If you use a thermometer, stop cooking just before the temperature reaches 180°F. If you don't have a thermometer, take a clean spoon and dip it into the custard. If the liquid clings to the back of the spoon, and you can run your finger across the coated spoon without the custard running back together, you are done. Never let this custard boil. When it is thick enough, immediately pour the custard into a clean bowl and cool it in the ice water that's ready to go in your sink.

If all goes well, instead of just making scrambled eggs, you are controlling how the eggs cook. The proteins must denature without coagulating. This is the first secret to custard-making. Think of it this way. The egg proteins will denature as the hot milk cooks the protein. You want this to happen. But instead of the egg proteins rapidly going from a denatured, unwound state to the coagulated curd of scrambled eggs, you have controlled the process.

The liquid surrounding the proteins slows down the transfer of heat. As you stir, you also are exercising some control over the heat. Stirring blends the convection currents evenly and doesn't allow pockets of heat to build up and overcook those egg proteins. All is fine in custard land as long as you do not exceed 180°F. At that point, you begin to make curds from your denatured proteins, just like you do in scrambled eggs. And no amount of stirring can rescue things once the cascade of coagulating proteins starts.

So, what causes the thickening? The thickening power of stirred custard occurs as proteins unwind, separate, and trap liquid between them. The combined effect of denatured protein floating around in the liquid, along with the fat and proteins of the milk or cream, decreases the ability of the water to flow as freely as it could in the uncooked state. This is similar to the way that a gelatinized starch thickens sauces by impeding water movement. But unlike cooked starch, which goes through retrogradation, forming a solid as it cools, proteins in stirred custard do not retrograde. So, this means that the vanilla sauce you made yesterday and kept in the refrigerator overnight is still the right texture and ready to use the next day. This is the beauty and functionality of well-made stirred custard. Of course, adding different flavorings is the art of the technique. If you can master the science, the rest is a piece of cake.

Lab Project

For vanilla custard sauce, heat 1 cup of milk and 1 cup of heavy cream in a saucepan. Add half of a split vanilla bean, if desired. Whisk 6 large egg yolks and 10 tablespoons (5 ounces) of granulated sugar together in a bowl. Temper the egg yolks with a portion of the hot milk, and then pour all of the egg mixture into the saucepan. Cook the sauce over medium heat, stirring constantly, until it is thick enough to coat the back of a spoon. Do not allow it to boil. Strain the cooked sauce into a clean bowl and chill over an ice bath. If you did not use a vanilla bean, add 1 tablespoon of vanilla extract at this time.

Pastry Cream

A thicker variation of stirred custard is called pastry cream. Pastry cream is used as the filling for éclairs, fruit tarts, and all sorts of French confections. This custard should be more pudding-like than pourable. So, how do you get a stirred custard to thicken like a pudding but not look or taste like scrambled eggs?

Food for Thought _____

Another variation on custard is called *sabayon* in France or *zabaglione* in Italy. For this version, egg yolks, wine, and sugar are whisked vigorously over a water bath. Wine replaces the milk or cream, with marsala being the traditional flavor. The action of whisking and the gentle heat of the water bath denatures the egg proteins. The whisking introduces air, which creates a light, frothy custard. Savory sabayon can be made by removing the sugar and incorporating vegetable purée or stock as an ingredient. In this case, the dessert custard becomes a savory sauce, much like hollandaise.

The safety factor is the addition of cornstarch or flour to the basic stirred custard. In fact, starches not only give you a safety margin for not making scrambled eggs, the process even involves boiling the mixture to create additional thickening. You know you could never boil basic stirred custard without starch, so what's going on here?

Lab Project _____

For vanilla pastry cream, sift ¼ cup of cake or pastry flour with ¾ cup of sugar and set aside. Whisk ½ cup of whole milk with 6 Large egg yolks in a large bowl, and then add the flour mixture and whisk until completely smooth. Meanwhile, heat 1½ cups of milk in a saucepan. As soon as the milk simmers, whisk part of it into the egg mixture to temper the eggs. Pour the eggs into the saucepan of milk and return to medium heat. Stir constantly until the custard thickens. As it thickens, the custard will go through a lumpy stage; keep stirring vigorously and it will smooth out and thicken just before coming to a boil. Allow the custard to boil for about 1 minute, stirring constantly. Pour the custard into a clean bowl (without straining) and add 2 tablespoons of butter and 1 tablespoon of vanilla. Fold the flavorings in gently. Place a piece of plastic wrap directly on the surface of the cream and chill in an ice bath.

Starch prevents the egg proteins from coagulating by getting in the way of the denatured proteins. The gelatinized starches prevent egg proteins from coagulating and collapsing upon themselves. Just like the little bit of sugar you used to make your sweet stirred custard gave you some measure of protection by coating the proteins, gelatinized starches give maximum protection, even at a boil. Pastry cream is formed as proteins and gelatinized starch hook up into a protein-starch connection. The starches reinforce and stabilize the threads of denatured protein. The end result is pudding-like custard.

Lovin' in the Oven

This brings us to the second variation in the custard connection. *Baked custard* is one that is thickened in the oven rather than directly on the stovetop. Doing it this way does something different to the egg proteins. The finished custard will be firmer and less creamy; it can be cut, not poured.

The secret for successful baked custards is the use of a water bath. Because water's temperature won't exceed 212°F, it slows down heat transfer. So, in effect, you are surrounding the cooking process in a protective layer of water, thus tempering heat flow to the egg proteins.

Water can protect from overheating because it has a high *specific heat*. This means that water can absorb more heat without increasing in temperature than just about any other liquid on Earth. That is why you use water as part of the coolant in your automobile. It soaks up excess engine heat.

> **Chef Sez**
> A baked custard is cooked to a gel-like consistency in an oven using a water bath. **Specific heat** measures the number of calories needed to raise the temperature of 1 gram of a substance by 1°C. Water has a particularly high specific heat, meaning that it absorbs a great deal of energy (calories) before the temperature rises.

You are water-cooled, too, which means that all the water inside you absorbs much of your body heat, moving it away from your tissues. This is good because it keeps you from cooking. Imagine if you were filled with oil instead of water. Can you say fry, baby?

Baked Custard

So, what's the basic technique for these baked custards? Begin by making the custard base and portioning it into your containers, usually small ovenproof ramekins or custard cups. Arrange the cups in a cake pan or roasting pan. Allow room between the cups so that they can be surrounded by water. Place the pan on the oven rack and carefully pour water into the pan. The water should come to about halfway up the side of the custard cups. Be sure to avoid splashing or spilling water into the custard. Sometimes you cover the pan with aluminum foil to create a steam bath; sometimes you don't. It depends on what you are making. Now carefully slide the oven rack and pan into the oven and close the door.

The oven temperature is usually about 325°F. Low heat is another measure of control. Covering the pan with aluminum foil gives you more protection as it keeps the tops of the custard from over-browning. Remember, you do not have the luxury of stirring these custards, so the heat needs to be as gentle as possible. As egg proteins are gently denaturing in the oven, they are thickening the liquids, just as they do in stirred custard.

Baked custard may be either sweet or savory. The addition of other ingredients also adds a measure of protection from curdling by shielding the egg proteins and allowing them to cook slowly. But it is important that you don't overcook baked custards. Egg proteins will begin to coagulate when the temperature reaches about 180 to 190°F. If you overshoot the mark, the proteins will fully coagulate. This means that they go through the same changes as scrambled eggs. The clumps of coagulated proteins, now inside your nice little custard cups, release water. The water is trapped as pockets of moisture between the curds. You can actually see this moisture running out as the custard is sliced or unmolded from the container. But by then it's too late.

Accurate timing is the best way to prevent overcooking and to get perfect baked custards. Remove baked custards from the oven when the outer edges are just set but the center still jiggles slightly. Carryover-cooking will finish the job. Let the custard cool gradually. Another way to test for doneness is to insert a thin knife about halfway between the edge and the center. If it comes out clean, the custard is done. Either way, it's all a matter of heat, timing, and water.

Lab Project

For old-fashioned baked egg custard, bring 1 quart of whole milk to a simmer. Meanwhile, whisk together 4 whole eggs, $\frac{1}{2}$ cup sugar, $\frac{1}{2}$ teaspoon salt, and 1 teaspoon vanilla. Slowly whisk the hot milk into the egg mixture. Strain the liquid and divide it into 8 to 10 lightly buttered custard cups. Sprinkle nutmeg over the custards and bake in a water bath at 325°F for 45 to 60 minutes.

The Least You Need to Know

- ◆ Eggs contain proteins that denature when cooked and thicken liquids into custard.
- ◆ Temperature control and the presence of sugar or starch affect the consistency of the custard.
- ◆ Creamy stirred custards are cooked on the stove top, but must never be boiled.
- ◆ Starches from flour or cornstarch are used to make a stirred custard called pastry cream.
- ◆ Baked custards are cooked in a low temperature oven in a water bath to slowly denature the egg protein and produce a sliceable gel.

Part 6

Hitting the Sauce

The art and the science of cooking meet in sauce-making. Nothing adorns a plate of food as nicely as a well-made sauce. It's the artist's accent on cooking. But it is also the chemist's cauldron because sauces are precise mixtures. Lest you be afraid of diving into the sauce pot, remember that long before there were food chemists explaining how sauces work, there were grandmas making them.

Sauces can be simple or complex, sweet or savory, animal or vegetable based. They can be thickened with starch or butter or eggs, and then flavored with whatever suits your taste. Just remember that "too hot, too fast, or too much means too bad," and all your sauces will be a success. Taking a peek at sauce science will obviously help you become a more accomplished cook.

23

Stocking Up

In This Chapter

- ◆ The Bone Ranger
- ◆ Going slow and easy
- ◆ Light or dark
- ◆ Fish vs. fowl vs. beast vs. plant

When I was a kid, I kept a shrine to my mom's rabbit gravy in my bedroom. It was a gravy boat with votive candles on either side. I nearly rubbed the etchings off our blue-flowered Corningware plates, sopping up that stuff with a piece of homemade bread. We've lost a bit of confidence in making sauces and gravies like that because we think we need to slave over the stove like we think Mom did. Actually, a little advanced planning and some knowledge of fundamentals is all we need.

Great French chefs are probably weaned on that foundation of classic cuisine—*stock*. They called it a *fond de cuisine*. It's where good cooking becomes great cooking. Classical sauces begin with good stocks. And a special sauce can become any chef's personal signature.

As we've said before, it's all about the water. If you can simmer water, you can make a stock. And if you can make a stock, you can make a sauce from scratch. Many classic sauces are simply thickened stocks. Adding a starch or *reducing* the water content of the stock through evaporation causes this thickening. The end results should have a look, flavor, and mouth feel that complement the food you are eating. Such sauces are the *real* real thing.

To make many, though certainly not all, of those sauces, you need to begin with stock. To make a stock—any stock—you need four basic ingredients: water, bones or vegetables, mirepoix, and seasonings and aromatics.

How you select, combine, and cook these ingredients determines whether you have a rich brown stock; a light, jelly-like white stock; a functional vegetable stock; or worthless dishwater stock. So, pay attention.

Not Bad to the Bone

Let's start by learning about basic meat stocks. All meat stocks have one thing in common: They are made from bones, not meat. If you are a meat eater, then you have no doubt had chicken or steak with a bone in it. Gnawing on that bone can be a treat, right? The meat around it, and the occasional joint where smaller bones come together, is packed with flavor.

Dogs love bones. Now, the fact that Fido will spend hours chewing on an old bone that appears to be barren should tell us something. What it tells us is that there is lots of good stuff somewhere inside that bone. Unfortunately, humans don't have the right teeth or jaw power to break through most large animal bones and enjoy the flavorful marrow, but we can simmer bones in water in order to extract those magic flavors.

The kind of bones used in making stock affects the final product. Bones change in size and composition as an animal grows up. We are softer when we are young; so, too, are bones. Bones contain a substance called *collagen*. The bones of younger animals are softer and contain more collagen than those from mature beasts. Veal bones, derived from young cows, are the gold standard for stock-making. Finding veal bones in the corner market's meat case can be a real

> **Chef Sez**
> **Fond** is the French term for a stock. A **stock** is a clear, unthickened liquid flavored with meat, poultry, or fish bones, aromatic vegetables, and seasonings. Simmering a liquid to remove some of its water content by evaporation is called **reducing**. The end product is called a reduction.

> **Food for Thought**
> A stock that is made from bones and meat is called a broth. Broths are used to make soups. Stocks made from bones are generally used to prepare sauces.

> **Chef Sez**
> **Collagen** means "glue-like" and refers to a connective tissue found in bones and skin. Gelatin is derived from collagen by boiling bones and collecting the jelly-like extract.

challenge for those of us working in a home lab, however. Chicken bones are much easier and cheaper to obtain, and they still make great stock. Once you learn to make a good, dark, rich chicken stock and you have the method down, then go looking for veal bones, beef bones, or Tyrannosaurus Rex bones, if you like.

Slow and Steady for Success

Bones seem tough and hard. After all, they keep animals upright against the forces of gravity, right? Down deep inside, however, bones are nothing but softies. Collagen actually melts, just like ice cream but in a slightly different way. With enough heat and the right amount of acidity, gelatin will form from collagen in our water extract, right on the stovetop. And that's a good thing because that gelatin helps make great sauces.

Of course, all of the bone doesn't disintegrate. Because you want the stock to be as clear as possible and not cloudy, you need to be careful when making stocks from bones. Always start with fresh cold water. Cold water enables you to bring the temperature of the stock up more gradually. If you add hot water you will literally cook some of the proteins on the bones and these particles will float into the water. This is what causes a stock to become cloudy.

Never boil stocks, either; you only want them to simmer. When you boil stock, the bones start to break apart. The rolling movement of the boiling liquid creates eddies and currents that crash pieces of tissue into one another. As these little pieces break down, they can also cloud the stock. No amount of straining can correct the problem. So, go slow and easy.

One other thing, have a ladle handy, and once every hour or so, skim off the stuff that floats to the surface of your stock. That stuff looking like foam you see on the seashore is protein that has cooked out of the bones. Skimming it away helps keep your stock nice and clear.

Food for Thought

When purchasing bones for use in stocks, be sure to handle them with care. You can introduce harmful bacteria from improperly handling of the bones you are going to use for your stock. It's a good idea when you first get home to rinse the bones in the sink with cold, fresh, running water, drain them briefly, and then cover and store them in the refrigerator until it's time to use them. You can wrap your bones in freezer paper and keep them frozen for up to four months. Before using frozen bones, thaw them in the refrigerator. Remember to put them in a pan to collect any water given off as the bones thaw.

White vs. Brown

Stocks can either be light (white) or dark (brown) in appearance. The final color depends on what you do to the bones before simmering them. Just as you can roast a chicken to get a deep, rich, brown color, you can roast the bones to darken them. When you roast stock bones, the resulting liquid will have a richer, deeper flavor. If, however, you want the stock to be lighter and more delicate, simply simmer the bones without roasting them. So, stock can be rich and dark like a nice, rich Guinness stout, or light like a good pilsner. It's your call, but if you are making a sauce to go with a rich roast beef, we suggest roasting the bones.

The color of the stock also depends on other ingredients that you use. All stocks contain a mixture of raw vegetables. The trio of vegetables used most often is onions, carrots, and celery. The French call this mixture *mirepoix*. A nice thing about making mirepoix for stock is that you don't need to chop the veggies finely. They just get discarded when the stock is done anyway. Merely peel the carrots and onions and cut them into about 1-inch chunks. For celery, lop off the bottom and tops, and slice the stalks into 1-inch pieces. Of course, you should rinse all vegetables before adding them to the stockpot.

Chef Sez _____

Mirepoix is a mixture of two parts chopped onion, one part chopped carrot, and one part chopped celery. It is another foundation of French cooking.
Aromatics are things such as mirepoix, dried bay leaf, whole peppercorns, or springs of fresh herbs that are added to a food to enhance its aroma and flavor.

How much mirepoix do you need to make stock? Well, the French who wrote the rules on this would say that for every 8 pounds of bones you use, you need 1 pound of mirepoix. This means about 8 ounces of onion, 4 ounces of celery, and 4 ounces of carrot. Now, I don't know if you would ever buy exactly 8 pounds of bones, but you might go to the market and pick up a single chicken. The average grocery-store chicken weighs about 3 to 5 pounds, so let's split the difference and say 4 pounds.

Now, in most birds, bones and other parts of the carcass make up about half of the weight. So, for the average chicken, you'll have about 2 pounds of bones. So, if you bring a whole chicken home, take off the meat, and are left with bones for stock, you need only make up about $1/4$ pound of mirepoix. That's about the same size as a Big Mac. So, one nice medium onion peeled, one smallish carrot, and a stalk of celery is all you really need to make some chicken stock. Not much to ask for, is it?

To complete the stock recipe, you'll need to add some additional *aromatics* to the water, bones, and mirepoix. For a single chicken carcass, this means you need to add one bay leaf, two sprigs of fresh thyme, and three or four whole peppercorns. Throw in a couple of sprigs of fresh parsley, and you have it. By the way, never add any kind of salt to your stock. Stocks will eventually be reduced. This means that water will be cooked away. As the water evaporates, the flavors are concentrated, meaning you'll have more salt in less liquid. So, if you add salt now, by the time you reduce the stock and make your sauce, it will be much too salty.

Adding aromatics while simmering the stock is akin to steeping a nice cup of tea. The aromas from the herbs and pepper perfume the stock and give another level of flavor to the bone extract. If you do not have access to fresh herbs, some dried herbs such as thyme also work well for stock-making. Dried herbs contain much less water, so their fragrance and taste are much more concentrated. Because of this difference, you'll use much less of a dried herb than you would of its fresh counterpart. A good rule of thumb is to use about one third as much of a dried herb as a fresh herb. This makes for a handy kitchen conversion. There are 3 teaspoons per tablespoon, so 1 teaspoon of a dried herb will replace 1 tablespoon of a chopped fresh herb.

Now You're Cooking

The flavor of a dried herb is generally more intense than that of its fresh counterpart. When substituting dried for fresh in a recipe, use only one third to one half as much. In other words, use 1 teaspoon of dried herb for each tablespoon of fresh herb specified. Remember, you can always add, but it's pretty difficult to remove.

Lightly Does It

Let's go through the stock-making procedure step by step. We'll begin with white stock, and then progress to the brown version. Finally, we'll spend some time with fish and vegetable stocks to complete the lesson.

First, of course, you'll probably need to go shopping. Bring home a whole chicken and remove the meat for other uses. Or have your butcher do that for you. Or, just buy about 2 pounds of chicken and/or turkey wings and use them, flesh and all. Rinse the bones to clean off any blood or other stuff. Keep the bones cold while you chop the mirepoix.

Get yourself a 3-quart stockpot. Put the mirepoix and bones in the pot and just cover the bones and vegetables with fresh, cold water. Be careful to use cold, not hot, water. Clear, cold water makes the finest, clearest stock. And don't put in more than enough water to cover the bones or your stock will be too thin. Throw in your assorted aromatics, bring the liquid to a simmer, and cook it gently for two hours. Go have cup of coffee or take a break.

Going Deeper

To make a brown stock, you'll need to roast the bones and vegetables first. To do so, rinse off the bones and chop up the vegetables (mirepoix). Put everything in a lightly oiled roasting pan. Roast for about 30 minutes at 425°F. Take a peek after 15 minutes and notice that they are starting to brown nicely. It's important to allow the bones and mirepoix to develop a nice, caramel-brown surface. This is how your stock will get all of its color and much of its flavor.

Brown stock is usually made with beef or veal bones rather than chicken bones, which means one more thing is important. You must take at least four, and preferably six, hours when making stocks with these larger bones. Beef and veal bones are just more dense than chicken bones and do not give up their collagen easily. Part of this time is in the roasting of the bones, but it takes another four hours minimum (five is better) of simmering. The wait will be worth it, though, because you now have a very flavorful, rich, brown stock.

French chefs have a trick to make the stock even deeper in color and flavor. They found that adding a tomato product makes for a much better stock. You know how deep-red and succulent a well-made tomato sauce is. Tomatoes roasted in the oven become richer and darker as their natural sugars and acids cook. Now you could chop some tomatoes and roast them with the other things in the pan. But most tomatoes have a bit too much water to cook down quickly enough along with the bones. It's probably better to use simple ol' canned tomato paste for stock-making. Most of its water has already been removed, making it thicker. Just add 2 ounces of tomato paste to the roasting pan about 15 minutes after the bones or veggies begin to roast. Slather the paste all over the bones or the veggies. This exposes more of the surface area so the paste will brown better.

The acid in the tomatoes does another important thing in a stock. When water is added the acid will help dissolve collagen from the bones into gelatin. So, tomato paste does two things for you: It adds color and body through gelatin formation. Not a bad tradeoff for a little bit of paste. When everything is roasted to a nice color, put the bones in the stockpot and cover with fresh, cold water. Don't add the oil from the roasting pan to the stockpot if you can avoid it, however. Now complete the stock just like you did in "lightly does it" above. Add your aromatics; bring the stock to a gentle simmer. Remember to skim away anything that floats to the surface, as it's our old enemy, wasted protein. Oh, and have that cup of coffee, too, while you wait.

The Common Touch

After your stock (whether white or brown) has simmered nicely for about an hour, come back and skim off the foam that you'll see rising to the surface. When the stock is done, strain away the bones and vegetables. Straining can be a bit tricky and must be done with care. Never simply pour the stock from the pot into another container. For one thing, it's dangerous lifting a heavy pot of hot liquid and attempting to pour it safely. And just as important, consider what would happen to the contents if you did. Much of the debris and bad stuff has settled to the bottom of the saucepot. If you carelessly tip over the pot, you will mix up all of this sediment into the clear stock you worked so hard to make.

For a small batch, the best way to strain the stock is to line a mesh strainer with some cheesecloth. (You can buy cheesecloth at any fabric or craft store.) Fold the cloth into a double layer and make sure it covers the strainer and overlaps, so you don't have it fall into the strainer as you transfer the liquid. A good way to do this is wet the cloth, wringing out the excess water so it clings better.

Once your strainer is set, take a large ladle and gently transfer the stock from the stockpot, ladling it through the cheese-cloth-lined strainer and into a clean receiving container. If you get chunks of bone or mirepoix into the strainer, don't push on them to extract the juice; this will cloud your stock. If they build up too much, just empty the strainer into the trash every so often and continue straining. Don't worry about getting all of the stock off the bottom of the pot. Like we said, this last little bit has some sediment you don't want anyway.

Now, if you are planning on becoming a really, really, really big-time stock-maker, you can invest in a stockpot with a spigot on the bottom like the pros use. Inside the pot is a screen, so when the stock is done, you gently open the spigot and strain stocks this way. But usually for most people, investment in a large stockpot like this is not in the budget. But don't let that stop you from making stock; this liquid gold is really worth the effort, even doing it the old-fashioned way.

Stocks come off the stove very hot, somewhere between 170 and 190°F optimally. But once they are removed from the heat, the temperature quickly falls into the bacterial danger zone of 140° to 40°F if you simply let your stock cool without an ice bath. In fact, as little as one gallon of stock can remain in the danger zone for 10 to 12 hours even sitting in the refrigerator. This amount is just too much to cool quickly enough. And since stocks contain lots of the stuff that bacteria love, it won't take long before bacteria start frolicking in your pool of stock.

So, how do you cool stocks safely? First, make sure that you transfer your stock into a clean container that can conveniently fit into a sink or even a bathtub. Then stopper the sink, and put the stock container in it. Pack ice around the container until it comes about one third of the way up the side. Run some cold tap water over the ice, being careful to not splash any water into your stock. Now you have an *ice bath* that will chill the stock relatively rapidly. Stir the stock periodically to make it cool faster. When the stock has cooled to 40°F then, and only then, cover it and refrigerate.

Chef Sez

An **ice bath** is a combination of plenty of ice and a little cold water into which you can submerge a bowl or stockpot in order to cool the contents quickly. It's easy to build one in your kitchen sink, but it may mean emptying out your ice-cube maker.

When you look at your cold stock, it can appear as a deeply colored liquid that is very fluid, such as water. Or, it can be somewhat thick and jelly-like. Its appearance depends on how much collagen you were able to extract when you simmered the bones. One thing you will notice after the stock gets really cold—its surface will be covered with a layer of yellowish fat. Just take a spoon, scrape it off, and discard it. (Or use it to season some green beans or fried potatoes.)

If you don't use the stock within three days, put it back on the stove and simmer it for 20 minutes. Then rechill it in an ice bath and use within the next four days. A good rule of thumb is to keep stock for no more than one week in the refrigerator, with the proviso that you reheat it at about day three. You could also freeze the stock for up to six months. Once thawed, the same seven-day rule applies.

Whether from Land, Sea, or Air

Making stock from fish bones is different than using bones from chicken or four-legged beasts. Fish bones are relatively soft, and lucky for the fish. Having heavy bones would make swimming and avoiding predators pretty hard. Not so good for fish evolution. So, when you make stock from fish bones, you need to do so quickly but gently. Whereas a good chicken stock simmers for, say, two to three hours, and good veal or beef stock might cook for six hours, fish stock is done in about 20 minutes. So, here is another reason to eat more fish. Not only can you make a good fish stock in less time than it takes you to watch the latest episode of *Sex and the City*, you'll also be eating healthy food that's good for your heart and your brain.

What about French cuisine for vegetarians, you might ask? Is it possible to enjoy stock-making and fine sauces without the use of animal products? Well, just as collagen is the glue that holds animal tissue together, plants have their own glue substances. Jellies, jams, and preserves are examples of what happens when you cook fruits in a little water. The sweet substances create a sticky, gel-like mixture that most of us find appealing. Vegetables have glue-like substances such as the pectin and cellulose that hold the plant together. You can extract some of these for flavor, color, and texture. While the taste of vegetable stocks can be clean and refreshing, don't expect its body to be as sturdy as that of a stock made from animal bones. And a lighter stock will, of course, make for lighter sauces.

You can make a vegetable stock by simmering together just about any mixture of vegetables. Highly pungent veggies, such as cauliflower or Brussels sprouts probably aren't the best choice for a basic stock, and too many different ingredients can result in an odd, muddy flavor. So, keep it simple and start with basic mirepoix. For every pound of mirepoix, about 1 quart of water works. Throw in some aromatics and *voilà*: vegetable stock. Roasting or grilling the vegetables first will add flavor and color, kind of like browning bones does. And if you feel like adding about 2 ounces of tomato product, such as tomato paste, go right ahead.

Vegetable stocks need to simmer for only a short period of time. Cooking them too long, for more than about one hour, may produce a rather flat taste. You can skim the vegetable stock just like you did for the meat stocks, though you will likely find much less foam and debris. The straining process is identical, too. So, once you've mastered the stock procedure, you have it down for always and forever.

You don't even have to be a vegetarian to enjoy good vegetable stocks. They're great to use when you want to lighten up any sauce recipe. They have a lighter taste and lighter body on your tongue. This is because they are completely free of animal gelatin. And because the stock is of 100 percent vegetable origin, it's appropriate for vegetarian or vegan dishes. You now have a vegetarian option to help make light sauces, soups, or any entrée calling for stock.

Too Hot to Handle

Any stock, whether fish, fowl, or vegetable, can be an attractive playground for dangerous pathogenic bacteria. It is important to cool all stocks to below 41°F quickly using an ice bath. Then cover your stock well and store it in the refrigerator or freezer. Handling stocks safely will make your cooking safe and nutritious. Bon appétit!

The Least You Need to Know

◆ Simmering the bones of one chicken, a chopped onion, a carrot, a rib of celery, and some fresh herbs and peppercorns in 2 quarts of cold water for about two hours will make a small quantity of chicken stock.

◆ Never add salt to stock. Salted stocks cause overly salty sauces.

◆ Always use cold water and simmer—never boil—the stock so that it stays clear. Skim away any scum that forms on the surface to help keep the stock clear.

◆ Strain the stock into a clean container using a fine mesh strainer. Chill the stock and store it well covered in the refrigerator or freezer.

◆ Stocks can be made from bones or vegetables. Match the flavor of the stock to the sauce you intend to make.

◆ Make a variety of stocks on your day off. Freeze them to have a supply ready for cooking as needed. This impresses your dinner guests and highlights your culinary skills.

◆ Be proud and happy if your stock gels up when it gets cold. That's collagen in action.

Chapter 24

Sauces: Through Thick and Thin

In This Chapter

- Flour, fat, heat, and water
- Mother sauce: Who really wears the pants?
- Lumpless gravy and other pan sauces
- Gels and sols—the science of sauce

One of the most intimidating aspects of cooking is making sauces. Not gravy, sauce. Mom makes gravy; the French chef at Chez l'Hermitage du Maison makes sauce, right? The starting point for many great sauces is good stock, which you learned about in Chapter 23. Whatever type of stock you have, you can transform it into a whole family of classic French *sauces* with just a little more work.

To transform your stock into a classic sauce, you have to (1) thicken the liquid stock to the proper consistency, (2) strain out any particles that might interfere with the appearance or mouth feel of the sauce, and (3) do a little seasoning to suit your taste. That's it.

Roux-ed Awakening

The simplicity of thickening some sauces is based upon very natural ingredients in your kitchen: flour and fat. Your homemade stock supplies the other ingredient, a liquid base. When you combine flour and a fat you make a *roux*. Good old all-purpose flour works well. The type of fat can be any vegetable oil that you happen to have available. If you want to do it like the great French chefs, you can get a bit fancier and make clarified butter.

> ### Chef Sez
> **Roux** is a mixture of equal parts fat (oil or butter) and flour, cooked to either a light pale brownish blond or deep dark brown color. Roux is like hair color; we all have our favorite shade, and cooks have a shade for every occasion. A **sauce** is a thickened liquid used for seasoning food. Classic sauces all have a specific texture and appearance, each with its own unique flavor.

Butter Up

To make clarified butter, take a pot that can hold about 1 pound of whole, unsalted butter and melt it. Cook the butter gently, and as you do, some of the solids will float to the surface as foam, and some solids will settle on the bottom of the pan beneath the liquid butter. In the process, you are also getting rid of water (so what else is new; it's all about water anyway) hidden within the solid butter. What is left when you finish will be concentrated butterfat.

Using a large serving spoon, skim off and discard the surface foam after about every 20 minutes or so. These are the proteins casein and whey (just like Miss Muffet, by the way). The butter is ready when it clears up or "clarifies." It should have the appearance of clear, yellow, vegetable oil. You can tell when it's done (it takes about an hour) because you should be able to see the bottom of your pot where some of those solids have settled out. They appear like the surface of brown toast on the bottom as you peer down. All you need to do now is gently ladle off the butterfat, which is now about 90 percent pure fat, leaving the water and solids behind. After removing the water and the solids, you should end up with about 12 ounces of clarified butter from each pound of whole butter. You can store this clarified butter in the refrigerator, and use it as needed.

> ### Food for Thought
> Heating a quantity of whole, unsalted butter in a saucepan over medium heat until the melted fat separates from the milk solids makes clarified butter. Clarified butter is also called "ghee" in Indian cooking and is great as a condiment with spicy rich foods or sweet succulent lobster.

Why would you want to clarify butter anyway? Well, there are two reasons. First, clarified butter smokes less than whole butter. That doesn't mean it just kicked the habit by wearing a patch; it means that when you heat the butter in a frying pan, it takes longer for the butter to burn and smoke. Good for you if you do lots of frying and live in a small apartment with poor ventilation and serious fire alarms.

The protein is what would burn, so, since you skimmed it all away as the butter clarified, you get less scorching. A second reason to use clarified butter is that without the milk protein solids it is smoother. When we use it to make our roux, or use it to make Hollandaise sauce in Chapter 25, it gives a finer, better-blended sauce. But let's save that for the next lesson.

Roux Power

Once you have your clarified butter (or vegetable oil) and some flour, you're ready to make roux. For this lab experiment, measure equal parts of fat and flour into two separate containers. It is often easier to weigh the ingredients of a roux rather than do liquid measures, but using tablespoons works just fine. Remember, refrigerated clarified butter will be solid.

Measure out 4 tablespoons of butter or, using a kitchen scale, weigh out 2 ounces of butter or oil. Yes, liquid vegetable oil can be weighed, but just remember to subtract the weight of the container from the final weight on the balance to get an accurate reading. Now measure 8 tablespoons of flour or weigh out 2 ounces of flour. (Yes, that's correct; flour only weighs about half its volume.) Take a saucepan or small frying pan, add the oil, and heat it gently. Then add the flour all at once while you stir. Stir until the flour is absorbed into the butter. This works best using a wooden spoon or heat-resistant rubber spatula. Keep the mixture over medium heat, stirring as it cooks. Cooking for two to three minutes gives you what is called a pale roux with hardly any color. If you continue to cook the roux for an additional three to four minutes, it will turn a darker shade of brown. This is a blond roux. (There is no truth to the myth that blond roux has more fun.) If you cook the roux further, it turns a deep, dark chestnut brown, and then you'll have a brown roux.

Any leftover roux can be cooled and then stored in an airtight container for later use. Not surprisingly, it will turn from a liquid to a solid in your refrigerator, but that's no big deal.

For most sauces, we rarely need to go darker than a pale or blond roux. In fact, if you are making a white sauce, never cook the roux beyond the pale stage. Just cook it enough to take the starchy, floury taste out, which is what we are doing with the heat anyway. So, heating is the final step to making a well-balanced roux.

Food for Thought

Cajun and Creole cooks often use dark-brown roux to thicken their classic dishes such as gumbo. You can make a very dark roux by cooking the oil and flour slowly for about an hour on the stovetop, taking care not to burn it. Another way to get a brown roux with less chance of burning (and less time) is to bake the all-purpose flour first. Spread the flour out on a cookie sheet and toast it in a moderately hot oven (375°F) until it turns light brown. Now when you use the flour to make the roux, it starts out browner and takes less time to cook on the stovetop.

Roux as Roadblock

Heating the flour and fat is also important to create the chemistry of the roux. The melted fat coats the starches in the flour. Starches are nothing more than long chains of sugars, glucose to be exact, hooked together. These long chains are arranged in microscopic granules. The granules are like tiny little time capsules waiting to release their starch. The capsules of starch are strung together much like a pearl necklace. When you combine the starch and melted fat, fat coats the starch necklace. The fat-coated starch now forms the basis of the roux. Roux, when added to a hot liquid stock in this coated form, begins to dissolve from the heat. The fat coating makes the granules of starch dissolve more slowly than they would if you just plopped raw flour (sans fat) into the pot. The end result is that roux gives you more control of the thickening process.

As we continue to heat the stock, now combined with the roux, more tiny starch time capsules release their starches. As they do, the liquid thickens progressively because the starches spread out into the liquid, creating a mesh or net of sugars suspended in the fat and stock. Think of it this way: If suddenly tomorrow morning you jumped into your car and headed for work but found barrier after barrier on each and every street, it would take longer to get from home to the office. You would have to navigate around those barriers, right? Your flow to work would be slower.

By adding roux, our stock now has to navigate around sugars, which are like tiny barriers suddenly released into the neighborhood. It takes longer for the liquid to go from point A to point B; as the flow slows, it is seen as thickening. Some stock even gets trapped inside the barrier maze of sugars, which further thickens the liquid, along with the melted fat. Now that you understand how a roux thickens a liquid, you can use this knowledge to make sauces.

Mother's Helper

When two of the big daddies of French cooking, first Antoine Carême, and much later in history Auguste Escoffier, developed the Holy Grail of sauce-making, they did so to save time in the kitchen. What the great chefs pioneered was the concept called the *mother sauce*. If you can make a batch of something that you can keep handy to whip out when you need a sauce for dinner, this has to be a timesaver, right? So, by learning to make stocks, which keep well in the freezer, and learning the concept of roux, which also keeps well, two thirds of your work is done.

Classical French cooking includes a group of five basic sauce preparations known as mother sauces. These five sauces are used to produce a myriad of other sauces known as small sauces. The five mother sauces are velouté, espagnole, béchamel, hollandaise, and tomato. Two of the classic mother sauces are based on stocks and roux: velouté and espagnole. Béchamel is created by thickening milk with roux. Tomato sauce can be made with or without stock and with or without roux. Hollandaise is based on the incredible egg, a handy little science project in its own right. Velouté and espagnole are covered here; the others will be explained in the following chapters.

If you've been keeping up, you've made both a good chicken stock and some pale roux, so you have the makings of the first of the great mother sauces of French cookery, the velouté. Velouté means "velvety" in French. To make velouté sauce, thicken a white stock (chicken, fish, or veal, depending on what's for dinner) with a pale roux. Take a pot that holds at least 2 quarts, measure in $1\frac{1}{2}$ quarts of chicken stock, and bring it to a simmer.

In the meantime, measure 8 tablespoons or weigh out 4 ounces of roux and heat it in a small pan. Whisk the warm roux into the simmering stock. Whisk constantly and at a steady pace. You will see an almost instantaneous change in the color and texture of the stock. As you cook this gently for the next hour, a skin (or scum, it's sometimes called) will form on the surface. Use a large spoon or ladle to skim off the scum and discard it. This is the cooked-out flour we mentioned earlier.

Taste the velouté occasionally as it slowly cooks. At first you will notice that it tastes rather starchy, and when pressed to the roof of

Lab Project

For a velouté sauce, bring $1\frac{1}{2}$ quarts white chicken stock to a simmer. Meanwhile, heat 8 tablespoons of pale roux in a small saucepan. Gradually whisk the warm roux into the simmering stock. Whisk constantly to avoid lumps. Allow the sauce to simmer for one hour, skimming the skin off the surface periodically. Cool the sauce in an ice bath and refrigerate for later use.

your mouth, it is sticky or grainy. After about an hour of gentle cooking, it will taste much smoother and creamier. Now when you press it to the roof of your mouth, it feels slippery, not starchy. Mouth feel is an indicator that it is done. Pour the sauce through a mesh strainer into another pot and either season as desired for dinner, or cool it down like you did for stock, and store it away for later use. Velouté can also be frozen for up to two months.

Mother's Offspring

Once you have a batch of velouté, it becomes the base from which many *small sauces* can be made. It's easy to understand if you think of a mother sauce as one with lots of different-flavored offspring. So, how do we use the velouté in our dinner entrée?

> **Chef Sez**
> A **small sauce** is made by adding flavoring ingredients to a mother sauce. Flavors may come from vegetables, spices, herbs, meat products, and so on. Small sauces are grouped together into families based on their mother sauce.

Let's say you just roasted a nice chicken. You want to serve it with one of the small sauces called Sauce Supreme, which goes especially well with chicken. All you need are some mushrooms, and some heavy cream. Slice about 6 ounces of 'shrooms (as chefs sometimes call them) and add 1 cup of cold water. Simmer this uncovered until only half the water is left. You've now made an extract called mushroom cooking liquid (which happens to be another one of those fond de cuisine things we have been making all along.)

Now heat up 2 pints of your velouté sauce, add the hot mushroom cooking liquid (with or without the mushroom slices, according to your taste), and add about 8 tablespoons of cold heavy cream. Stir well, bring this mixture to a low simmer again, and season to taste with salt and pepper. When the liquid reduces (this is simply cooking away some of the water) to the point that it is about as thick as heavy cream, it is done.

> **Lab Project**
> For a sauce supreme, simmer 6 ounces of sliced mushrooms in 1 cup of water until the liquid is reduced by half. Heat 4 cups (1 quart) of velouté sauce in a separate pan. Stir the mushrooms and their cooking liquid into the hot velouté. Add 1/2 cup (8 tablespoons) of cold heavy cream and return the sauce to a simmer. Cook, uncovered, until the sauce thickens slightly. Season to taste with salt and white pepper, and strain out the mushrooms if desired. Swirl in 1 tablespoon of whole butter immediately before serving.

So, you're thinking about all those good bits and pieces of stuff in the bottom of the chicken roasting pan. Or maybe another time, in a different recipe, you sautéed some meat and have that nice-looking meat residue in the pan. Julia or Emeril would scrape that stuff up and use it in their sauce, right? Well, all right, you want to get fancier and add that to Sauce Supreme the real French way? It's pretty simple.

Pour off the fat from the roasting pan. Take 4 ounces of good drinkable white wine (a nice chardonnay or Riesling perhaps?) and add it to the pan. With the pan on the stovetop over medium heat, use a wooden spoon or spatula to scrape up the bits from the pan surface. The wine helps lift the bits and pieces of chicken off the bottom of the pan. Reduce this liquid down until half (water!) of it disappears. This burns off the alcohol, too, because alcohol vaporizes much more readily than the water that remains. You've now succeeded in extracting the flavor from the bottom of your roasting pan into this reduction. The bits and pieces are now expendable. Strain this reduction directly into your mushroom cooking liquid.

Now you are ready to proceed by reducing the velouté combined with the mushroom cooking liquid (with your roasting pan reduction in tow) until you get about a third less volume in the pot. Then add the cream to finish, cook slowly for about five minutes more, and voilà, a real classic sauce the modern way. If you really want to be politically correct (the French way), strain the final sauce one last time and stir in a dollop of butter. The heat of the sauce will melt the butter, giving it a rich flavor and a nice shine. Maybe add some fresh chopped parsley or a bit of thyme, and enjoy your Roasted Chicken with Sauce Supreme.

Chef Sez

Deglaze means to add a liquid to a pan that has cooked bits and pieces adhered to it in order to remove or resuspend the pieces into the liquid. This extract intensifies the flavors of whatever we add it to in our sauce making process. To deglaze, we heat the liquid while scraping the pan to loosen up the pieces stuck on the bottom, and then strain off this extract.

Food for Thought

Sometimes you might read or hear instructions to *finish* or *mount* a sauce with butter. Finish means to add that final little touch, perhaps some cream or fresh herb seasonings to set off the flavors. Mounting a sauce, or more correctly in French *monte au buerre*, means swirling in some butter just as the sauce comes off the heat. It adds flavor and a little eye-appealing shine. Hey, you're the chef, so you decide what goes. Just remember not to boil the sauce after adding this butter, or the fat will float to the surface like a bad oil slick.

Variations on the Theme

If you are fortunate enough to get veal bones or beef bones, and make a brown stock as we described in Chapter 23, you can tackle one more of the grand mother sauces, the Sauce Espagnole, a.k.a Brown Sauce. This sauce is usually based on a brown veal stock.

To make an Espagnole sauce, cook some mirepoix (two parts onion, one part carrot, and one part celery, remember?) with 1 tablespoon of tomato paste in a small bit of butter in a 3-quart sauce pot. You want to simmer the vegetables and tomato paste until they give up their water and begin to take on a brown, caramel-like color. If you like the taste of bacon or ham, add a couple of tablespoons of diced meat as you simmer the mirepoix. Then add 2 quarts of your veal stock and bring it back to a simmer. When just about to the boil, stir 4 tablespoons of roux into the stock and vegetable mixture. Once combined well, simmer all of this for an hour. You should skim the scum from the surface, just as you did when preparing velouté, in order to remove the cooked-out flour proteins.

When the hour is over, strain the brown sauce, and cool it in an ice bath. You now have the makings of a base that can be used just as we did the chicken velouté. Like most of our preparations in stock and sauce-making, brown sauce can be kept frozen for two months, if covered for protection from the freezer aroma demons.

But say you still want to go further and push the envelope of sauce-making ecstasy? Who are we to hold you back? Go for what the French call demi-glace. Some call it black gold because, once you make it, taste it, and use it in sauces, it will be more valuable than Jed Clampett's Texas tea.

To produce demi-glace, combine equal parts of your Brown Sauce and the home-made veal stock you stored away, and simmer for about an hour. This will reduce the volume by half as it removes water, concentrating the collagen and flavor extracts intensely.

After an hour, strain the sauce again to remove any solid particles. You have now succeeded in extracting maximum flavor, color, and collagen from the bones and vegetables, and have created a lacquer–like sauce base. Demi-glace is so powerful as a seasoning that it can be used directly to deglaze roasting pans. By deglazing with the mother sauce, you have succeeded in elevating the flavor over water alone. This makes a more complex and usually pleasing addition to the sauce. Demi keeps well in the freezer, too, preferably under lock and key.

Gravy 101

Say the word "gravy" and lots of people conjure up memories of Sunday dinner with Mom. It's comforting, like the food you imagine it gracing. Yet, for others it can trigger a deep fear. Those are the people who have tried valiantly, yet failed to master their mother's lessons about how to fashion the perfect meat gravy.

A gravy is derived from meat juices. So, gravy goes with roasted meats like Sally goes with Harry. The meat can be beef, pork, chicken, elk, deer, rabbit, or moose, for that matter. What matters is not necessarily the meat that you cooked but the end products left in the pan.

Déjà Roux

Let's say you just roasted a 27-pound turkey (My, that is a big one!) and that you have plenty of pan drippings to transform into gravy. As you look at this situation, you see liquid with fat swimming around it. Your goal is to separate the fat from the liquid and recombine just enough of each to transform these drippings into that gracefully delicious gravy.

It's often easiest to pour the contents of the roasting pan carefully into a clear measuring cup large enough to hold all of the liquid and fat. Because fats float, you will see a yellow film develop atop a brown liquid. This may take a few minutes but the wait is worth it. After the liquids separate, measure about 1 to 1$^{1}/_{2}$ tablespoons of fat back into the roasting pan. You can skim off and discard the rest of the fat, but reserve all the precious liquid from below the fat.

Roux is the thickener of choice for classic gravy. Instead of making a roux from scratch, however, you are going to use some of that flavorful fat from the roasted meat to make your pan gravy's roux. So, you now have a tablespoon or two of fat in the bottom of the roasting pan. Just add an equal amount of flour to create a paste and then cook this for two to three minutes to produce your roux. Don't try to make the roux without first pouring off all the pan drippings, of course. The water would interfere with the fat-flour bonding action and leave you with lumpy gravy.

Stirring is important to the making of a good gravy. Don't just add back liquid and cook. You need to disperse the roux in the liquid evenly and completely. Use a wire whisk and constant arm action. Improperly dispersed roux results in a problem technically known as lumps. If lumps do develop, you can always cheat and strain the sauce through a mesh strainer.

Once the roux is made, add the liquid, stirring vigorously to mix everything together and loosen all that good stuff off the bottom of the pan. While your 27-pound turkey probably produced plenty of pan drippings, other meats might not be so generous. If the pan drippings didn't give you enough liquid to form the gravy you'll need back-up, which can be some nice, rich, homemade stock. It can also be canned broth or even lightly salted water. Whatever liquid you choose, you'll need about 1 to 1½ cups. Whisk it in as described above and bring the gravy to a simmer. The combination of roux and reduction will lead you to just the right consistency within five minutes or so. Adjust the seasonings to suit, and serve it up with your beautiful bird.

Lab Project _____

For the perfect roast turkey gravy, pour all of the pan drippings and fat into a large measuring cup. (Yes, you should remove the bird from the pan first.) Place the roasting pan over a burner on the stovetop. Spoon 4 tablespoons of fat from the pan drippings into the roasting pan, and then stir in 4 tablespoons of flour. Cook over medium heat, stirring to make a thick paste, but do not allow the roux to brown. Spoon any extra fat off the collected drippings and discard. Add stock or water to the remaining liquid as needed in order to produce a total of 1 quart of liquid. Slowly pour this liquid into the pan with the roux, whisking constantly. Scrape up any cooked-on particles from the bottom of the pan. Simmer for a few minutes until the desired thickness is reached. Season with salt and pepper, whisk in a tablespoon of butter, and serve with pride.

Breakfast of Champions

This brings us to another reason for learning to make gravy properly: the breakfast standby of biscuits and gravy. Some call this sausage gravy. Traditionally it's made by frying up some ground sausage and using the rendered fat to make your roux. Nothing new here; still 1 tablespoon of fat to 1 tablespoon of flour. Simple. Gradually add a cup or so of whole milk, whisking well. Stir in the cooked sausage, add cracked black pepper and get plenty of piping hot biscuits.

Food for Thought _____

One gravy that clearly does not have roots in classic French cuisine is the elixir made with the fat and pan drippings left after cooking country ham. Red-eye gravy, also known as "frog-eye" gravy, is made by adding a little water and some strong coffee to the pan in which you've just cooked ham. Scrape up all the bits of cooked meat and reduce for a few minutes. No starch thickener found here; this is cowpoke cookin' at its finest. Serve piping hot with ham, biscuits, and grits.

Slurry Up

Another way to thicken sauce or gravy is to use cornstarch. I can remember my mom standing over a pan of simmering liquid, stirring in cornstarch slurry. Usually it was juices from a braised dish liked beef or game. I remember her turning that thin liquid into a shiny delicious concoction; at the time it seemed like magic. But it wasn't magic at all; she just was applying some basic thickening principles.

Cornstarch, like flour, is made up of long chains of sugars hooked together like beads on a necklace. Unlike flour, though, cornstarch does not contain any protein. Because cornstarch does not have protein, when you use it to thicken a liquid, the finished sauce tends to be clearer and has a nice shine. And because it's all starch, you'll need less cornstarch than flour to thicken a cup of liquid. The rule of thumb is that cornstarch has twice the thickening power of wheat flour. So, you'll only need 1 tablespoon of cornstarch to get the same thickening power as 2 tablespoons of flour.

When you stir cornstarch into a cold liquid, you are making a *slurry*. Scientifically speaking, you are forming a *sol*. The tiny starch granules are like time-release capsules. They keep their shape in cold water or cold stock, although they usually turn the water a milky white. As the liquid is heated, it flows into the starch granules, making them swell. The granules burst, releasing their sugars into the liquid stock. Voilà, just like a roux, sugars hook up and form a maze.

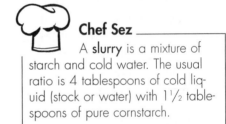

Chef Sez _____

A **slurry** is a mixture of starch and cold water. The usual ratio is 4 tablespoons of cold liquid (stock or water) with 1 1/2 tablespoons of pure cornstarch.

One important thing you need to keep in mind: Always add cold liquid to cornstarch before stirring it into hot liquid for thickening. That's because cold water won't prematurely burst our little time capsules of starches and sugars. When you add the cold slurry to the hot stock to thicken it, it is a more controlled process. Imagine making a slurry using hot, rather than cold, water. The hot water would burst the capsules, releasing the starches. The slurry would be almost like congealed gelatin and too thick to add to your stock. So, to maintain maximum control over the thickening process, go slow and cold with your cornstarch slurry.

Like roux, cornstarch has its preferred place as a thickener. Typically, you use cornstarch to thicken a sauce when prolonged cooking on the stovetop is not necessary, such as thickening meat juices from a braised dish. Roux is the better choice when you are preparing the sauce ahead of time and will have plenty of time to cook out the starchy flavors.

Food for Thought

A number of starches from plant roots can be used for thickening. All of them work on the same principles as cornstarch, but differ in the strength of their thickening power. Potato starch and arrowroot, derived for the cassava (manioc) plant, thicken at three times the strength of cornstarch. This means that if you use 1 tablespoon of cornstarch for every cup of liquid, you would use 1 teaspoon of arrowroot to get the same thickness. This is because root starches have very long chains of sugars.

These longer chains form bigger mazes. So, if you use too much arrowroot, you end up with a tangled mess of sticky starch and your sauce will be gummy. A positive side effect is that sauces or dishes thickened with root starches freeze better than those thickened with other starch, and they are clear when set, so your sauce will have a glossy finish.

So, what about gels? Well, when you thicken a liquid with cornstarch properly, the liquid still flows, but much more slowly than water. A standard to measure this flow is to compare it with cold, heavy whipping cream. This is the consistency you're looking for in the finished sauce. Funny thing is, when you put your leftover thickened sauce into the refrigerator, it will become as thick as jelly. The liquid has become immobilized in the solids, which is called a *gel*. What happened? When the sauce was hot, all those sugars were tumbling around, doing their maze thing. Once the heat was removed and they found themselves in a cold refrigerator, the sugars settled down for a long winter's nap. No longer tumbling around, they actually get compacted together. In fact, those sugar mazes get so closely stacked together as they cool down that, in the process, any water that was trapped in the maze of the warm sauce is now squeezed out. What you see when you first peek at the jelly-like sauce in the refrigerator is water on the surface. So, we might say that a hot liquid sauce thickened with cornstarch is a softer form of a gel that can flow freely, while one taken from the refrigerator the next day is a firmer gel. Of course, when we reheat the firm gel for a leftover hot roast-beef sandwich, the soft gel reforms as the hard gel melts. The heat forces our starch chains apart once again, recreating our fluid sauce.

Chef Sez

A **sol** is a solution-like mixture of microscopic particles (such as a starch) suspended in a liquid. Sols are not rigid; they flow. When a sol is properly heated, the starch will gelatinize, making the liquid thicken. Then when it cools, the sol becomes rigid and is called a **gel**. A gel is a soft, spongy solid that holds its shape. Scientists say that the liquid is now trapped within the solid.

Starches gelatinize when cooked. That means that the starch granules release their sugars. These sugars form a mesh-like network that does the work of thickening. Flour and cornstarch gelatinize between 140 and 160°F, which is below the temperature at which water simmers. The maximum temperature at which most of the starch has completely gelatinized and your sauce is thickest is about 200°F. As sauce cools on your plate during dinner, you'll notice that it quickly begins to thicken. One way to avoid serving a gummy sauce is to make sure it is just a bit on the thin side in the kitchen. By the time it reaches the table, it will be thicker.

In a sol, microscopic particles are separated from one another. The liquid flows easily. In a gel, these particles cling together in interlacing strands, and the mixture becomes soft but rigid.

Sol   Gel

Too Hot to Handle

Before you get any bright ideas about using unflavored granulated gelatin to thicken your sauce, stop! Don't be misled by our use of the terms gel and gelatinize. Although the theory is similar to what happens when you make a box of cherry dessert gelatin, that stuff won't work to thicken your warm sauce. Those gelatins are protein-based extracts (remember collagen) that must be dissolved in cold liquid, and then heated, and then cooled to thicken a liquid. If granulated gelatin is added to a hot sauce, you'll just end up with a stringy, gloppy mess. So, save your granulated gelatin for cold aspics and congealed fruit salads.

The Least You Need to Know

♦ Roux is a cooked mixture of equal parts of fat and flour. Velouté is a classic mother sauce made from white stock, thickened with roux.

♦ Sauce Supreme is a velouté sauce flavored with mushroom extract and heavy cream.

♦ Combining roux with veal stock, tomato paste, and mirepoix creates the basis for Brown Sauce or Sauce Espagnole.

♦ Many different small sauces can be prepared from each mother sauce by adding different seasonings or varying the cooking techniques.

- Gravy is meat drippings thickened with flour. Combine flour and fat from the roasting pan to make a roux and then whisk in defatted pan drippings to make gravy.

- Stirring is an important part of good gravy-making because it prevents lumps from forming.

- Always dissolve cornstarch in a cold liquid (a slurry) before adding it to a hot liquid for thickening.

Chapter **25**

Egg Sauces: Emulsions Forever?

In This Chapter

- ◆ Emulsify that mayo
- ◆ Making mayonnaise safe
- ◆ Heat it up for hollandaise
- ◆ How would you like your eggs?

The egg is an amazing thing. If I were stranded on a desert island and could pick 10 things I would have to have, a big fat chicken would be one of them. So many foods and so many cooking techniques owe their existence to the science of the egg. Mayonnaise and hollandaise sauce are just two such products. See, both of these sauces are made by doing the impossible—mixing oil and water. The miracle ingredient that makes it possible is egg yolk.

Hold the Mayo: A Cool Sauce

Mayonnaise is made by combining lemon juice or vinegar (water!) with vegetable oil and egg yolks. Thick, creamy mayo is possible because egg yolks contain protein and substances called *emulsifiers*.

Chef Sez

An **emulsion** is the complete mixing of two or more liquids that normally would not stay together, such as oil and water. Emulsions form when the liquids are combined along with an emulsifier and energy. That energy can be heat or good old-fashioned muscle power in the form of whisking. An **emulsifier** is a substance that helps bridge together two liquids that otherwise would not mix. Emulsifiers are the optimum unifier because they happily live in either fat or water.

Mayo and hollandaise are known as emulsified sauces; emulsified sauces can be cooked or uncooked, hot or cold. Mayonnaise is one nice, white homogenous mixture that is versatile enough to take on many different flavors and be used as a dipping sauce, a sandwich spread, a salad dressing, or a general condiment.

An oil-in-water emulsion in which emulsifiers form a protective barrier around individual oil droplets keeping them apart.

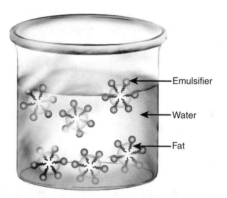

Emulsifier

Water

Fat

The mayo you buy at the grocery store is technically known as "bomb proof." Unopened, it can happily sit on your shelf for a very long time without deteriorating. Once opened, of course, mayo must be refrigerated, yet it stays in the refrigerator as happily as it did on the shelf. Look at it today and it's thick, creamy, and white. Look at it six months from now and it's thick, creamy, and white. Commercial mayonnaise is as stable and true as a convent full of nuns. When you make homemade mayonnaise, however, you will find that it is not as stable as the commercial stuff. At best, it lasts for only a couple of days. Why the big difference? We will answer this question as we prepare the mayonnaise.

When commercial companies make mayonnaise, they not only take advantage of the natural emulsifiers found in egg yolk, such as lecithin and cholesterol, they also add a few of their own. Commercial mayonnaise contains large, complex sugar molecules in the form of starch. These come mostly from plants. Just as starch works to help thicken a sauce, these starches help keep the water and fat together for long periods of time after mixing. Of course, the big companies who produce mayo also use some heavy-duty mixers that whip these ingredients into frenzy. After going a few rounds with a big mixer, no self-respecting egg yolk is going to dare separate. You, on the other hand, do not have a ready supply of commercial emulsifiers in your home lab. Nor do you have industrial-strength mixing machines. So, you must rely on the natural chemistry of the egg and some of your own strength to mix up a perfect mayo.

Making a good mayo is not very difficult, but it is impressive and the flavor can't be beat. Imagine taking homemade mayonnaise to the next company picnic. They'll be calling you "chef" for weeks afterward.

 **Too Hot to Handle**

Food safety is as important when using eggs to make homemade mayonnaise as when using eggs in general. Use fresh eggs and keep them refrigerated. Use clean bowls for separating yolks and whites, and never handle eggs at the same time as other foods such as while chopping vegetables or cutting meat. And most important, avoid cross contamination by washing your hands and cleaning up your work area before and after making mayonnaise.

Food for Thought

Separating eggs is an essential culinary technique and mandatory for making mayonnaise. An easy way to do this is to crack the egg and let it fall into your cupped hand, resting on your curved fingers. The whites will slip through the spaces between your fingers, and fall into a bowl placed underneath your hand. Marvel at the egg yolk resting in your hand; consider how nature fashioned this food supply so perfectly. Those thick white cords are called *chalazae* and are there to hold the yolk in place within the white. Treat them just like you would the rest of the egg white. The yolk is the food source for the future chick. The eggs you purchase are not fertile, by the way, but they do contain about 75 calories of digestible protein, fat, and vitamins.

The Basic Steps: Mayo 101

Take a nice, fresh, large egg and let it sit on your kitchen counter for about 20 minutes. (Notice again that we always use large eggs in cooking; just seems to be one of those constants like the speed of light in physics.) Next, measure out 1 cup of vegetable oil and squeeze the juice from half a fresh lemon (red wine, apple cider, or white-wine vinegars work nicely, too). You'll also need a pinch of salt and some ground white pepper. If you want to add a bit more punch to the mayo, you can add a tablespoon of Dijon mustard.

First things first, though. Separate the egg and plop the yolk in a nice, clean bowl. Add the pinch of salt and the lemon juice. Without an acid such as lemon juice or vinegar, the proteins in the egg yolk won't unwind or denature properly and you'll have less control when you start to from the emulsion. Failure is not an option! Take your whisk and stir this ever so slightly until you see tiny little bubbles forming.

Now add a couple of drops of oil as you keep whisking. Once that oil is incorporated, add a couple more drops of oil. Continue this on-and-off process until you see the mixture change appearance from the thin yellow egg yolk to a lighter, slightly thickened mixture. Once you get to this stage, you can add the oil in an almost continuous slow stream as you whisk. Just be careful to whisk constantly as you add the oil.

Mayo will thicken considerably even before you add the full cup of oil. Adding the full cup of oil will give you the perfect 8:1 ratio, even if it seems a bit too thick. You still need to adjust the flavor with mustard or more lemon juice, both of which tend to thin the final product. So, it's better to start thick in order to end up with the right consistency. You can also add a bit more salt and just a touch of white pepper to suit your taste. Use white rather than black pepper to keep your mayo a nice light shade with no black freckles.

Notice that your homemade mayo is more yellow than most commercial varieties? You can magically change the color if you prefer a whiter product by whisking in 1 tablespoon of boiling water after the seasonings.

Lab Project

For a basic mayonnaise, whisk 1 Large egg yolk with 2 tablespoons of lemon juice or vinegar, 1 teaspoon of Dijon mustard, and a pinch of salt in a small bowl. Slowly add 1 cup of canola or corn oil, whisking constantly. Add the oil a few drops at a time, increasing the speed with which you add the oil after the mixture thickens and the emulsion forms. After all of the oil is whisked in, adjust the flavor with additional lemon juice, mustard, salt and/or pepper, to taste. You can also whisk in 1 tablespoon of boiling water to lighten the color.

The Basic Science: Mayo 101

Now that you have successfully made your mayonnaise from scratch, what was so important about each step in the process? Why, for example, do we warm up the eggs before beginning the mayo odyssey? It's best to take the chill off the fat and emulsifiers before combining them with other ingredients because warm proteins make better emulsions. Think of it this way: You feel more relaxed after a nice warm bath because your muscles are relaxed. So, warming up the egg proteins, just like warming up your muscle proteins, makes them relax. And relaxed proteins form better combinations.

And what was so darn important about adding the oil slow and easy at first? Why not just dump it in there and get on with the show? Well, what you are doing is breaking the oil into many smaller drops as you whisk. As the drops get smaller and increase in number, they begin to spread out within the egg-yolk base. You are also adding some air, which increases the volume of the mixture. As you whisk and pour alternatively, you are basically dividing the oil from one large drop into a million smaller ones. These smaller drops of oil fit between the egg yolk proteins as they unwind. If you get hasty and add the oil too quickly, you'll overwhelm the egg's emulsifiers, lecithin and cholesterol.

The emulsifiers can handle the oil in small bites rather than one large big one; it gives them more spaces to fit into and they can do their job better. They do this by using their chemical charges to keep the drops of oil suspended from each other. Try as the little drops of oil might to get back together into one big drop, they are blocked by both emulsifier and the energy of whipping. You have succeeded in overcoming *surface tension* by combining energy with emulsifiers.

> **Chef Sez**
> **Surface tension** is the tendency of like molecules to stick together. Like attracts like, and molecules that are similar will be attracted to one another. Surface tension is demonstrated by adding oil to water without mixing. The oil floats on the surface, with water happily existing below it in its own neighborhood.

And the final coup de grace is the addition of the boiling water at the end to change the color. This is an optional step, of course. The hot water will cook the proteins slightly and set the color a bit lighter. But the heat of the water is not just for looks. Hot water does one other important thing. It helps stabilize the fat with the emulsifiers, giving your mayo a longer life in the fridge without separating. So, here's yet another reason to learn to boil water.

If you don't use all of your fresh mayo immediately, you must refrigerate the leftovers. It keeps for a couple of days, but you will notice that it may separate or become mottled in appearance. This brings us full circle to explaining why commercial varieties withstand storage but your homemade version does not.

It's all a matter of surface tension. Homemade mayo does not contain all of the emulsifiers of commercial products. When it sits for any length of time, the globules of fat (the oil that you whisked in) begin to get back together. Without the energy you supplied when mixing to keep the oil and water apart, the oil begins to migrate and join forces once again.

Food for Thought

Some people like the taste of olive oil. If you're one of these people, go ahead and make your mayo with olive oil. One cautionary point though. When you whisk olive oil, it tends to taste bitter. You end up breaking down some of the fats, and since olive oil tends to be more acidic than other oils, you can sometimes taste this effect. A compromise mixture of about 50/50 olive oil and vegetable oil will solve that problem. If you do prefer all olive oil because it's good for your health, you have created a special mayonnaise called *aioli*. Of course, you should also stir in some minced garlic, because a real aioli is nothing without garlic.

Once this happens, the drops of oil grow. All of those millions of tiny droplets run together like so many small streams forming a large river. Larger pools of fat now begin to appear. There are so many emulsifiers chocked between the fat droplets in commercial brands that this migration is greatly reduced, sort of like flood gates that keep the fat at bay.

Chef Sez

Breaking refers to the separation of fat and liquid (water) from an emulsion. This separation is simply the process of surface tension, where like molecules seek out each other. A broken sauce can sometimes be fixed by adding back energy or changing the temperature to encourage the molecules to re-emulsify.

Another big reason why commercial mayo is so stable has to do with the mixing process itself; because commercial varieties have mixed the fat into tens of billions rather than millions of smaller drops of fat, it simply takes longer to *break* or separate.

So, why not just use a commercial mixer or blender or even a trusty food processor to stabilize mayonnaise? After all, it would save your muscles from overwork. The answer is that you can create blender mayonnaise very nicely. These mechanical devices work especially well with larger batches of mayonnaise.

Mechanical blenders and mixers are not as efficient for one-egg mayo recipes simply because the volume in the bowl is so small that good mixing does not take place. If you are using at least four egg yolks and 1 quart of oil, just begin by adding small amounts of oil to the slightly beaten egg yolks and lemon juice, and then follow the procedures outlined above.

There is one danger in using a blender or a mixer—over-beating. Once your emulsion is complete and perfect, if you continue to mix you can break the system down and reverse all of your efforts.

Basically you are destroying the arrangement of proteins and emulsifiers that you worked to intersperse between your tiny fat droplets. It's kind of like having built and framed a nice home, but suddenly removing all of the supporting beams. Everything is still there, but the weight-bearing elements have been weakened, and the structure collapses. Your weight-bearing beams, so to speak, are all of those proteins and emulsifiers. The mayo breaks because all those tiny bubbles of fat rush together, seeking their common ground of surface tension. So, if you do use the blender or mixer, stop when the mayo is done and use only medium speed throughout the process.

So, what if your homemade mayonnaise breaks? Should you dump everything out and start over? Actually, you can rescue a broken mayonnaise and not waste any of your efforts. Leave your broken mayo, which now is very runny and starting to leak oil, sitting in its bowl. Place a large egg yolk in a clean bowl and add a little lemon juice and salt. Using some fresh oil, slowly start making a fresh mayo. At the point when the mixture begins to thicken, switch from the pure oil to your broken mayo. Add in all the broken mayonnaise goop just as if it were oil, by whisking (or blending) it in slowly. All you are doing here is combining the nonemulsified sauce into one that you have started to emulsify. Then go back to the pure oil and slowly whisk that in. Voilà, a double batch of mayo without missing a beat.

But Mom, Is Mayo Safe to Eat?

What about the dangers of eating raw egg products? The risk of getting a food-borne illness from salmonella bacteria, which is common in eggs, is always a possibility. The contemporary handling of eggs by the poultry and food industries has greatly reduced this risk. Yet, there are ways to make a homemade mayonnaise with cooked eggs if you prefer.

Cooked mayonnaise can be made using hard-boiled yolks. Cooking the egg yolk naturally destroys nasties such as salmonella. It also changes the protein structure, so that when you make this mayonnaise you need to use a slightly different approach. Because the proteins of cooked egg yolk are now essentially solids and have less water because some has evaporated, you need to add back moisture before adding any oil.

Cambridge is a cooked-egg mayonnaise from the classics repertoire. To make this type of mayo, take a couple of hard-boiled egg yolks and add 1 tablespoon white-wine vinegar and a teaspoon of Dijon mustard. Mix this preparation in a bowl until it is the consistency of raw, uncooked egg yolk. Add a bit of water to make it more fluid if needed. Then proceed just as if you were making regular mayo, by rapidly whisking in the oil drop by drop. When the emulsion is formed, adjust the seasoning with some fresh, chopped herbs and, if you wish, some anchovy.

You will notice that this style of mayo is coarser. This is because of the cooked egg-yolk protein. You can smooth out the consistency by scraping it through a fine-mesh strainer. As before, 1 tablespoon of hot water can be added to help stabilize and lighten the color of the sauce. If the sauce breaks over night in the fridge, whisk in 1 tablespoon of hot water. This will help revive the sauce by helping to form the emulsion once again.

Hollandaise: A Little Heat Will Do

Few things in life are as satisfying as enjoying a thick juicy steak with a sauce béarnaise or some fresh, steamed asparagus dipped in hollandaise sauce. And what would Sunday brunch be without eggs Benedict? The unifying ingredient here is the hollandaise family of sauces. Hollandaise is a warm, creamy, rich blend of butter and eggs flavored with lemon and, in the case of béarnaise, some tarragon.

Like mayonnaise, hollandaise is an emulsion of water, egg yolks, and fat—always clarified butter in this case. But unlike common mayonnaise, hollandaise sauces are emulsified with the aid of heat energy. Since you've already mastered preparing clarified butter, making hollandaise will be a snap. And yes, hollandaise is another of the classic French mother sauces.

The important thing to remember about making hollandaise is reciting the mantra: "Too hot, too fast, too much, too soon is too bad." Scientifically speaking, this sauce is only difficult if you have too much energy in the form of heat, or have butter that is too hot, or try to add too much butter, or add the ingredients too fast.

The Basic Steps: Hollandaise 101

Classic hollandaise is made with a *reduction*. Some folks dispense with this step in the hope of simplifying things. The fact is, however, eliminating the step makes it more difficult because the reduction is an acidic mixture that helps guard against failure. And the reduction adds flavor that is lost if you leave it out.

To make the hollandaise reduction, place ½ cup of cider vinegar (or white-wine vinegar) in a small pan along with one bay leaf, one sprig of thyme, and a few black peppercorns. Simmer this until the liquid almost totally disappears. Then add ½ cup of cold water. Swish this around and strain it into a clean bowl. Pop the reduction into the refrigerator for 10 minutes to further chill it down. You can make the reduction days ahead and store it in the refrigerator.

Remember the clarified butter you prepared in Chapter 24? Heat 1 cup of that liquid gold to about 105°F. This is not very hot. Remember that your body temperature is 98°F. If you don't have a thermometer handy, take a drop and put it in your wrist. This should make you say AHHHHHH-HHH. You'll need a double boiler to make a hollandaise, but don't worry if this isn't part of your lab equipment yet. You can make one by simply using any saucepan that your metal mixing bowl fits over properly. The idea is for the bowl to hang on the edge of the pan, suspended over hot water. The bowl should not sit directly in the water. Place about 2 inches of water in the saucepan and heat it to a simmer; despite the name, the water should not boil.

Chef Sez _____

A **reduction** is made by heating a liquid to evaporate its water content. Chefs speak of reducing a mixture by one half, one third, or some other fraction, meaning that the finished product is one third less than what you began with. If heating continues until the pan is nearly dry, it is called *au sec*. A reduction is a way to concentrate flavors.

As the water heats, place four egg yolks and the reduction (or $^1/_2$ cup of it, if you happened to make a bunch of this stuff), in the bowl. Whisk this mixture together, and then place the bowl over the simmering water. Place a plain old dishtowel between the bowl and the pan of water to hold the bowl steady and keep the steam from burning your hand as you whisk. Have half of a lemon nearby, along with a bit of salt and some white pepper (remember, we want the sauce to be light, not freckled, so use white pepper).

Whisk the mixture until it thickens and begins to look like light cake batter. Remove the bowl from the heat. It's a good idea to set the bowl on your work surface with a fresh towel underneath.

Add the warm butter in a slow, steady stream, whisking all the while. The towel will keep your bowl steady and prevent it from walking away as you work. The easiest way to add the butter is with a small ladle. Because you are using four egg yolks, you need to add 1 cup of clarified butter (the ratio for classic hollandaise is 2 ounces of butter for each large egg yolk.) Don't go too fast, or add too much too soon. Keep chanting the mantra. Hollandaise should be satiny smooth and pourable; it will be much thinner than mayonnaise.

A good hollandaise should taste first like butter but have lemony finish. Add a bit of lemon, some salt and white pepper (just a pinch!!!), mix, and taste it again. Your tongue has its own preferences, so you're on your own here. Don't add so much lemon that it is too acidic—just enough to sharpen the butter taste. Some contemporary versions of the sauce also include Tabasco or cayenne pepper. Hey, if you like a little kick, by all means, go for it. As we say, different strokes for different folks, right?

Lab Project

For a hollandaise sauce, simmer ¹/₂ cup of vinegar, 1 bay leaf, a few pepper-corns, and a sprig of thyme until it is reduced *au sec*. Pour in ¹/₂ cup of cold water, swirl it around, and strain this liquid into a clean bowl. Refrigerate the reduction. Meanwhile heat 1 cup of clarified butter to 105°F. Set up a double boiler and place 4 Large egg yolks and ¹/₂ cup of chilled reduction in the bowl. Whisk together, and then place the bowl over the heat and whisk until the egg-yolk mixture begins to thicken. Remove the bowl from the heat and slowly drizzle in the warm clarified butter, a few drops at a time, whisking constantly. When the sauce thickens, add the butter slightly faster. Once all of the butter is incorporated, add a pinch of salt and white pepper and about 1 tablespoon of lemon juice. Adjust the flavor as desired, and serve.

The Basic Science 101: Don't Break My Heart

When you make hollandaise, you are applying the same principles of emulsification that you did with mayonnaise. In this case, you are not only using manual energy (whisking) to break down large fat globs into smaller ones, you are also heating the mixture to change the protein structure in the egg yolk. As you heat the egg yolks gently, you are denaturing protein without coagulating it. That's another reason why you cool the reduction down; if it is too hot, you will cook your egg yolks prema-turely. The difference is a perfectly made hollandaise or a bowl of scrambled eggs.

Scrambled eggs are denatured and coagulated; well cooked, in other words. We talked about how meat proteins coagulate when we make a steak. Egg proteins do the same thing. Here is where the reduction does its magic. The water and the acid do two things.

First, the liquid buffers the heat and allows the protein to denature *slowly*. Unlike scrambled eggs where you plop the beaten eggs directly onto a frying pan at high temperatures, for hollandaise the egg yolks are cooked in the presence of water. Water helps slow heat transfer.

Second, the acidic reduction causes the proteins to unwind or denature slowly. This adds a safety net so you're less likely to make scrambled eggs. And finally, whisking in the liquid butter slowly gives you a chance to break up the fat into many tiny bubbles with the whisk. If you add the butter all at once, you'll see the process of surface tension in action. So, that's why we say to go slow and easy.

By now you might be asking, "What if I go too fast and the mixture prematurely coagulates?" Well, all is not lost because this happens even to the best of us some-times. If you break the sauce, just do what we did for a broken mayo. Keep the bro-ken sauce nearby. Set up all the preparations as if you were making half of the above formula for hollandaise. That means put two egg yolks and ¼ cup of reduction in the bowl. Repeat the process right through to the point where the egg-yolk mixture has thickened over the heat. Now, when you remove the egg from the double boiler, whisk in the broken sauce slowly instead of using clarified butter. This should rescue everything. Just have a little warm clarified butter handy in case you need it to adjust the consistency.

Food for Thought

Hollandaise can be seasoned with many different things to produce variations on the theme. All of the sauces are made exactly the same way; don't change the methods—just change the flavorings. The classic béarnaise sauce is one example. Make a hollandaise and then add chopped fresh tarragon at the end. If you want even more flavor, substitute a pinch of dried tarragon for the thyme in the reduction recipe. Like a tomato hollandaise? Well, after making the béarnaise variation, whisk in some chopped tomatoes or a spoon of tomato paste and voilà, you have a sauce Choron. A great accompaniment to lamb is sauce Paloise. It's made by adding chopped fresh mint to a hollandaise. Once you've mastered the techniques, the rest is simple; just get creative and do your own thing.

You can strain your finished hollandaise into a clean, warm container that will fit in a pan of warm, not hot, water. Use the hollandaise within a couple of hours or throw it away. Why? Well, first, it breaks easily, and second, because of the eggs, it is a highly perishable food. So, go do a steak and some asparagus and invite the neighbors over for some classic French fare. Feel like experimenting with some chilled hollandaise? Go right ahead; just realize that the butter will solidify if it gets too cool and the sauce cannot be easily re-warmed. You'll have some delicious butter that can be used as a spread or melted over grilled fish, but it'll never be hollandaise sauce again.

The Least You Need to Know

- Emulsified sauces use egg-yolk proteins to bind water and oil together; they may be cooked or uncooked.
- A classic mayonnaise is uncooked and composed of one egg yolk, juice from half a lemon, a pinch of salt, and 1 cup of vegetable oil.
- Hollandaise and other variations are a form of a cooked-egg-based sauce using clarified butter instead of oil.
- Warm sauces made with raw eggs should be used within two hours or discarded.
- Repeat the mantra "too hot, too fast, too much, too soon is too bad" when making egg-based sauces.

Chapter 26

Quickies: How to Cheat and Get Away With It

In This Chapter

- Milk, fat, flour, and heat
- Vegetarian thickeners and natural sauces
- Pan juices, heat, starches, and aromatics
- Butter and cream—two sides of the same coin

If you aren't yet ready to tackle making a stock and the sequence of steps needed to make brown sauces, or pumped up enough to take on cooking a hollandaise instead of scrambled eggs, there is one mother sauce that might be just what you're looking for. It's based on simple, natural milk and, most important, it can be put together in an hour or less. This base sauce is versatile enough to be served with down-home suppers or, with a touch here and there, can participate in some of the finest dishes in French cuisine.

Milk and Roux: A Beautiful Friendship

Béchamel is the classic mother sauce that results from milk, fat, flour, and heat. If you can go to the grocery store and purchase some fresh, whole milk, then you are half way there. Also buy one yellow onion, some whole cloves, and some ground nutmeg if you don't already have these in your kitchen lab. The only other thing you need is all-purpose flour and some oil or clarified butter. That's right; you are using our old friend Mr. Roux again. Because you already know from Chapter 24 how to concoct a pale roux, the béchamel sauce really goes together quickly.

The ratios of a classic sauce béchamel are 4 ounces (about $1/2$ cup) of pale roux for every quart of whole milk. This means cooking 4 tablespoons of clarified butter or vegetable oil with 4 tablespoons of flour. Vegetable oil works just as well as clarified butter, so if you really want to speed things up and skip the clarification step, this is fine with us. By the way, canola or corn oil works well for béchamel. Olive oil with its unique flavor and higher acidity does not go as well with the flavor of milk.

> **Chef Sez**
>
> **Infuse** means to extract flavors into a liquid by steeping. The easiest way to accomplish this is to heat the liquid, add the aromatics, cover, and remove from the heat. Allow it to steep for 15 to 30 minutes. Just like making a cup of tea.

The first step in making béchamel is to *infuse* your milk with some aromatics. The aromatics that we use are a yellow onion, whole cloves, and bay leaf. Pour the quart of milk into a pot that is big enough to hold the milk comfortably. Bring the milk to a simmer over medium heat. Peel the onion and cut it in half, leaving the end core attached so that the onion doesn't fall apart. Stick two whole cloves in each onion half and add both pieces of onion to the milk.

Add a bay leaf and a scant pinch of nutmeg. When the milk reaches a low boil, remove the pot from the heat, cover it and let it steep. The aromatic oils from the onion, cloves, and bay leaf will infuse into the milk, latching onto fat and proteins. This gives the unique flavors of the béchamel base. It takes about 20 minutes to get the hint of the infusion. At this point you can remove the aromatics and proceed with the thickening step. Of course, if you want a richer flavor from the aromatics, nothing says you can't leave them in the milk until the sauce is completely finished. It's your call.

As the milk infuses, turn the oil and flour into roux. Once ready, bring the milk back to the boil and whisk in the roux. It's important that you whisk well as you combine the roux and milk so that roux does not fall to the bottom of the pot, where it tends to burn. Adding warm roux to hot milk will start the thickening process almost instantly and can help prevent lumps from forming and settling to the bottom of the pot. Once the roux and milk are well mixed, turn the heat down and begin to cook the sauce.

Béchamel needs to cook for about 30 to 45 minutes. It is very similar to the process for making a velouté (refer to Chapter 24). You are using the thickening power of the roux along with the liquid, proteins, and fat in the milk. In the process, you are skimming off cooked flour proteins. You need to skim the surface every 15 minutes or so and discard the skin. Some of the classic daddies of cooking say that you should stir the béchamel every so often to keep the bottom from burning. If you do this, be sure to skim the surface first, or you will introduce the scum back into the béchamel. You can omit the stirring; just keep the béchamel cooking on a medium-low heat.

The béchamel is done when it loses its flour or starchy taste. Taste the béchamel at the beginning by pressing it on the roof of your mouth to gauge the texture and smoothness. When the béchamel is done, strain it through fine-mesh strainer and cool it down. Béchamel keeps well in the freezer if well covered. You now have succeeded in making one of the classic French mother sauces. Congratulations!

Lab Project

For a béchamel sauce, pour 1 quart of whole milk into a large saucepan. Peel and cut one onion in half. Press two whole cloves into each piece of onion and add the onion to the milk. Add a pinch of nutmeg and a bay leaf to the milk and then bring it to a simmer. Cover and remove from the heat; set aside for 20 minutes.

Meanwhile, make a pale roux with 4 tablespoons of clarified butter or oil and 4 table-spoons of flour. After the milk has infused sufficiently, reheat it to a low boil and whisk in the roux. When the roux is fully incorporated, reduce the heat and simmer for 30 to 45 minutes. Skim the surface of the sauce every 15 minutes, discarding any skin that forms. Strain the finished sauce through a mesh strainer and cool in an ice bath before refrigerating.

A béchamel base can be used to make a host of very classic French small sauces. The most basic of these is the cream sauce. To fashion this one, all you need is the base and some heavy whipping cream. You heat the béchamel and add some heavy cream, typically about one part cream to four parts béchamel. Then you reduce this down about 20 percent, so that if you start with 1 quart, you'll end up with close to 3 cups. You can even infuse the cream with any aromatics that fit the dish you are serving, such as fresh herbs or citrus zest. Your imagination is the limit here.

Sauce from the Garden

So far we have talked about sauces that use animal products as a part of the thickening process. Animal-based stocks, milk, and eggs have saturated fats, proteins, and natural emulsifiers that help us achieve the right consistency for each sauce. That consistency gives us a mouth feel that is pleasing to the palate and will match the food we want the sauce to complement. While vegetable stocks and sauces based on them will never have the same mouth feel and texture as animal-derived sauces, they can be used to accent food. Making them is not rocket science.

Probably the easiest vegetable sauce to understand is based on the thickening power of the humble tomato. Yep, you guessed it; tomato sauce is one of the classic mother sauces. Of course, chicken stock is a component of a truly classic tomato sauce. But nothing says that you can't achieve an unctuous tomato sauce *sans* chicken stock. We'll just call it a marinara, or lighter tomato sauce.

After all, have you checked out canned tomato paste lately? No animal product in there. Yet it is thick and rich. Why? Well, it's all about water. Slowly cooked tomatoes give off a lot of moisture. What's left is the *essence* of the product. That's because what you are getting down to is pectin and cellulose, the glues that hold plants together. Just like collagen is the glue of animals, and the substance we extract to make animal stocks, sauces based on plant reductions depend upon pectin and cellulose for some thickening power. Since over 90 percent of a tomato is water, you have to start with lots of tomatoes to make a thick paste or a rich marinara sauce.

Chef Sez

A **purée** is made from vegetables or fruits that are mashed, strained, or finely chopped into a smooth pulp. An **essence** is an extract of an aromatic vegetable made by cooking or stewing it in a very small quantity of liquid. The resulting liquid can be used as a flavor component in sauce-making.

Any vegetable (or fruit for that matter) that is cooked down thickens as water evaporates—if you leave the lid off the pot so the steam can escape, that is. Grandma's old-fashioned applesauce is an example, but hopefully we can move beyond that as we learn some simple rules. The basics are all the same: Cook the vegetable or fruit, *purée* it, strain if desired, and thicken by reduction.

Purées are generally lighter, which isn't necessarily a bad thing if you just want something light on your pasta. Purées should still be full flavored and well seasoned, however. You need not be boring when making vegetable purées for sauces. For example, red or yellow bell pepper sauce will add a brightness to plates, which appeals to both the sense of sight and taste. Pepper purées can be prepared just like the tomato marinara sauce described later. Vegetable purée sauces possess one other important virtue. They can be higher in fiber. The fiber that is in there contributes to the texture, but even more important, it does the body good.

Often it's better to combine several vegetables and use a vegetable stock to get maximum flavor for a vegetable-based sauce. Mixtures of veggies complement one another because each has its own flavor profile that creates more interest in the sauce on your tongue. And using some higher fiber veggies such as peas or beans, along with lighter ones such as celery and onions, gives you the health benefits of more fiber in addition to great taste.

To make the simplest of tomato marinara sauces, you need some flavorful rich tomatoes, like romas. Roasting the tomatoes along with onion, garlic, and fresh herbs deepens the flavor through the process of caramelization. For every 5 pounds of tomatoes, use one onion, a nice bunch of herbs, and one entire head of garlic. Oil a roasting pan with a little olive oil, slice the tomatoes in half, and toss them in the pan to coat with the oil. Add the crushed garlic cloves and fresh basil. Chopped onion can be distributed around the pan. Sprinkle liberally with fresh cracked black pepper and kosher salt. Roast all of this in a 400°F oven until the tomatoes have just begun to soften and char slightly. They almost look melted. The sugars and the proteins cook together from all of these ingredients, giving a broad-based sweetness and depth.

Purée all of the contents of the roasting pan through a food mill. A food mill is better for this than a blender because it gently cuts the cells of the vegetables rather than completely pulverizing them. This will help keep a more appealing color. Using a blender introduces so much air in the process that you oxidize all those color molecules, essentially taking off their shine.

Puréeing tomato sauce with a food mill.

Once you have your purée, just cook it on a low simmer until the consistency thickens. You can also add a full-flavored vegetable stock to the tomato purée before you begin the reduction process. If the tomatoes lack acidity, add some red-wine vinegar to taste. A touch of sugar balances acid, as does salt. Fresh, cracked black pepper is added for pungency. Season the sauce at the beginning of the cooking process, in the middle, and at the end to finish.

Lab Project

For a tomato marinara sauce, coat a roasting pan with olive oil. Put 5 pounds of halved roma tomatoes, 1 chopped onion, $1/2$ ounce of fresh basil, $1/4$ ounce of fresh oregano, and 1 head of garlic (peel and crush the cloves) in the pan. Sprinkle on a liberal amount of kosher salt and freshly ground black pepper. Toss everything together and cook at 400°F until the vegetables are softened and slightly charred, about 40 minutes. Purée everything through a food mill and place the purée in a large saucepan. Taste and adjust the acidity with red-wine vinegar or sugar as needed. Add 1 cup of vegetable stock and bring the sauce to a simmer over medium heat. Simmer gently until thick. When the sauce is a thick as you'd like, adjust the flavor again with salt and pepper, and with sugar or vinegar.

Mushrooms, both the wild exotic kind and the more common ones, make rather sexy and elegant sauce bases. You used mushroom *essence* previously to make a classic sauce suprême. Mushrooms need not be fresh to serve as a sauce. In fact, there is an intense, flavorful compound found only in dried shiitake mushrooms after hydrating them. It is called *lenthionine* if you must know. Next time you plan to sauté veal or beef medallions, pick up some dried shiitakes also. When you get the 'shrooms home, rinse them quickly, remove and discard the tough stems, and place the caps in a small bowl with just enough Madeira to cover them. Allow them to rehydrate for about 20 minutes, and then heat this infusion for 10 minutes on a low simmer to drive away the alcohol. Now, take out the mushrooms and chop them up. Use the mushroom cooking liquid to deglaze the sauté pan after cooking the meat. Then add the chopped mushrooms, swirl in a little whole butter, and call us in the morning.

Jus Like Me, Jus Really Like Me!

The simplest sauce a meat lover can make is *jus*. Think about all the pan drippings you are left with after cooking meat. When the cooking method is roasting, the juices left are dark, rich, and flavorful. Your nice, brown and somewhat crusty roast goes perfectly with this meat extract. If you are a loner with only one mouth to feed, usually there are plenty of drippings in the pan to feast upon. Simply take the roast out of the pan, cover it, and allow it to rest while you fashion your jus into a sauce.

If you have a fair amount of liquid, you can put the roasting pan on a burner and turn up the heat. The fat will break from the heat (this is one situation where you want high heat to break the fat from the liquid) and you can take a spoon and skim off the fat.

Then scrape the bottom of the pan to loosen all those nice crunchy bits, strain it all into a sauce pan, and reduce this extract down until it thickens slightly. As the liquid reduces, more and more bubbles start to form around the edge of the pan. You will notice it turning into a syrupy consistency as the water evaporates. If you dip the backside of a spoon on the surface of the liquid, it should cling there. Run your finger across the spoon and see if you divide the syrupy coating into two areas. If you can, then it is just right. By now it is so rich that only a tablespoon or two per person is needed. Just season with some salt and pepper and serve.

> **Chef Sez** _____
>
> **Jus** is French for "juice" and refers to the natural meat juices remaining in a roasting pan after cooking. These pan drippings are full flavored and are the basis of a natural sauce. When a dish is served with these juices, we say it is served *au jus*.

If you have a couple of mouths to feed, cooking the jus down to a tablespoon often leaves one guest left out and unhappy. So, we need to extend things a bit. In this case, or when you have very little drippings to start with, you need to add a flavorful stock or lightly salted water to the roasting pan. Scrap up the tasty bits, de-fat the liquid and strain it, and then reduce it in another pan. Make a bit of cornstarch slurry (or use arrowroot) to thicken the jus slightly. This will add the texture you want without evaporating so much that you cannot feed your guest. Of course, you still need to season well with some salt, pepper, and maybe just a splash of fortified wine (port or Madeira) to give the flavor a final pop.

> **Too Hot to Handle** _____
>
> At the risk of overstating the obvious, pan juices evaporate quickly when heated on the stovetop. It is also very easy to scorch them, or even completely burn away the contents of the pan, leaving you without any sauce for your supper. Keep the pan over medium or low heat and never walk away to answer the phone or engage in a heated debate (or otherwise) with your partner while reducing a jus.

Aromatics can also come into play with jus. First, as we mentioned in roasting of meat, you often use a mirepoix as the bed for the roast. The vegetables release their flavors during the roasting process and are captured when you make your jus into a sauce. Another place you can introduce aromatics is during the sauce-making process. Before you deglaze your roasting pan with stock, water, or wine, add a few chopped shallots and a sprig of thyme. Cook this mixture until it sizzles and the shallots have taken on a shine, maybe two minutes or so. Now deglaze, de-fat, or strain, and de-fat again. Now reduce to a nice syrupy consistency, or thicken with starch and season. You will notice a difference in the taste of this simple jus.

Sauce from the Dairy Case

If a chicken were a chef's first choice for a desert island companion, the cow would be his second. This may sound a little strange, but we just take our cooking and eating seriously. A cow is going to keep us supplied with cream and butter, which, along with eggs, define the French style. It all goes back to mouth feel and the simple fact that fat makes things taste good.

Butter and cream possess physical characteristics that are essential for many classic sauces. In fact, cream is the gold standard used to determine one of the properties of a well-made sauce, namely texture. Butter is a water-in-fat emulsion, while cream is a fat-in-water emulsion. This may not be as hard to imagine as it sounds. You already know that an emulsion is the oneness achieved when two nonmixable liquids get together in harmonious bliss.

Picture this in your mind before you started to churn the cream. The water was top dog and had surrounded the fat. This is why the cream flowed; water could move around from place to place with the fat tagging along for the ride. When you churn cream, which is 30 to 40 percent fat, you are breaking up the fat into millions of small fat droplets. Now imagine a point as you are churning when you have created so many fat droplets that they overwhelm the water. The fat now becomes top dog and the tables turn. Now the fat, broken into millions of small spheres, outnumbers the water. The water can no longer go where it wants to go without running into a sphere of fat.

The butter you just whipped and churned has becomes a solid. All the water is still in there; it just is trapped inside the fat. Now you have your water-in-fat emulsion. We can also thicken cream without whipping in air by reducing it, to evaporate some of the water. When you reduce a quart of cream by half (to a pint, that is), you will find that the consistency has thickened dramatically.

So, what does all of this food science have to do with you and sauce-making? Well, if you neglect to make stocks, refuse to make a hollandaise, balk on making a vegetable purée, but still want to serve an impressive sauce, there is hope for you yet. Go to the market, buy some heavy whipping cream, one that is 35 to 40 percent butterfat, some unsalted butter, and some aromatics, if you don't already have a supply at home. For this lesson, it would also be nice to have a couple of center-cut pork-loin chops handy.

Taking Cream to the Limit

One of the best ways to use cream in cooking hot foods is to first cook it a bit. Cooking the cream ahead of time thickens it by evaporating some of its water content. This improves the texture of the sauces that you make and can save you time when you want to use it in a pinch.

Reducing cream is an easy task if you keep some important things in mind. Cream is not called heavy for nothing; it's a thick liquid because of all the fat it contains. Unlike water that boils away to steam, heating cream causes a different response. In its haste to bubble away as it boils, the water part of cream runs into all of that fat. The water can literally push the fat up and out of the pan, which makes for a very messy stovetop. But you don't have to allow that to happen. What you do is use a pan that is about four to five times deeper than the volume of cream you are heating.

That way, as the cream rises and the water escapes, you've created a safety zone for the cream to expand into. And never cover the pan. That will only make it boil harder. Just use medium-high heat, and give the cream a stir once in awhile. Stirring will help release some steam pressure and keep the milk proteins and fat from settling on the bottom of the pan and burning. Reduce the cream until about half of the original volume remains. You have now succeeded in making reduced cream. Once cooled, you can keep it tightly covered in the fridge for making quickie sauces.

Reduced heavy cream is also a great medium for an infusion. Take a variety of aromatic herbs, hot peppers, peppercorns, fresh ginger, lemon zest, or anything that can release *essential oils* for flavor. The essential oils are often found in the skins or seeds of plants. You can demonstrate them by squeezing a piece orange or lemon peel. Notice that fragrant spray and smell? That's the good stuff you may want in your cream to flavor it. They are volatile, which means that they can carry their aromas over long distances. The high fat content of your cream, though, traps these flavors into the cream and

> **Food for Thought**
> Even wonder about cartons of cream labeled **ultrapasteurized?** Milk products undergo pasteurization; a sterilizing heat treatment used to destroy pathogenic bacteria and enzymes that cause spoilage. But cream's high fat content means it will spoil easily, so packagers put it through an especially high-temperature treatment called ultrapasteurization. Ultrapasteurized cream must still stay refrigerated, but it does have a much longer lifespan.

> **Chef Sez**
> **Essential oils** are the volatile oils that give plants their distinctive fragrances. These oils can be extracted from some flowers, leaves, seeds, or skins.

captures their inherent essence before they can escape. This is a great technique for adding a layer of depth to your sauces with very little effort.

Now that you have some reduced cream, you can try it out in a quick recipe. Heat the oven to 325°F and take a sauté pan that has a tight-fitting lid. It's a pretty good idea to make sure the pan you are using has a handle that can withstand the heat of the oven. This means that the handle should be oven-proof. Put a tablespoon of olive oil and a couple of smashed cloves of garlic in the pan. Infuse the garlic into the oil without burning it, and then remove the garlic cloves. Season your pork chops well on both sides with salt and freshly ground black pepper. Of course, it's your pork, so add more seasonings if you like; curry powder, for example, is nice.

Rub all the seasonings into the chops. Sear the chops over high heat for two to three minutes on each side. Put the garlic back in the pan, and add ⅓ cup cold water. Be careful; the pan is hot and the water will sputter, but it's worth the trouble. Place the lid on the pan and pop it into the oven. Cook the pork for 15 minutes. You can check for doneness as we described for meat cookery; either press it to check for firmness or, better yet, measure the internal temperature with a thermometer probe. Remember that tender cuts of pork are best at 145°F, which allows for a little carry-over cooking.

Lab Project

For pork chops in a curried cream sauce, heat 1 tablespoon of olive oil in a sauté pan. Add 2 crushed cloves of garlic and cook over medium heat until the garlic is tender and translucent. Remove the garlic and set aside. Meanwhile, sprinkle 2 center-cut pork chops with salt, pepper, and curry powder. Increase the heat to high and sear the pork in the sauté pan, cooking about 2 minutes per side. Return the garlic to the pan and carefully add ⅓ cup of cold water.

Cover the pan and place in a preheated 325°F oven. Cook for approximately 15 minutes, or to an internal temperature of 145°F. Remove the pan from the oven and move the pork from the pan to a plate, cover with a piece of aluminum foil, and let it rest while you prepare the sauce. Put the sauté pan on medium high heat and reduce the pan juices, skimming away any excess fat. Add the juice from half a lemon. Reduce the liquid until it looks a bit syrupy, and then add 6 tablespoons of reduced cream and cook slowly for another minute. Whisk in 1 tablespoon of unsalted butter. Pour the sauce over the pork and serve.

When the pork is done, remove it from the pan to a plate, cover with a piece of aluminum foil, and let it rest while you prepare the sauce. Put the sauté pan on medium-high heat and reduce the pan juices. Skim away any excess fat. Add the juice from half a lemon. Reduce the liquid until it looks a bit syrupy, and then add 6 table-spoons of reduced cream and cook slowly for another minute. Whisk in 1 tablespoon of unsalted butter and enjoy a *jus* that is enriched with butter and reduced cream. What could be simpler?

The Butter Connection

Butter is the ultimate finisher for a sauce, be it with cream or just a plain jus. Unsalted butter is a must because the flavor of salted butter is very difficult to control. It is easier to add salt to taste than to use a salted butter.

For a super simple butter sauces just melt some butter in a small pan. Just like when you made clarified butter, the solids and water will cook out. The butter foams during this process as water is released from the proteins and fats. Once the solids fall to the bottom of the pan, they begin to brown. When the butter has taken on a light brown shade and smells a bit like nuts, remove it from the heat. Let it cool three minutes and then add a squeeze of lemon juice and some chopped fresh parsley. You've succeeded in making a brown butter sauce, or, as the French say, *beurre noisette*. This is a classic sauce that is based on the process of breaking the emulsions that normally keep butter happy in your refrigerator. If you were to cook the butter until it gets a bit browner, but not burned, and then were to cool it and add white-wine vinegar instead of lemon juice, you would have a *beurre noire*—black butter. Both of these broken sauces are great with fish, or some lightly salted steamed vegetables.

So, you still aren't convinced you can make a classic sauce and want something even simpler? Okay, we have one more possibility. Bring a pound of unsalted butter to room temperature. Put the flat paddle attachment on your mixer and plop the butter in the bowl. Beat the butter into a nice, creamy consistency. Add a couple of spoonfuls of chopped fresh parsley and squeeze the juice from half a lemon into the butter. Season with some salt and white pepper and, voilà, you have a compound butter that can be used as a sauce. Its fancy French name is *maître d' butter*, just like the guy in the tux at a restaurant. If you're feeling crazy, mix some finely chopped shallots into the butter also. Classic compound butters are served with big steaks. They also function well on broiled or grilled fish. Or you can use the butter to swirl into soup, or finish one of the sauces that you have so far refused to make. Compound butters can be infused and flavored with many different things, from nuts to red peppers. Your imagination is the only limit.

> **Chef Sez**
> **Maître d' butter** is a compound butter flavored with lemon juice, parsley, white pepper, and salt.

The Least You Need to Know

◆ Béchamel is a classic mother sauce made by thickening onion-infused whole milk with pale roux.

◆ Vegetable purées, stocks, and essences can be used as sauces. A tomato marinara is one example.

◆ The most basic sauce derived from roasted meats is the jus. In its simplest form, it is reduced pan drippings.

◆ Butter and reduced cream can be used to thicken a simple jus, or to finish and enrich a reduced sauce.

◆ Flavored butter, known as compound butter, can be used as a simple sauce for grilled meat, fish, or poultry, or on steamed veggies.

Chapter 27

Salad Years: Green in Judgment

In This Chapter

♦ The basic training vinaigrette

♦ Flavor exercises—training your tongue

♦ Lettuce: standing tall and firm

Everyone seems to be eating salad these days. You find them in supermarket delis and fast-food joints. Oddly enough, the desire to eat salad because of the health benefits found in low-calorie, high-fiber, fresh veggies is being destroyed by folks who immerse their greens in rich, thick, commercial salad dressings. This is even more of a mystery considering how easy it is to make an endless variety of your own dressings with as little (or as much) fat as you prefer.

Next time you're grazing on greens, take a peek at the label of your favorite commercial dressing. You will see that it's chock full of ingredients that you probably can't pronounce. Just like the purveyors of mayonnaise make it "bomb proof," the same companies need to add a bunch of emulsifiers, gums, and stabilizers to make your dressing look healthy and beautiful while sitting on your shelf for months on end. And, we might add, at a considerable cost to you. With a little basic training you can make dressings that are healthier, more flavorful, and less costly, with very little effort.

Vinaigrette Boot Camp

Like a mayonnaise, the basic *vinaigrette* is an emulsion. You'll recall that an emulsion occurs when you succeed in mixing two or more liquids that normally would not be happy together, such as oil and water. You force them together with a bit of energy and a chemical catalyst called an emulsifier. The chemical emulsifier acts like a good mediator, bringing the parties together so that they mix and mingle without separating. All emulsions are temporary, which means that they will separate after sitting for a length of time. A vinaigrette is the most temporary of emulsions. Withdraw the energy source (your whisking power), and within mere minutes you can watch the emulsion break.

Chef Sez

Vinaigrette is a basic oil-and-liquid emulsion typically used to dress salad greens.

The vinaigrette is the best emulsion to illustrate the principle of surface tension. Here's a lab project that will help you understand how to combine a liquid with oil, and why the order of additions is so important. Of course, if you are not such a purist, and just want to dump everything in a blender and mix it as if it all didn't matter, be our guest. But there is a right way to do it, which helps guarantee your results every time.

Measure out a $^1/_4$ cup of oil and $^3/_4$ cup of white-wine vinegar. If you use olive oil that has a nice green shade, the visuals will be easier for you to see. Take your favorite clear 16-ounce measuring cup and pour in the vinegar. Then pour in the oil. You will see the oil form a slick atop the vinegar; voilà, surface tension at work here.

Next, take the same ingredients and reverse the process. Now add the oil first, and then the vinegar (water again!) atop it. Oil will still climb to the surface, but what happens here is a bit different. Now the oil forms a bunch more droplets. You might even see a few of these suspended within the liquid. By the way, you can reserve the ingredients from these experiments and fashion them into a vinaigrette. Your effort and expense is not wasted, but more on that later.

The lab experiment illustrates what your goal is in making an emulsion. You want to achieve the mixing of the oil in the water phase, not by creating just a few droplets of oil in water, but millions of tiny droplets. Imagine, if you can, the oil slick suspended totally within the vinegar, each droplet separated by some vinegar. Now, instead of one big drop on the surface of the pond, you have many tiny drops in the pond. The liquid is no longer just liquid, but takes on part of the consistency of the smaller drops of oil, and the texture thickens.

Over time, the oil droplets will begin to float to the surface and join together again into one slick. Because most homemade vinaigrettes have no appreciable amounts of emulsifiers to hold the oil in suspension and tug the drops to the center, the oil floats to the surface quicker than say, your mayonnaise. Of course, some commercial vinaigrettes have solved this problem by adding stabilizers and other fun things, but a few packaged vinaigrettes allow the oil/water mixture to separate on the grocery shelf. Guess the manufacturers think it looks more natural that way.

So, if you're ready to put this science into action, let's get started. Remember, the order in which you add the ingredients when whisking a vinaigrette together by hand is very important. First, take a clean bowl and place it atop a towel on your work surface. The towel keeps the bowl from moving around on you. Add 4 tablespoons of your favorite vinegar to the bowl. Measure out $^3/_4$ cup (12 tablespoons) of oil—olive, corn, salad, whatever you prefer. With the oil in your left hand (sorry, assuming right-handed persons here) and the whisk in your right, begin to add a few drops of oil to the vinegar. Whisk like mad. Add a few more drops and whisk again. Think of our mantra as you proceed: too much, too fast, too soon means too bad. Now begin to add the oil in a nice steady stream as you whisk. See how this procedure is just like making mayonnaise, only without the eggs? As you add more and more oil, the vinaigrette thickens. Once all of the oil is added, you should have a relatively viscous liquid.

You add oil over the water (vinegar) so that you can control the break-up of the fat droplets in the oil. It's a lot easier to beat small globs of oil into smaller globs of oil. When you are dealing with a more viscous liquid, it will take less of your energy to attack a small part of it than to attack the whole thing.

High Notes and Low Notes: Flavor Training

Once you have the basic components and mixing procedures down for vinaigrette, it's time to consider your seasoning options. Salt and pepper are obvious additions, but chopped fresh herbs and other goodies from your home lab can also be used.

A less-than-wonderful vinaigrette may either taste flabby or sharp. Flabby means it tastes too oily while sharp gives the impression of an acid finish on your palate. The best vinaigrette, as in most food, is well balanced. It should not be so flabby that it causes you to yawn, nor so sharp that you are left gasping for breath. Since a vinaigrette is eaten with salad, you should taste it with a piece of lettuce or other salad greens. Vinaigrette that may taste a bit too sharp *au natural*, may be just right when accompanying salad greens.

Obviously, vinaigrettes take on the character of the oils, vinegars, and seasonings that you choose to use. A vinaigrette made with extra-virgin olive oil will taste decidedly different from one made with canola oil. And the world of olive oil offers a large variety of styles and acidity levels. Other flavorful, albeit more expensive, oils include walnut, avocado, hazelnut, sesame, and pumpkin seed. Pick whichever turns you on.

Combining a bland oil with a highly flavored one may be just the combination you're looking for; likewise for vinegars. Some, such as distilled or white-wine vinegar, provide acidity with little real flavor; others offer specific flavors to complement your salad. If you do any amount of cooking at all, your home lab will soon contain a selection—raspberry, red-wine, balsamic, sherry, tarragon, malt, and cider vinegar are just a few of your choices. And, despite the name, the acidic ingredient in a vinaigrette need not even be vinegar. Diluted lemon or lime juice works just fine, also.

The ratio of acidic liquid to oil tends to be a constant. Classic vinaigrette contains three parts oil to one part acid. In other words, ³/₄ cup oil to ¹/₄ cup vinegar. Using one part, more or less, of oil adjusts the flabbiness factor up or down.

When it comes to specific flavor notes, you can fashion a virtually limitless variety of vinaigrettes using one basic procedure. If, for example, you want to add the flavor of fresh herbs or chopped shallot, add 1 teaspoon of finely chopped fresh herbs or shallots to your ¹/₄ cup of acidic liquid before adding the oil. Whisk in the oil like we explained above, and then adjust the seasonings to suit. The finished product should be seasoned with salt, white pepper, black pepper, or even sugar to taste. Sugar and salt soften acidity and can be used to balance the vinaigrette at the end. Fresh herbs whisked in just before serving vinaigrette add freshness. Finally, you can infuse vinegars with herbs, and use the flavored vinegars to make more robust and rich vinaigrettes.

> **Now You're Cooking**
>
> Just about anything that would add a great flavor to your salad can be used in your vinaigrette. It's best, however, to start with a small amount of each flavoring ingredient and add more only if the taste test proves it's really needed. Some examples to get you started include roasted garlic, crumbled blue cheese or feta cheese, Dijon mustard, lemon zest, and poppy seeds.

Look back at your oil-in-water and water-in-oil experiments from the beginning of this chapter. Notice that both contain the proper 3:1 ratio of oil to vinegar. All that's missing is for you to add some flavoring ingredients, such as a tablespoon or so each of Dijon mustard and honey, plus some salt and white pepper. Now, whisk both "experiments" together and get out the greens.

Don't Wilt Me

Salad greens are alive. They, along with their kissing cousins fresh fruits and vegetables, and some fresh shellfish, are some of the few foods we consume while they are still living and breathing. Mixing the vinaigrette with the living tissue of salad greens affects how the greens look and taste. This is simply the biology of the plant cell taking control.

Plant cells breathe. They circulate oxygen, carbon dioxide, and water. Since plant tissue approaches 95 percent moisture, you can imagine that water is located just about everywhere in a plant cell. When it was still in the ground, the plant's plumbing system transported water from the soil through the stems to the leaves. Water was continuously replenished as needed. The pressure of the water inside the plant pressing out against the cell tissue kept it upright.

You no doubt have observed what happens when you go on vacation and forget to give your petunias a drink of water before you leave. When you return, the plant is a little droopy. It has run low on water pressure. The plant used up some of its water through metabolism and some just evaporated away. This loss of water is a process called transpiration. Give it a drink and watch it perk right up again, just like a good little soldier.

In other words, a plant wilts because it has lost too much moisture. So, keep fresh greens in a high humidity environment to decrease the chance of losing water. That's what a good vegetable crisper does in your refrigerator. And did you ever notice those automatic sprayers in the vegetable section of your market? They periodically give the vegetables a spray of water. It coats the leaves and cools them off, creating a higher localized humidity and delaying water loss. By the way, the water doesn't soak into the plant very well by this method. The waxy cuticle on the plant skin causes most of the water to bead up. But it does protect against water loss. Once the plant loses water, it is less healthy and susceptible to diseases and molds. It becomes sickly and unattractive.

Lettuce, like most plants, prefers to drink its water through its roots. Now, in nature, lettuce can be pelted with rain without wilting. Because lettuces, and all plant cells, have a skin called a cuticle the water runs off. The cuticle is waxy and protects the plant from water soaking through.

So, unless it starts to pour down rain containing Italian dressing, our lettuce is relatively safe in the garden. In your salad bowl, it's another question. When we add salad dressing to a lettuce leaf, we are exposing it to an acid, some liquid, and heavy fat.

The heavy fat has a fondness for the waxy fat of the lettuce leaf, because like molecules are attracted to each other. Try as it might, the lettuce cannot keep the oil and the acid from being drawn into it. Once that occurs, the tissue breaks down. The epidermis, or outer skin layer, of the lettuce cells becomes leaky. There is literally a chemical abrasion of the skin happening now. You know what happens on your skin when you touch something abrasive or caustic like acid? There is pain and often a change indicating injury: It burns. The same thing happens in a plant.

In this case, the waxy cuticle, epidermis, and first layers of tissue underneath the epidermis called the *parenchyma* start to take up the oil and acids. The invasion spreads to more cells; it's like tipping over a set of dominoes now. More acid and fat enter, and as more cells break apart, they spew out their own acids. Soon you have a cauldron of wastes around all of the lettuce tissue. You have a virtual digestion of the greens going on right on the plate. The greens visibly wilt.

> **Chef Sez** ___
>
> A **tossed salad** is one where the greens and other ingredients and vinaigrette are freely mixed and then served. A **composed salad** is one where greens and other ingredients are arranged on the plate and then dressed.

How can you deal the inevitable wilting of a dressed salad? It's all about timing. It's also about quantity. A good rule of thumb is to use no more than about 1 tablespoon of vinaigrette per serving. A second, common-sense rule is to mix the greens with the dressing immediately before serving them. If you compose your salads, drizzle the vinaigrette over them right before serving. In other words, wilting is inevitable; the best you can do is delay the process until after your salad is served.

The Least You Need to Know

- Vinaigrette is a temporary emulsion composed of a liquid and an oil; if vinaigrette breaks, whisking or mixing the ingredients will restore the emulsion.

- The basic ratio for making classic vinaigrette is three parts of oil to one part of acidic liquid.

- Vinaigrettes can be made with a variety of oils and acidic liquids depending on the style and the flavor profile desired.

- Never use aluminum utensils or storage containers for making vinaigrettes. The color of the food can be affected and the acid may leech toxic aluminum into the food.

- Salad greens should be dressed as close to serving time as possible to prevent premature wilting.

Appendix A

Glossary

albumin   See *egg*.

aromatics   Ingredients such as *mirepoix*, bay leaf, peppercorns, or springs of fresh herbs that are added to a food to enhance its aroma and flavor.

baking   A dry-heat cooking method that cooks food by surrounding it with hot air in an enclosed chamber such as an oven. The same process may be referred to as roasting, depending on the food item being cooked. For example, meat and chicken are roasted; cakes, bread, and fish are baked.

barding   Tying a thin piece of fat or bacon across lean meat or poultry, especially game. The fat adds moisture and tenderness during cooking.

basmati   An aged aromatic long-grain rice from the Himalayan foothills. Its sweet, delicate flavor and creamy color are widely preferred in Indian cuisine.

batter   (1) A mixture of flour and water that forms a pourable, semi-liquid state; (2) A pourable mixture usually made from flour, milk, and eggs that can be used to coat foods for deep-frying.

beans   Plant species that have seedpods. For some varieties, the entire pod is eaten fresh; for others, only the seeds are eaten. Some seeds are eaten fresh, but many are dried and then rehydrated during cooking.

biotechnology   The manipulation of living cells and their components. Food biotechnology is the application of techniques such as genetic engineering to modify foods or processes.

blanch   To plunge fruits or vegetables into hot water or fat for a very short period of time. The food may be *shocked* or refreshed by immediately placing it in ice water to stop the cooking process. Blanching is used to firm texture, remove skin, or set color.

breading   A three-step process of dipping food into flour, and then into a liquid egg-water mixture, and then coating the food with crumbs. Breading adds flavor and texture, and coats and protects delicate foods being fried or baked.

breaking   The separation of fat and liquid (water) from an emulsion. A broken sauce can sometimes be repaired by adding back energy (rewhipping) or changing the temperature.

brine   Heavily salted water used in the curing of food.

broth   Stock made from bones and meat. Broths are generally used to make soups.

bulgur   Wheat berries that have the bran removed and are then steamed, dried, and cracked into small pieces; it can be cooked like rice and is the basis for tabbouleh.

capon   A castrated male chicken fed to produce a larger bird with a higher proportion of white meat.

caramelization   A browning process caused when sugar reacts to very high temperatures. A specific type of caramelization is called the *Maillard* reaction, in which protein and fat react with sugars to aid in the browning process.

carbohydrates   Organic nutrients including sugars and starches. They may be single molecules—monosaccharides such as glucose; they may be two molecules hooked together—disaccharides such as sucrose; or they may be several molecules hooked together—oligosaccharides.

carryover cooking   The effect of residual heat contained within cooked food items. This heat continues to cook the food even after it is removed from the oven or other heat source.

ceviche or **seviche**   Raw fish and/or shellfish marinated in lemon or lime juice. The acids partially denature and cook the proteins.

cold smoking   The process of smoking food at temperatures below 100°F. The food is not cooked during this process.

collagen   Word meaning "glue-like" and referring to connective tissue found in ligaments, tendons, cartilage, and skin. Gelatin is derived from collagen through moist-heat cooking.

composed salad   One in which the greens and other ingredients are arranged on the plate and then dressed.

connective tissue   Tissue that holds muscle fibers together and holds meat to bone. Collagen, elastin, and reticulin are the three types of connective tissue.

cooking   The application of energy, usually in the form of heat, to food. This energy alters the food's molecular structure, changing its texture, flavor, aroma, and appearance.

couscous   Small spheres of high-protein semolina dough that are rolled, dampened, and coated with a finer wheat flour. Couscous is a staple of North African diets.

couverture   Professional quality chocolate that is extremely smooth and glossy. It contains a minimum of 32 percent cocoa butter.

curing   A process of treating a food to preserve it. Salting, brining (pickling), and drying (dehydrating) are all forms of curing. Smoking can be added to enhance flavors and to aid in the curing process.

custard   A liquid thickened by the denaturing and coagulation of egg proteins. Stirred custard is cooked to a creamy, pourable consistency by stirring it in a pan on the stovetop. Baked custard is cooked to a gel-like consistency in an oven using a water bath.

DNA (Deoxyribonucleic Acid)   The genetic material that passes information from one generation to the next. It works with cell RNA to make proteins.

dough   A stiff mixture of flour and water that is pliable and workable as a soft solid.

drawn   Fish that has been gutted but still has its head and gills attached.

egg   The hard-shelled reproductive body produced by a bird. It consists of the egg white (albumin) and egg yolk. Egg white is the clear translucent part of an egg. It is comprised of three different albumin proteins, vitamins, and minerals. Egg yolk is the central yellow part of an egg. It is a thin membrane filled with proteins, lipids, vitamins, and minerals.

emulsion   The mixing of two or more liquids that normally would not stay together, such as oil and water. Emulsions form when the liquids are combined along with an *emulsifier* and energy.

emulsifier   A substance that helps bind together two or more liquids that otherwise would not mix. Lecithin is a commonly used emulsifier found in egg yolks.

enzymes   Proteins that regulate production of a biochemical reaction and allow biological reactions to occur within a cell at an efficient rate. Enzymes have a profound effect on the way food looks or tastes because they affect the production of all food molecules.

essential oils   The volatile oils that give plants their distinctive fragrances. These oils can be extracted from some flowers, leaves, seeds, or skins.

étuvé   To cook in a covered pot with a minimal amount of liquid.

fat   A general term used to describe a class of organic nutrients including *lipids*, triglycerides, sterols, and phospholipids. Fats and oils that are separated from plant or animal cells such as lard, butter, or shortening are called *visible fat*. Fats and oils that we consume as part of a basic food such as nuts, meat, milk, or eggs are called a *constituent fat*.

fermentation   See *yeast*.

fiber   The nondigestible part of a plant-cell wall; it is comprised of cellulose and pectin substances.

field or **dent**   The type of corn grown for livestock fed. Sweet corn and popcorn are used for human consumption.

fillet   A boneless piece of flesh cut from the entire side of a fish. *Roundfish* have two fillets; *flatfish* have four.

flatfish   Category of fish characterized by a backbone in the center, with muscles above and below the bone and both eyes on the top of the body. Dover sole and halibut are examples. See *roundfish*.

fletch   Pieces of fish muscle from flatfish. There are four fletches from every flatfish.

foam   Gas (such as air) dispersed in a liquid. Whipped cream is an example of a foam, as is ice cream.

fond   French for base; used to refer to *stock*.

game hen   (a.k.a. Rock Cornish game hen) The young offspring of Cornish chickens, or a genetic cross between a Cornish chicken and a White Rock chicken. A whole game hen is a small single-serving-sized portion.

gelatinization   The process by which starch granules cook. When placed in a liquid and heated, starch will absorb moisture, and then swell and soften. Gelatinization occurs at different temperatures for different starches, but for most food starches this occurs between 135° and 160°F.

gelato   A creamy Italian-style ice cream that is denser and softer than American ice cream because it contains less *overrun*.

gene   The portion of a chromosome that makes a particular protein.

genetic engineering   A technique of modifying, moving, or adding genes to living organisms. It is also called gene splicing, recombinant DNA technology (rDNA), or genetic modification (GM).

genome   The entire blueprint of genes located in an organism's chromosomes.

germination   Sprouting of a dry seed caused by its absorbing water.

gluten   An elastic network of proteins formed when water and wheat flour are combined. Wheat is the only grain with sufficient quantities of the specific proteins—glutenin and gliadin—needed to produce gluten.

GMO   (genetically modified organism) An organism altered using techniques of *genetic engineering*.

granita   A very grainy frozen dessert also known as an ice; made with water, sugar, and liquid flavorings such as fruit juice or coffee.

gravy   A *sauce* made by thickening the pan drippings or juices produced when roasting or baking meat or poultry.

hot smoking   The process of smoking foods at temperatures above 180°F. The combination of heat and time cooks the food at the same time that it smokes it.

hybrid   The offspring of plants or animals of different breeds, varieties, or species that are bred selectively to improve qualities such as yield, flavor, or resistance to diseases.

ice bath   A combination of ice and cold water into which a bowl or stockpot is submerged in order to cool the contents quickly.

imitation chocolate   Solid chocolate made with vegetable fats rather than pure cocoa butter.

infuse   To extract flavors into a liquid by steeping.

invert sugar   Sucrose that has been partially broken down (inverted) into glucose and fructose by an acid. Inversion prevents crystallization and makes smoother candies, frostings, and confections.

ionizing radiation   Very high-frequency waves of energy (millions of trillions of cycles per second); ultra-violet and X-rays are examples. Non-ionizing radiation uses a much lower frequency of energy waves (around 2500 million cycles per second); microwaves and radio waves are examples.

jus   French for "juice"; refers to the natural meat juices remaining in a roasting pan after cooking. These pan drippings are the basis of a natural sauce. A dish served with these juices is served *au jus*.

lactose   The natural sugar found in milk; it is a disaccharide.

larding   Inserting strips of fat into lean meat to increase its moistness and tenderness during cooking. A larding needle or a sharp, thin knife will assist with this process.

leaveners or **leavening agents**   Anything that causes a baked good to rise; it includes steam, air, and products that create carbon dioxide gas such as baking soda and *yeast*.

leavening   The process of adding gases such as air, steam, and carbon dioxide to dough or batter though chemical, biological, or physical means.

legume   The seed portion of a bean. The legume family includes peas, lentils, soybeans, and peanuts.

lipid   Any substance that dissolves only in solvents such as alcohol-based compounds, but not in water. All *fats* are lipids, but not all lipids are fats.

Maillard reaction   A specific type of *caramelization* in which protein and *fat* react with sugars to aid in the browning process.

maître d' butter   Compound butter flavored with lemon juice, parsley, white pepper, and salt.

marbling   Thin bits of fat located within or between muscle fibers. This fat is desirable because it adds flavor and juiciness to meat.

marinade   A highly seasoned liquid usually containing an acid. Food is marinated (soaked) in marinades before cooking in order to add flavors and improve its texture.

microwave cooking   A heating method that cooks food with *radiation* generated by a special oven. The waves' non-ionizing radiation agitate water molecules in the food, creating friction and heat; this energy then spreads throughout the food by conduction.

milling   The process in which grains are cleaned, hulled, cracked, and sifted in order to break down the seed into the germ, bran, and endosperm.

mirepoix   Classic name for a mixture of two parts chopped onion, one part chopped carrot, and one part chopped celery.

molecule   The smallest particle of any compound that has all the chemical attributes of that compound. Elements such as hydrogen, oxygen, carbon, and nitrogen are bound together into molecules because of their negative and positive magnetic-like charges.

mother sauce   Any of five classical French sauce preparations, which are used to produce a myriad of other sauces known as *small sauces*. The five mother sauces are velouté, béchamel, espagnole, hollandaise, and tomato.

muscle   Contractile tissue used for locomotion and movement. A muscle fiber is the basic building block or cell of a muscle. A muscle fibril is a filament or thread-like part of a muscle fiber.

myocommata   Thin layers of connective tissue found between fish muscle groups.

myoglobin   Protein that gives red meat its color.

myotomes   The bundles of muscle-fiber cells of fish.

organic   The process of growing food, both plants and animals, using no chemical herbicides, pesticides, hormones, or GMOs.

oven finishing   The process of completing the internal cooking of food in an oven after it has cooked sufficiently on the surface through another method, such as searing, grilling, or sautéing.

overrun   The percentage of air churned into ice cream. A 100 percent overrun means that the final product will be 50 percent air.

pan-dressed   Fish that are *drawn* and have fins, head, and tail removed. Smaller fish such as trout may be pan-dressed with the head and tail attached.

pan-frying   See *sauté*.

pastry cream   Rich, creamy starch-thickened custard cooked by the stirring method. It is used to fill tarts, éclairs, and other pastries.

pellicle   The dried outer surface of food that has undergone dry cures and air dehydration.

photosynthesis   The process by which plants use carbon dioxide to produce sugars for food; oxygen is produced in the process.

pigment   A natural substance in plant or animal cells that imparts a color characteristic. Pigments are grouped into classes based upon their light-reflecting properties.

pilaf   A cooking method in which grain is lightly sautéed in fat before a hot liquid (usually stock) is added. The mixture is simmered until the grain absorbs the liquid.

primal cuts   Large specifically defined divisions of muscle, bone, and connective tissue produced by the initial butchering of an animal carcass. Retail cuts are the smaller, even, individual-portion cuts, that are sold in retail markets.

pulse   A dried *legume* seed.

purée   Mashed, strained, or very finely chopped vegetables or fruits. The term is used as both a noun (the raspberry purée) and a verb (to purée the raspberries).

radiation   The transfer of energy by electromagnetic waves.

reduction   Heating a liquid to evaporate its water content. Chefs speak of reducing a mixture by one half, one third, or some other fraction, meaning that the finished product is one-third less than what you began with. If heating continues until the pan is nearly dry, it is called *au sec*. Reduction is a way to concentrate flavors.

render   To cook a fatty piece of meat until the fat melts out and the meat crisps.

retrogradation   The movement of water in a gelatinized starch from the interior to the exterior, as a gel is formed. The starch becomes less soluble and more crystalline. A process involved in staling.

rigor mortis   The loss of extensibility of a muscle.

risotto   (1) A cooking method for grains (especially rice) in which the grains are first lightly sautéed in fat, and then liquids are gradually added. The mixture is simmered with nearly constant stirring until the still-firm grain merges with the liquid, creating a creamy but toothsome dish. (2) The finished dish prepared by the risotto method.

roundfish   Category of fish characterized by a backbone on their top or dorsal area and an eye on each side of the head. Trout is an example. See *flatfish*.

saturated solution   One that contains the maximum amount of a substance that can be dissolved and still have a stable solution.

sauce   A thickened liquid used for seasoning food.

sauté   To cook in a pan over very high heat using a very small amount of fat as the cooking medium. *Pan-frying* uses a similar process but the food is cooked in more fat.

savory   A food that is not sweet.

scale   To remove the scales from fish using a fish scaler or knife.

searing   A dry-heat cooking technique in which the surface of a food is browned quickly over very high heat; often done to add color and flavor as the first step in a combination cooking method.

seviche   See *ceviche*.

sherbet   A frozen dessert made with fruit juice, sugar, water, and some milk or cream. It is not as smooth as ice cream, nor as granular as sorbet.

shocking   The technique of plunging *blanched* or par-boiled food into ice water to stop the cooking process.

shellfish   A diverse group of freshwater or saltwater aquatic animals that have some form of shell.

simple syrup   A mixture of sugar and water. Syrups may be light, medium, or heavy, depending upon sugar concentration.

slurry   A type of *sol* made from cold liquid (stock or water) and cornstarch.

small sauce   Any of a large variety of sauces made by adding flavoring ingredients to a *mother sauce*. Small sauces are grouped together into families based on their mother sauce.

smoke   A solid dissolved in a gas.

smoke point   The temperature at which a fat burns. Saturated animal fats tend to smoke at lower temperatures than vegetable oils.

sol   Microscopic particles of a solid suspended in a liquid.

solubility   The ability of one substance to dissolve into another substance. Water is usually the standard used to determine solubility.

sorbet   A frozen dish made with puréed fruit or fruit juice and sugar. Because it contains no dairy products, sorbet forms ice crystals that are larger than those in ice cream; it is slightly gritty or granular.

specific heat   A measure of the number of calories needed to raise the temperature of one gram of a substance by 1°C. Water has a particularly high specific heat, meaning that it absorbs a great deal of energy (calories) before the temperature rises.

sponge method   A two-stage process for making bread in which a batter is first made with part of the flour, liquid, and yeast. This batter ferments, and then the remaining ingredients are added to complete the formula.

starch   A polysaccharide composed of hundreds of thousands of connected sugar molecules.

steaming   A moist-heat cooking method in which food is cooked by direct contact with the hot steam rising off of a boiling liquid; the food is placed in a basket or rack above a boiling liquid in a covered pan.

steer   A castrated male calf that is raised for beef.

stock   A clear, unthickened liquid flavored with meat, poultry, or fish bones, aromatic vegetables, and seasonings.

straight dough method   A one-stage process for making bread in which all of the ingredients are simply combined and mixed.

surface tension   The tendency of like molecules to stick together. Surface tension is demonstrated by the way oil naturally floats on the surface of water.

tossed salad   One in which the greens and other ingredients are freely mixed before serving.

toxin   A substance that is poisonous when consumed in sufficient quantities.

venison   The flesh from any member of the deer family, including antelope, elk, moose, reindeer, red-tailed and white-tailed deer, mule deer, and axis deer.

Vibrio vulnificus   A pathogenic bacteria that can colonize shellfish and cause severe gastroenteritis in humans who then consume the raw shellfish.

vinaigrette   An oil-and-liquid emulsion typically used to dress salad greens.

volatile compound   One that will evaporate or vaporize rapidly at room temperatures. Examples include alcohol and the flavor oils in citrus rind.

wheat berries   Whole kernels of wheat. When the berries are broken into different-size fragments, they are called cracked wheat.

yeast   Microscopic fungi that eat sugars and produce carbon dioxide and alcohol through a process known as fermentation.

yolk   See *egg*.

Appendix B

Charts for Quick Reference

Common Measurement Equivalents

dash = $^1/_8$ teaspoon

3 teaspoons = 1 tablespoon

2 tablespoons = 1 fluid ounce

4 tablespoons = $^1/_4$ cup (2 fluid ounces)

$5^1/_3$ tablespoons = $^1/_3$ cup ($2^2/_3$ fluid ounces)

16 tablespoons = 1 cup (8 fluid ounces)

2 cups = 1 pint (16 fluid ounces)

2 pints = 1 quart (32 fluid ounces)

4 quarts = 1 gallon (128 fluid ounces)

2 gallons = 1 peck

4 pecks = 1 bushel

1 gram = 0.035 ounce ($^1/_{30}$ ounces)

1 ounce = 28.35 grams

454 grams = 1 pound

2.2 pound = 1 kilogram (1000 grams)

1 teaspoon = 5 milliliters

1 tablespoon = 15 milliliters

1 fluid ounce = 28.35 milliliters

1 cup = .24 liters

1 gallon = 3.80 liters

Measurement Conversions—Formulas for Exact Measures

	When You Know:	Multiply By:	To Find:
Mass	ounces	28.35	grams
(Weight)	pounds	0.45	kilograms
	grams	0.035	ounces
	kilograms	2.2	pounds
Volume	teaspoon	5.0	milliliters
(Capacity)	tablespoon	15.0	milliliters
	fluid ounces	29.57	milliliters
	cups	0.24	liters
	pints	0.47	liters
	quarts	0.95	liters
	gallons	3.785	liters
	milliliters	0.034	fluid ounces
Temperature	Fahrenheit	5/9 (after subtracting 32)	Celsius
	Celsius	9/5 (then add 32)	Fahrenheit

It is important for foods to reach the right internal temperature to kill pathogenic microorganisms that might be present. The following internal temperatures are recommended by the USDA.

Recommended Cooking Temperatures

Food	Internal Temperature
Beef/Veal/Lamb (steaks or roasts)	145°F
Chicken/Duck/Turkey	180°F in thigh; 170°F in breast
Eggs	145°F for 15 seconds if prepared immediately before consumption or until yolk and white are both firm
Fish	145°F or until it is opaque and flakes easily
Ground Meats	160°F
Ground Turkey or Chicken	165°F
Leftovers	165°F for 15 seconds
Pork	145°F for 15 seconds
Stuffing	165°F

Appendix C

Further Reading

Part 1: Cooking in the Raw: Past, Present, and Future Food Basics
General Subject Matter

CAST. *Pesticides and Safety of Fruits and Vegetables*. Ames, IA: Council for Agricultural Science and Technology, 1990.

Fennema, Owen R., ed. *Food Chemistry*. New York: Marcel Dekker Inc; 1996.

Labensky, Sarah R. and Alan M. Hause. *On Cooking: A Textbook of Culinary Fundamentals*. 3rd edition. New Jersey: Prentice Hall, 2003.

McGee, Harold. *On Food and Cooking—The Science and Lore of the Kitchen*. New York: MacMillan Publishing Co; 1988.

McSwane, David, Nancy Rue, and Richard Linton. *Essentials of Food Safety and Sanitation*. 2nd edition. New Jersey: Prentice Hall, 1998.

Biotechnology

Grace, Eric S. *Biotechnology Unzipped*. Washington, D.C.: Joseph Henry Press, 1997.

Lambrecht, Bill. *Dinner at the New Gene Café*. New York: Thomas Dunne Books, 2001.

Pence, Gregory E. *Designer Food*. Lantham, MD: Rowan and Littlefield Publishers Inc., 2002.

Rifkin, Jeremy. *The Biotechnology Century*. New York: McGraw Hill, 2001.

Part 2: Eat Your Veggies ... and Other Stuff

Gross, J. *Pigments in Vegetables: Chlorophylls and Caratenoids*. New York: Van Nostrand Reinhold, 1991.

Lorenz, K.J. and K. Kulp, eds. *Handbook of Cereal Science and Technology*. New York: Marcel Dekker, 1991.

Robinson, T. *Organic Constituents of Higher Plants*. Boca Raton, FL: CRC Press, 1991.

Waters, Alice. *Chez Panisse Vegetables*. New York: Harper Collins Publishers, 1996.

Weichmann, J. *Postharvest Physiology of Vegetables*. New York: Marcel Dekker, 1987.

Part 3: Muscle Mania—The Handling and Cooking of Meat

Bechtel, P.J. *Muscle as Food*. New York: Academic Press, 1986.

Forrest, J.C., E.D. Eberle, H.B. Hedrick, M.D. Judge, and R.A. Merkel. *Principles of Meat Science*. San Francisco: W.H. Freeman, 1975.

Jones, D.A. and J.M. Round. *A Textbook of Muscle Physiology*. London, UK: Manchester Univ. Press; 1990.

Lawrie, R. ed. *Developments in Meat Science*. London, UK: Applied Science, 1981.

The Meat Buyers Guide. Reston, VA: National Association of Meat Purveyors, 1990.

Meat Nutrient Update. Chicago, IL: National Livestock and Meat Board, 1994.

Webster, Harold W., Jr. *The Complete Venison Cookbook*. Brandon, Miss.: Quail Ridge Press, 1996.

Part 4: The Aquatic Cook

Peterson, James. *Fish and Shellfish*. New York: Morrow, 1998.

The NFI Culinary Handbook for Seafood. Arlington, VA: National Fisheries Institute, 2002.

Sylvia, G., A. Shriver and M.T. Morrissey, M.T. (eds.). 1994. *Quality Control and Quality Assurance for Seafood*. Corvallis Oregon: Oregon Sea Grant, 1994.

The Seafood Handbook. Portland, ME: *Seafood Business Magazine*, 2002.

Part 5: Beautiful Baking

The Agricultural Handbook: Composition of Foods; Dairy and Egg Products. Washington, D.C.: Agricultural Research Service, 1976.

Eggcyclopedia. 2nd ed. Park Ridge, Ill.: American Egg Board, 1989.

Eliasson, A.C. and K. Larsson. *Cereals in Breadmaking*. New York: Marcel Dekker, 1993.

Jaspersohn, William. *Ice Cream*. New York: Simon and Schuster, 1988.

Labuzza, T.P., G.A. Reineccius, V. Monnier, J. O'Brien, and J. Baynes, eds. *Maillard Reactions in Chemistry, Food, and Health*. Boca Raton, FL: CRC Press, 1995.

Lineback, D.R. and G.E. Inglett, eds. *Food Carbohydrates.* Westport, CT: AVI, 1982.

Mathlouthi, M. and P. Reiser, eds. *Sucrose, Properties, and Applications.* Glasgow, Scotland: Blackie, 1995.

Part 6: Hitting the Sauce

Bailey, A.J. and N.D. Light. *Connective Tissue in Meat and Meat Products.* New York: Elsevier Applied Science, 1989.

Peterson, James. *Sauces: Classical and Contemporary Sauce Making.* New York: Van Nostrand Reinhold, 1991.

Sokolov, Raymond. *The Saucier's Apprentice.* New York: Knopf, 1976.

Zobel, H.F. "Molecules to granules: A comprehensive starch review." *Starch/Starke.* 40:44–50; 1988.

Index